SEVEN
GAMES

ALSO BY OLIVER ROEDER

The Riddler: Fantastic Puzzles from FiveThirtyEight (editor)

SEVEN
GAMES

A
HUMAN
HISTORY

Oliver Roeder

W. W. NORTON & COMPANY
Celebrating a Century of Independent Publishing

For information about permission to reproduce selections from this book, write to
Permissions, W. W. Norton & Company, Inc., 500 Fifth Avenue, New York, NY 10110

For information about special discounts for bulk purchases, please contact
W. W. Norton Special Sales at specialsales@wwnorton.com or 800-233-4830

Manufacturing by Lakeside Book Company
Book design by Beth Steidle
Production manager: Beth Steidle

Library of Congress Cataloging-in-Publication Data

Names: Roeder, Oliver, author.
Title: Seven games : a human history / Oliver Roeder.
Description: First edition. | New York, N.Y. : W. W. Norton & Company, 2022. |
Includes bibliographical references and index.
Identifiers: LCCN 2021038188 | ISBN 9781324003779 (hardcover) |
ISBN 9781324003786 (epub)
Subjects: LCSH: Board games—History. | Card games—History.
Classification: LCC GV1312 .R64 2022 | DDC 794—dc23
LC record available at https://lccn.loc.gov/2021038188

ISBN 978-1-324-05102-2 pbk.

W. W. Norton & Company, Inc., 500 Fifth Avenue, New York, N.Y. 10110
www.wwnorton.com

W. W. Norton & Company Ltd., 15 Carlisle Street, London W1D 3BS

1 2 3 4 5 6 7 8 9 0

In memory
Shirley Tabor, who taught me to play
1928–2019

God is dead! And we have killed him. . . .
What festivals of atonement, what sacred games
shall we have to invent? Is not the greatness
of this deed too great for us?

—FRIEDRICH NIETZSCHE,
"THE PARABLE OF THE MADMAN"

I'm a machine and you're a machine
and we both think, don't we?

—CLAUDE SHANNON,
WHEN ASKED WHETHER
MACHINES COULD THINK

CONTENTS

SEVEN
GAMES

PROLOGUE

"Making music, were you?" they cried.
"Very well; now dance!"

—AESOP

ESOP TOLD A FABLE about two neighbors, an ant and a grasshopper. One warm summer day, the grasshopper emerges from his home and stretches his hind wings. Basking happily in the sun, he decides to spend the day at play. The grasshopper sets off merrily through the field and comes across the ant, who is scurrying back and forth, muttering to himself. The ant is hard at work stockpiling seeds for the winter.

"Hey, ant," the grasshopper says. "Come and play with me!"

"No," the ant mutters in solemn reply. "There is work to be done. Winter is coming and I need food."

The grasshopper laughs. "But you have plenty of food right now. Come on, let's play!"

The ant refuses again and returns to his toil. The grasshopper continues on his way, alone but happy, inventing and perfecting his games in the meadow. Days pass, and then weeks and months, and eventually winter does come. The meadow freezes over and food becomes scarce. The grasshopper, seedless, goes hungry. The ant eats well from his stockpile. The end.

In this fable, the grasshopper is supposed to be a cautionary figure; the ant is the diligent hero.

The diligent hero of *this* book, however, is the grasshopper—the player of games.

INTRODUCTION

The view we take in the following pages is
that culture arises in the form of play, that it
is played from the very beginning. . . . It is
through this playing that society expresses its
interpretation of life and the world.

—JOHAN HUIZINGA, *HOMO LUDENS*

THERE IS AN ISLAND in a mangrove swamp in southern Mexico made almost entirely out of clamshells. Five thousand years ago, before the rise of the great Mesoamerican civilizations of the Olmec, Aztec, and Maya, a group of people fished and gathered shellfish on this island. As the generations passed, countless clams were cooked and eaten. Their shells were discarded and crushed into the ground. Perhaps growing weary of walking on broken shells, the people began to build clay floors. They installed racks to dry their fish. More shells were crushed, and the island continued to grow. Eventually, the people built something else, too—something that would puzzle the archaeologists who would discover the site millennia later. It was a simple thing: a curved pattern of small holes embedded in the clay floor above the shells.

Archaeologists tend to classify ancient discoveries into either the utilitarian (the clay floor, the drying racks) or the ritualistic (a temple, say). But the pattern on the floor stumped them, seeming, as it did, to belong to neither category. It was an ancient mystery, neither practical nor devout.

Or maybe, more profoundly, it was both.

It was a game, one of the earliest known. "For the fisherfolk of

Tlacuachero, game playing had apparently become one of the necessities of life," writes the anthropologist Barbara Voorhies, who has
studied the site extensively.

Ancient Mesoamericans weren't alone in their fondness for
play. Archaeologists have pondered ancient findings from countless places. In a grave site in Egypt, for example, dating from the
Neolithic period, before the pharaohs, diggers found a game called
senet with pieces molded of dried mud. They've found games from
ancient Persia, too, and ancient India, and ancient China—wherever
humans settled, games became necessities of life.

In each of these far-flung societies, games straddled the utilitarian and the ritualistic. Egyptian senet was played by both peas-
ants and kings. In secular terms, it required strategic planning and a
sophisticated understanding of probability, as players tossed casting
sticks (essentially ancient dice) to race a set of pawns around a board.
But senet also represented the connection between life and death,
and the movement of *ba*—a concept similar to the Western idea of a
soul. "The senet board effectively became the Netherworld," writes
the archaeologist Peter Piccione.

The Royal Game of Ur was first played in ancient Mesopotamia.
It is also a strategy game played with dice. It had at least one earthly
attraction—gambling—and a heavenly one as well: the spaces a
player's pieces landed on were thought to symbolize messages from
the beyond, declarations of her fate. A recent archaeological study
painstakingly traces the game's spread across the Middle East. It has
been found at hundreds of sites in many countries from across hundreds of years, essentially unchanged.

You know a version of this game today; it's called backgammon.
Another ancient game from Egypt, with versions later mentioned
by Plato and Homer, became modern checkers. An ancient game
from India, used for military training, became modern chess. One
from China, used for similar purposes, became Go. Playing cards,

and therefore games such as poker and bridge, can be traced back a thousand years, to the development of printing.

Games remain necessities of life today. For one thing, they're fun. They activate and satisfy psychological desires. Pleasure derives from immersing oneself in games' worlds, or in improving one's skills, or in benefiting from their systems of chance. The real world may from time to time offer us a chance to solve an elegant problem, and the satisfaction that comes with it, but games offer this chance constantly. While other art forms, like painting or film, might capture some visual aspect of the world, a game records a set of decisions and actions, packing them onto a small board, into a deck of cards, or onto a hard drive. In other words, games offer a space to enjoy *agency*. When playing games, "we can take up goals temporarily, not because we actually care about achieving them in an enduring way, but because we want to have a certain kind of struggle," writes C. Thi Nguyen, a philosopher at the University of Utah. "And we can do so for the sake of aesthetic experiences of striving—of our own gracefulness, of the delicious perfection of an intellectual epiphany, of the intensity of the struggle, or of the dramatic arc of the whole thing."

Games also offer simplified models of a dauntingly complicated world, with dynamics that we can grasp and master. Playing a game—entering what the cultural historian Johan Huizinga called the "magic circle," or the space created when players sit down to play—is adopting a unique way of seeing and acting in the world. We can take parts of ourselves into this magic circle, and we can take parts of the game back out with us. The border between the two is thin and often porous. Learning a game's intricacies and playing that game with others binds us with other humans, shaping our culture and, indeed, our perspective on the "real" world. "Any game can at any time wholly run away with the players," Huizinga writes. "The contrast between play and seriousness is always fluid. The inferiority of play is continually being offset by the corresponding superiority of its seriousness. Play turns to seriousness and seriousness to play. Play may rise to heights of beauty and sublimity that leave seriousness far beneath."

This book explores seven games in depth: checkers, whose reputation as a child's game belies its haunting depth; chess, the canonical and ubiquitous game of military strategy in the West; Go, the elegant and intricate surrounding game of the East; backgammon, the best and cruelest game played with dice; poker, the world's most popular card game in our capitalistic age; Scrabble, the canonical word game; and bridge, the pinnacle of strategic card games. Each of these games has developed its own unique personality. Competitive play has produced a voluminous tactical literature studied and revered by a unique subculture of masters. The games themselves are fascinating characters—each with its own virtues and its own flaws.

I, too, love these games. In graduate school, I studied game theory, wanting to spend as much time as I could thinking about the mathematical underpinnings of these pursuits. And when I got my first journalism job, I wrote a weekly column and countless other articles about games and puzzles, wanting to explore and proselytize about the rich worlds that games contain. To write this book, I competed in the World Series of Poker in Las Vegas and the North American Scrabble Championship in Reno, Nevada. I studied famous chess problems and volumes of theory, and I taught everyone I know to play backgammon, whether they liked it or not. I also met the games' elite practitioners. In an apartment on the Upper East Side of Manhattan, for example, a wealthy bridge player assembled his well-paid team of ringers. In the Las Vegas desert, a group of poker professionals underwent a moral crisis. In a hotel ballroom in New Jersey, the world's best backgammon player lamented the loss of a seedier time. And in Washington Square Park, a grizzled chess hustler tried to wring a few dollars out of me through the game of kings.

WHAT IS A GAME? This simple question has vexed great thinkers. The illustrious Cambridge philosopher Ludwig Wittgenstein, for example, failed to find an answer, deciding that there was no proper definition. All one could do, he said, was recognize certain "family resemblances" among games. "For if you look at them," he wrote, "you will not see something that is common to all, but similarities, relationships, and a whole series of them at that."

Others were unsatisfied with this analysis. Bernard Suits, a relatively obscure but aptly named scholar who spent most of his career at the University of Waterloo, in Canada, was perhaps the first true philosopher of games. He dismissed Wittgenstein for his cowardice and offered instead a definition; it hinges on what he called a *lusory attitude*, a state of mind required by a person playing a game. Derived from the Latin *ludere*, meaning "to play," a lusory attitude is that of the grasshopper. "To play a game," Suits wrote, "is to attempt to achieve a specific state of affairs [prelusory goal], using only means permitted by rules [lusory means], where the rules prohibit use of more efficient in favour of less efficient means [constitutive rules], and where the rules are accepted just because they make possible such activity [lusory attitude]."

Or, put more succinctly: a game is "the voluntary attempt to overcome unnecessary obstacles."

Suits's work, published mostly in the 1960s and '70s, is the clearest rubric we have for understanding what games truly are, and for how to think about them. The philosopher Thomas Hurka, who provided the summarizing bracketed phrases in Suits's definition, called it a "precisely placed boot in Wittgenstein's balls." The grasshopper is Suits's hero, too, and his argument about games, which takes the form of a parody of a Platonic dialogue, reverses the moral of Aesop's fable. Suits imagines a future world he calls Utopia. In Utopia, advanced technology has solved all the problems of scarcity—humanity is well fed, well clothed, and well housed. Such a future would be blandly pleasant, perhaps, but boring—without games, that is. "The notable institutions of Utopia, accordingly, will not be economic, moral, scientific, and erotic instruments—as they are today—but institutions which foster sport and other games," he writes. Perhaps the grasshopper is a sort of ant after all. "We thus call games 'pastimes,' and regard them as trifling fillers of the interstices in our lives," Suits concluded. "But they are much more important than that. They are clues to the future. And their serious cultivation now is perhaps our only salvation."

WHY DO WE PLAY GAMES? Imagine you're an early human. The world is harsh, and you have to hunt wild animals for food. You have a few options. One: you could hunt all the time. This, however, would put your life in regular peril and, therefore, endanger the propagation of your genes. Two: you could hunt only when you were hungry. But then you would be unskilled at hunting and run the risk of starving to death. Three: you could *practice*. You could invent a game that would motivate you to engage in this practice. For example, *first player to throw a rock and hit that tree wins*. This game improves your aim, which improves your hunting ability without the risk. According to this theory, adding structure to play—that is, inventing and playing *games*—is central to our developmental intelligence.

I first heard this account not from an anthropologist or archaeologist or evolutionary biologist but, rather, from a computer scientist. If games have been central to the development of human intelligence, they have been just as central to the development of artificial intelligence, the sort of technology, its creators hope, that could one day solve certain persistent problems of human society and bring about "Utopia."

As long as there have been computers, their programmers have harnessed human games. For two months in 1956, a cadre of computer scientists, mathematicians, and psychologists assembled for a workshop on a leafy Ivy League campus. The Dartmouth Summer Research Project on Artificial Intelligence is now considered a founding event of that field, and the document proposing the meetings is an urtext of AI. The authors requested $13,500 in funding and made their ambitions clear: "We think of machines performing the most advanced human thought activities—proving theorems, writing music, or playing chess."

Games attract AI researchers for the same reason they attract human players. They are fun, but they are also *practice*. Games are potent distillations of narrow elements of the real world. And by mastering these elements, computers master aspects of the human world. Indeed, games have become the most visible success story of artificial intelligence, with a dramatic series of "human versus machine" contests instilling in our species both humility of place and pride of invention.

For some of these researchers, the games were a means to an end—mere test beds for new approaches in computer science that they hoped would cross the porous border and be used later in "more serious" endeavors. For others, the games were the thing, and they hoped that their computer systems would reveal new truths, new strategies and tactics, new ways of thinking. Out of both of these camps of scientists came new creations, literally superhuman artificial intelligences, albeit limited in scope to the narrow band of their particular game. At the same time, these superhuman intelligences were also tools to play the game better. Inventing tools to augment skill is one of *Homo sapiens*' foundational behaviors. Therefore, "human versus machine" contests are also "human versus human" contests.

I, too, enjoy getting better at games, learning new truths about them. So I recently spent a long time playing games against these creations. I played chess and Go and backgammon and poker and Scrabble against opponents who couldn't talk but nonetheless destroyed me. I knew the programs were written in bloodless code, but I found that they had their own personalities. And I discovered the stories of their programmers. In the wilderness of Oregon, an astrophysicist and programmer pondered the mathematics of bridge. In an IBM office in rural New York, a small team built a supercomputer that became perhaps the world's best chess player. On the icy campus of the University of Alberta, a professor upended his family in pursuit of a solution to checkers. And in a Google office in London, an elite squadron conquered the most beautiful, and most complex, board game on the planet.

The seven games in this book belong to a rough hierarchy; each game on the list adds a strategic feature and, therefore, more closely hews to some aspect of the "real world." The aspects of each game crystallize a specific and potent form of agency. And when taken together, these aspects form a rough menu of intelligence. Computer scientists and their algorithms have been making their way through the list, on their way, perhaps, to truly general artificial intelligence. Checkers allows you to practice basic strategy—but its canvas is limited and its moves often rote. Add different pieces with more complex movements and you produce chess, a game that for centuries has been associated with intelligence itself. Or increase the number of pieces and the size of the board—like managing not just a small tribe but a giant civilization—and you have Go, the mathematically richest game played by humans. But life is random and is always throwing you some unexpected new development; practice for that with backgammon, which relies on chance. Poker models a world of hidden knowledge and deceit. Scrabble demands that a player make intertemporal trade-offs between satisfying desires today and saving up for tomorrow. Bridge, perhaps the most "human" of all the games in this book, offers a world of flourishing language, alliances, communication, empathy—and cheating.

Games have had a special cultural longevity. They appear among the ancient relics of humankind and in the code of cutting-edge software. The same ones that were played in ancient cities of bygone empires are played by supercomputers. They are a backbone both of our own species and of the ongoing creation of a new kind of being. Maybe Bernard Suits was right: their serious cultivation is perhaps our salvation.

Life itself contains both necessary and unnecessary obstacles, and both voluntary and involuntary attempts to overcome them. Perhaps, then, what matters is one's attitude toward overcoming these obstacles. Perhaps a ludic attitude is a valuable resource. Perhaps life is a game. Perhaps we're grasshoppers after all.

CHECKERS

The bird fights its way out of the egg. The egg is the world. Who would be born must first destroy a world. The bird flies to God.

—HERMANN HESSE, *DEMIAN*

ONE QUIET AFTERNOON IN 1990, a book collector named Jonathan Schaeffer stood in his office in Edmonton, Canada. He grasped a sharp pocketknife in one hand and a treasured volume in the other. Schaeffer, a sturdy man with open features and thick mop of curly dark hair, was contemplating dismemberment. With a wince, he made two surgical incisions in the binding, ridding the book of its cover. This freed the two hundred pages inside, which Schaeffer held carefully in his hands. He was overcome, he recalled, with morbid fascination.

Schaeffer, then thirty-three years old, specialized in rare, leather-bound volumes about Arctic and Antarctic explorers and disasters. He sensed magic in these books. Holding history in his hands, he would read the accounts of "the vain but heroic attempts to rescue the lost souls, of the bravado of a time long ago." In a large glass case in his living room floats a model of the HMS *Erebus*, a nineteenth-century naval ship that was icebound and abandoned in the Northwest Passage. Tiny plastic sailors stand on bergs around their motionless vessel, hundreds of miles from civilization. Schaeffer wanted desperately to be a part of history.

The mutilated volume Schaeffer held contained travelogues of a different kind. They described journeys into the cold mathematical depths of the game of checkers. The book detailed the moves made in 732 games played by Marion Tinsley, the greatest human checkers player who ever lived. Schaeffer was going to dissect them, one by one.

Tinsley was the Ernest Shackleton of the game—a legendary, bespectacled figure in a professor's suit and tie. Over a forty-year stretch of competitive play comprising more than a thousand serious tournament checkers games, he lost exactly three times. He won the U.S. national championship nine times and the world championship seven times (or maybe eight, but more on that later). He'd have won many more titles if he had not disappeared from the game's tournament scene for so long.

Schaeffer, on the other hand, by his own admission, was a checkers novice, aware of little beyond the rudiments of the game. But in addition to being an avid book collector, Schaeffer was—and is—a professor of computer science at the University of Alberta working in artificial intelligence. For the past year his academic work had involved building a computer program to play expert checkers. He intended to pore over Tinsley's moves in search of some hidden checkers secrets, some weakness in Tinsley's game. The research project had taken on the cast of a personal crusade, and the monomaniacal obsession with defeating the great man over the checkerboard would eventually dominate Schaeffer's career and personal life.

In his office, Schaeffer fed the flattened pages from the dismembered book through his university's state-of-the-art optical character recognition machine. The system scanned the printed text, digitizing the games of the great human master. Schaeffer then uploaded the digital records of the games into his artificially intelligent checkers system. In some parts of the world, checkers is known as "draughts" (pronounced "drafts"). Schaeffer called his system Chinook, after a warm wind that blows through Canada like California's Santa Ana. Chinook analyzed Tinsley's games—hundreds of them. The program ran on four machines simultaneously for two weeks straight. At last, Chinook finished, and Schaeffer examined the results. To his creeping horror, he discovered that Tinsley hadn't made a single mistake.

HUMANS HAVE BEEN PLAYING some version of checkers for millennia. Early in Plato's *Republic*, written around 380 B.C., Socrates goes to the philosopher Polemarchus's house to discuss justice. The conversation turns to checkers—πεσσός, or *pessós*. The classicist and translator Allan Bloom explains, "In Plato, [checkers] is often employed as a symbol of dialectic, just as housebuilding or architecture . . . frequently stands for lawgiving. In dialectic, premises—like pieces—are set down and are changed in relation to the moves of one's partners. The game can be played over, and one's moves can be improved on the basis of experience with the opponent's moves. It is a friendly combat and an amusement for its own sake."

Distant family relations of the game have been dated to the second millennium B.C. and unearthed in Crete, Cyprus, Egypt, Iran, Iraq, Israel, Jordan, Lebanon, Syria, and Turkey. A game called alquerque, a parent of modern checkers, is mentioned in the *Book of Songs*, a twenty-volume tenth-century work by an Arabic historian. Alquerque contained the basic movements and piece-taking of modern checkers. The variant described in the *Book of Games*, a thirteenth-century document commissioned by a Spanish king, introduced the concept of crowning—"king me"—in which those special pieces can move either forward or backward. In the seventeenth century, the rule that you have to jump an opponent's piece whenever possible was incorporated. Since then, modern checkers has flourished so successfully that no fuller explanation here of its rules is really necessary; they seem woven into human DNA. Checkers move diagonally, hopping over enemies to capture them, and becoming kings should they arrive at the far end of the board.

"Playing chess is like looking out over a limitless ocean," Tinsley once said. "Playing checkers is like looking into a bottomless well."

Marion Franklin Tinsley was born on February 3, 1927, in Ironton, Ohio, an industrial town across the river from the Kentucky county where his father was sheriff. His mother was a schoolteacher, and he had two brothers and a twin sister, Mary. When Tinsley was a young boy, the family moved to a farm, which they would lose shortly thereafter in the aftermath of the Great Depression. The exact moment Tinsley discovered checkers is lost in this history. He learned it at home, or at school, he claimed not to remember which. But it seems to have always been a part of him. His family eventually wound up in Columbus, Ohio, and welcomed into their home a boarder named Mrs. Kershaw. Tinsley regularly played checkers with his dad and his brother and Mrs. Kershaw. She'd beat him "and rub it in and laugh and laugh," Tinsley later recalled. "Oh, how she'd cackle as she'd jump my men."

Tinsley was a precocious student—he excelled at math and memorized poems and skipped four of the first eight grades. He attributed this acceleration to his mother's fear that as a result of "hard farm life," she might not live to raise her children. Education was seen as a path out of poverty. By age fifteen, he was enrolled at Ohio State University. In the library, a beginner's text called *Winning Checkers* caught his eye. "Having acquired a dislike for losing and a love of books, this discovery set the stage for a lifelong fascination," he'd recall.* For the rest of his college years, he devoted eight hours a day to the game. He had visions of beating Mrs. Kershaw, her cackle rattling in his brain. He wouldn't get the chance—she'd since left the family home. But the visions drove his obsession, as did

---

* These recollections are from a typescript by Tinsley, titled "God Can Use Checkers Too!," later published in the 1994 annual report of the International Checker Hall of Fame.

a nagging sense that he was the less favored twin, and that his parents smiled instead on Mary.

Tinsley entered his first checkers tournament, a minor event in Louisiana, in 1945. He won. He took the Ohio State Juniors that same year and was runner-up in the national championship the year after that, at age nineteen. A string of a dozen tournament and match victories came in the next five years, including his first national championship. A dozen more came in the five years after that, including his first world championship. Tinsley is said to have spent twenty thousand hours during the late 1940s and early '50s studying checkers. That was nothing. A hero of his, the former world champion Asa Long, is reported to have devoted a hundred thousand hours to studying the game. "That fact should answer a few questions about this 'simple' game," Tinsley wrote.

In 1958, at age thirty-one, he won his third world championship in blindingly dominant fashion, nine wins to one with twenty-four draws against the second-best player in the world. This feat cemented him as an untouchable great. At the peak of his powers, however, Tinsley disappeared from the game. He'd recently completed a PhD and begun teaching abstract algebra and combinatorial analysis, a branch of math concerned with counting complex combinations of objects. He'd also, through the competitive checkers world, found religion. This newfound calling would quickly occupy Tinsley's time and mind much as checkers had.

Tinsley's mother was religious, "baptized the way Jesus was" in the waters of a stream, but in college Tinsley was a "practicing and professing unbeliever." A checkers friend obstinately confronted this unfaith. He would present Tinsley with biblical prophesies, asking him, "Now how do you explain that?" Another checkers figure, Charles Walker, was the secretary of the American Checker Federation and the founder of the International Checker Hall of Fame in Petal, Mississippi. You couldn't spend more than a few min-

utes around him, Tinsley recalled, without him asking if you were
saved. The two became close, Tinsley and Walker regularly tes-
tifying their faith to other players and praying for the sick among
them. Walker later became Tinsley's promoter. Tinsley recalled that
upon his first visit to the Hall of Fame, they prayed for a comatose
woman whose family was awaiting her imminent death. Shortly
thereafter, he said, she awoke, asked for food, and lived for another
five years. Tinsley wrote that the "best part about winning tournaments and matches . . . was in sharing these accomplishments with
my mother." His faith became another thing he could share with
her. Along with their church, the two "gave sacrificially" to help
build a hospital in Zimbabwe. "All I am or hope to be I owe to my
darling Mother," Tinsley wrote.

Tinsley became a volunteer part-time minister at the Church of
Christ. He produced a biblical radio program. He taught the Book of
Revelation in a weekly class. He joined the charismatic movement,
which embraced the practices of Pentecostalism. He performed
intricate analyses of the Bible and, the *Orlando Sentinel* reported,
"worked for years making an outline of the Old Testament from
the New Testament perspective." He preached at a predominantly
Black church. (Tinsley is white.) He was once diagnosed with a rare
blood disorder and given, he said, not long to live. He had surgery to
remove his gallbladder and spleen. He fully recovered, and later told
friends that his religious healing sessions helped save his life.

During his absence from checkers, Tinsley also moved from
teaching at Florida State to teaching at Florida A&M, a historically
Black university. "I had thought of going to Africa as a self-supporting
missionary," Tinsley told *Sports Illustrated*, "until a sharp-tongued
sister pointed out to me that most people who wanted to help blacks
in Africa wouldn't even talk to blacks in America."

In 1970, after a twelve-year absence from competitive checkers, Tinsley returned. He was forty-three. This return was another

charitable act. Tinsley had been quietly playing casual games on the side and had become good friends with Don Lafferty, another one of the best players in the world. Tinsley was concerned about Lafferty's health, deteriorated as it was from a life of hard drinking. Lafferty offered Tinsley a deal: Lafferty would quit drinking if Tinsley returned to the game. Tinsley accepted—his own father had also battled alcoholism. Tinsley, at least, upheld his end of the bargain. Having returned, he dominated checkers as perhaps no one has dominated any competitive pursuit in the history of humankind. He won the next twenty-eight tournaments and championship matches he entered, none being particularly close. He defeated Lafferty himself in a world championship. At one point, he went a full decade without losing a single game.

During his historic return to championship play, Tinsley lived with his mother in a house south of Tallahassee. Shelves in an upstairs den held some two hundred checkers books. *The Modern Encyclopedia of Checkers*—his other bible, its margins filled with his notations and corrections—had to be re-bound after heavy use. (Note-taking appears to be compulsive among serious checkers players. The used copy I bought, a small volume bound in blue leather with gold embossing, is filled with dense marginalia and has typewritten game records taped inside.) The room was also littered with tall championship trophies, and a bespoke checkerboard sat at the ready on a cluttered table. Tinsley never married and had no children. "It is a very rare woman who can be married to a real student of checkers," he once said. At his bedside was a smaller, magnetic board for spontaneous checkers analysis. When studying checkers, he favored a soundtrack of Bach, Brahms, and Handel. Outside of checkers, he preferred spirituals.

But the books and boards in his house were little more than props; the real checkers work happened in Tinsley's mind. He could play twenty games at once blindfolded and win them all; he put himself through college playing such exhibitions for fifty dollars apiece, according to a profile in *Sports Illustrated*. Checkers ideas, and improvements on the moves documented in his collected books, would come to him "out of the clear blue sky." His insights into Scripture, he said, came the same way.

At tournaments, Tinsley favored a green suit with a red tie and horn-rimmed glasses; a tuft of white hair peeked over an otherwise bald head. In early photographs, he looks like a young Edward R. Murrow, with the checkerboard as an anchor desk. Later in life, the frail professor appeared to blend into the game itself, his jacket matching the board's green squares and his tie matching the red checkers. The phenom Bobby Fischer famously haggled over the $125,000 purse for his chess world championship. Tinsley, far and away more dominant than Fischer but anonymous to the American public, was playing for prize money that never exceeded $5,000.

"Checkers players tend to be a little humble," Tinsley said on the eve of yet another world title defense, held, as many of them had been, at Charles Walker's lavish Hall of Fame—a building completely out of proportion with the fame of its honorees—where Tinsley always stayed in the Crown Room, reserved for checkers champions of the world. "They realize the world does not think that much of them."

BETWEEN TINSLEY'S two legendary runs, in 1963, a blind checkers expert named Robert Nealey took a seat alone in front of a checkerboard in his home in Stamford, Connecticut. He'd been playing checkers seriously for decades, held the state's championship title, and was at that moment engrossed in one of a series of six games, intently studying its positions by feeling for the pieces with his hands. When he finally decided on his move, he typed it on a postcard and mailed it to an address twenty-five miles away at the IBM Watson Research Center in Yorktown Heights, New York. And then he waited.

Once the postcard arrived at the center in New York, Nealey's move was keyed by technicians onto a punch card and fed into an IBM 7094 mainframe computer, which then searched tens of thousands of checkers positions, as deep as twenty moves into the future, and selected its response. The computer's move was then duly recorded on a postcard and sent back to Connecticut, where Nealey played it on his board. Though he was not an especially notable player in the pantheon of master checkers players, Nealey triumphed for humanity—postcard by postcard, over five months—scoring one win and five draws.

Nevertheless, the program itself was an achievement and a watershed. It was perhaps the first computer program that ever *learned*. In its August 1964 issue, *Popular Mechanics* ran a photo of an IBM engineer named Arthur Samuel examining a 150-foot-long roll of paper printed out by the IBM 7094. It was a list of instructions for Samuel's checkers-playing program.

Samuel was born in small-town Kansas and talked his way, literally, into MIT and a job at General Electric. After earning his PhD, he found a position at Bell Telephone Laboratories, where he worked on various machines, including a "multicavity magnetron" and a "microwave klystron." He published many papers (e.g., "A Method of Obtaining a Linear Time Axis for a Cathode Ray Oscillograph") and was granted fifty-seven patents. But Samuel, seeking a better salary, decamped for the University of Illinois in 1946.

With tenure, he indulged in some of his more theoretical interests, particularly having to do with electrical charge. This research required the intricate numerical operations of calculus, which, in private industry, according to a history of Samuel's work in the *IEEE Annals of the History of Computing*, "would have been done by a staff of women computers using electromechanical desk calculators." Samuel did not have this human resource at the university; nor was he about to do these calculations by hand. "The thing to do was to buy or build a computer," Samuel wrote. He decided to build. His dean at Illinois arranged $110,000 for the project, and Samuel began barnstorming the country's finest institutions of higher learning, hosting lectures, and employing graduate students to hone his plans.

But by 1948, the project had stalled. Running out of money, he decided to stage a publicity stunt: build a bare-bones version of the computer and have it do something impressive. Samuel had heard that Claude Shannon, a mathematician back at Bell Labs, was talking about making computers play chess. "It ought to be dead easy to program a computer to play checkers," Samuel reasoned. So he began to write a checkers program for an enormous machine that did not exist.

Not long after, Samuel took a job at the International Business Machines Corporation. He began at IBM in 1949, when the company was in the midst of developing a large commercial digital computer, its first, which would come to be called the IBM 701. The company told its shareholders that this "Defense Calculator" would be "the most advanced, most flexible high-speed computer in the world." One of the first things it did was run Samuel's checkers program.

The 701s rented for $11,900 a month (more than $100,000 today) and were capable of "more than 2,000" multiplications per second. Each night, from midnight to eight a.m. on the factory floor, Samuel would load one version of his checkers program onto one of the huge machines and a second version onto another and have them play each other over and over again. Each version was programmed to learn differently, and Samuel could observe their results—he learned how machines learned.

"I became one of the . . . very first to work in the general field later to become known as 'artificial intelligence,'" Samuel wrote in an unfinished and unpublished autobiography. "In fact, I became so intrigued with this general problem of writing a program that would appear to exhibit intelligence that it was to occupy my thoughts during almost every free moment for the entire duration of my employment by IBM and indeed for some years beyond." He wasn't alone in his self-assessment. One computer historian wrote that Samuel's checkers player was clearly "the world's first self-learning computer program" and "the first functioning artificial intelligence program."

IBM didn't mind Samuel's late-night gaming in its factory—at least someone was testing its expensive machines. But it did not publicize his research. Then, as now, there was fear of AI. IBM salesmen did not mention the company's artificial intelligence research to their customers; nor did they speculate about the company's future innovations. When Samuel finally did write about his work for public consumption, in 1959, he offered the following conclusion: "A computer can be programmed so that it will learn to play a better game of checkers than can be played by the person who wrote the program." Samuel could have gone further. A computer can be programmed to play checkers like God.

So HOW DOES A COMPUTER play a game? Imagine standing at the base of a very tall tree, looking up. The tree is all the possible futures of a game. The trunk represents your next move, a big limb some possible move after that, the smaller branches some moves later, and the countless tiny twigs and leaves way at the top a continuation of possible moves in the distant futures of the game—the endgames.

Humans stare up at the tree and are reminded of trees we've climbed, trees we've seen, and trees our friends have told us about before. We have an innate, primal sense about which limbs can bear our weight and which branches will bend under pressure, and we know which twigs seem hardy. We remember the times we fell, and how we made it to the top. We write down which branches are safe and which are risky, and we share this knowledge with our fellow humans. We climb trees—that is, we play games—through our intuition, experience, community, and literature.

Computers, on the other hand, have no such intuition for the tree. But they can climb all over the place, very fast, like a colony of ants. This is called search. At each point on the tree that they happen to arrive, they perform a small calculation, assessing that location's quality and awarding it a score. This is called evaluation. Before any move in a game like checkers, a computer's ants might climb to millions of places on the tree, collecting calculations. If one route upward returns higher scores, that's where the computer will head. Computers climb trees—that is, they play games—by searching and evaluating, searching and evaluating, searching and evaluating.

Both search and evaluation present serious technical challenges. For one thing, there are 500,995,484,682,338,672,639, or about five hundred billion billion, possible positions in a game of checkers. Schaeffer offers this analogy: If the Pacific Ocean were empty, and you had to fill it with a small cup, the number of cupfuls you'd need is equal to the number of possible positions in the game of checkers. Try another: If the entire land surface area of the earth represented all the possible checkers positions, an individual position would be equal to a thousandth of a square inch. Searching efficiently, therefore, is critical. If, by brute force, we looked at each of these positions for a thousandth of a second each, doing something similar to what Samuel's machine did, looking at all of them would take longer than the age of the universe.

Evaluating any given game position, once we do look at it, is not trivial. In checkers, certain features of a position are desirable: having more checkers, having more kings, having control of the center of the board, and so on. And certain features are undesirable: having your checkers relegated to the sides of the board, having an unprotected back rank, and so on. The trick is to turn that tapestry of features, and the complicated nonlinear mathematical interactions among them, into a single number that your computer program can understand.

Marion Tinsley relied on human intuition and calculation, and his ability to digest and retain the checkers wisdom of the humans who came before him. He could look up nearly any tree and find the best path to the top, operating on the low wattage of the human brain. But as he began his second run, in 1970, the ants were multiplying—and gaining speed.

Now, one might be tempted to ask a computer scientist why she spends her valuable time and energy, and her grant money, creating computer programs to play board games. The computer scientist will invariably reply with one of the following stock answers: Games are test beds. Games provide benchmarks for the performance of artificial intelligence systems. Games allow computer performance to be easily compared to human performance. Games are simplified models of aspects of the "real world." Or, if she is being slightly more forthcoming: Games are fun. And those answers are fine, but none of them are really true.

The true motivation of a computer scientist developing a game-playing AI is not dissimilar to that of a parent spending valuable time and energy raising a child. It is an act of creation. Mary Shelley's Dr. Frankenstein, upon contemplating his creature, said, "A new species would bless me as its creator and source; many happy and excellent natures would owe their being to me. No father could claim the gratitude of his child so completely as I should deserve theirs." Jonathan Schaeffer felt this the first time one of his algorithmic creations beat him at a game. "I could create intelligent behavior," he wrote. "I was scared."

Schaeffer, born in Toronto in 1957, grew up playing games. In *One Jump Ahead*—Schaeffer's book describing his checkers odyssey, a bildungsroman for his computer program—he floridly describes his early fascination with chess, what with its "Arthurian pieces defending the honor of the king" and their "precisely scripted ballet." He likened his love of the game to that of a connoisseur of "fine art or music." When he was sixteen, he earned the game's master title. At the University of Toronto, he meandered from mathematics to physics to computer science, eventually lured to this last field by the promise that while *he'd* never be world chess champion, perhaps he could write a *program* that would be. He learned to code by dissecting a strong existing computer player, written in an early programming language called Fortran. At the University of Waterloo, he spent so much time programming computers to play the game that his dissertation wound up "in shambles." No matter. He turned the chess work into a dissertation instead, gave it the academia-approved title "Experiments in Search and Knowledge," and graduated in 1986.

Two years later, by then an assistant professor at the University of Alberta, he decided to take a detour into checkers. "This was going to be easy," Schaeffer thought, as Samuel before him had. After all, *it's only checkers.* Schaeffer had no love for the game, or any fascination with its deep strategic gems, which so captivated Tinsley. His interest was born of baser instincts. "I could give you a lot of valid scientific reasons, but deep in my heart I knew the true answer," he wrote. "I could win." Checkers came to dominate Schaeffer's life.

Work on what was initially called the Beast began on June 2, 1989. Schaeffer quickly staffed up, enlisting two colleagues who had accidentally steered him toward the game over lunch. He dusted off Samuel's papers, which were by then three decades old. And he posted a message—a cry for help, really—on a Usenet group devoted to chess. (There wasn't one for checkers.)

"Wanted," his statement read. "Checkers evaluation function or guidance on how to build one."

The only answer came from the Dominion Radio Astrophysical Observatory, in British Columbia, sent by a man named Norman Treloar, who was, at the moment, unemployed. Schaeffer invited him to Edmonton. Treloar—"a short, proper Englishman dressed in a conservative suit"—had read Samuel's work closely. It was deeply flawed, he argued, and he knew how to fix it. For one thing, Treloar, unlike Schaeffer and Samuel, was an expert checkers player.

The Beast became known as Chinook. It had its search guy in Schaeffer and its evaluation guy in Treloar and they were ready to build a machine that could climb the tree of checkers better than any human alive—better, even, than Tinsley.

In August 1989, Schaeffer sat at a table in the five-star Park Lane Hotel in London, biting his nails and shaking his leg. His checkers research budget wouldn't cover a room in the hotel, so when he needed to freshen up, he used the lobby bathroom. Every morning, he lugged Chinook to the Park Lane on the Underground. The bulky equipment sat by his side, running on a Sun Microsystems machine with a single processor and thirty-two megabytes of RAM. He and Treloar had already built a system that Schaeffer himself couldn't beat.

Man and machine were in London to compete in the inaugural Computer Olympiad. On dozens of tables across an enormous ballroom, computers, minded by human babysitters like Schaeffer, were playing each other in checkers and chess, as well as awari, bridge, Chinese chess, Connect Four, dominoes, Go, gomoku, Othello, renju, and Scrabble. The chatter of their programmers and the shuffle of games pieces were punctuated by the clack of keyboard keys.

Chinook's competition in the checkers division included programs named Colossus, Sage Draughts, Checker Hustler, Tournament Checkers, and, simply, Checkers. Checkers was the one to watch. Its creator was a software developer, a concert pianist, and the editor of *Hang Gliding* magazine. Nevertheless, Chinook bested all AI comers and won the gold medal in London.

Schaeffer and Treloar celebrated their victory, but they knew the London field had lacked checkers' most formidable player,

Marion Tinsley. By that time, Tinsley's second dominant run had lasted nearly two decades. "In many ways my mind was corrupted," Schaeffer told me recently. "How do you beat a Tinsley? You're not talking about a normal person. You're talking about—and I don't mean this in a negative way—you're talking about an aberration of nature. You're talking about a person who was blessed with an extraordinary set of skills. And I very quickly became terrified."

In addition to searching quickly and evaluating accurately, there were two key pieces that Schaeffer needed to build into Chinook if it was going to beat the master: openings and endgames. Every game of checkers begins the same way, with the twenty-four pieces deployed on their squares just so, a predictable quilt of possibilities. Most of these games end similarly, too, with the players' forces nearly depleted, and victory for the one side (or a draw) ensured. This frequency and familiarity generate a large body of published theory—shelves of books—about the *beginnings* of games and the *ends* of games. The beginnings are so familiar that they are given names: the Henderson, the Sicilian Defense, the Shusaku *fuseki*. And because by the endgame so few pieces remain on the board, it is often possible to perform exhaustive computational analyses of what will happen. In chess, for example, an endgame featuring a bishop and a knight versus a bishop is a theoretically guaranteed draw, a fact well known by good players. (In contrast, the middle game, the netherworld between the opening and the endgame, is the Wild West—lots of pieces, lots of possibilities. The calculations are too complex, and therefore little concrete theory exists.)

It would be too expensive, computationally speaking, to work out each endgame position in real time. Much better would be to work out the correct endgame plays ahead of time and bake this knowledge into Chinook. It's easy at first. With one piece on a checkerboard, a trivial endgame situation, there are just 120 possible positions—a checker could be on one of twenty-eight squares, a king could be on one of thirty-two squares, and the piece could be either white or black. With two pieces, though, there are seven thousand. With three pieces there are more than a quarter million. With four pieces, seven million; five pieces, one hundred and fifty million; six pieces, two and a half billion; seven pieces, thirty-five billion.

Schaeffer, in other words, needed to teach Chinook to do by brute force what the top human players could do through intuition and study. For two hours a day over the course of a month, Schaeffer had meticulously entered opening moves into his computer from a seven-volume checkers book. (That was nothing. Ken Thompson, the designer of the Unix operating system and a chess machine called Belle, once spent an hour a day for three years keying in lines from the *Encyclopedia of Chess Openings*.) For the endings, Schaeffer had set machines to work calculating the countless permutations of checkers and outcomes. After more than two months of calculation, the four-piece endgames had been finished just in time for the London tournament in 1989. At the time, these precious databases were stored on magnetic tape, like a huge audiocassette. Schaeffer traveled with this singular object to competitions around the world. A single bit of corrupted data in his massive file—a single 1 rather than a 0— would render the entire database useless.

Work on the endgame database quickly became Schaeffer's priority, and the vexatious endeavor would occupy and plague the project for years to come. For example, during one eventual grueling ten-month stretch working on the database, with a baby at home, Schaeffer would spend each evening checking not on his child but his machines, only to wake again at two a.m. to check them again, staying up all night if necessary. He'd forget Valentine's Day, lamenting that night instead about a particularly tough loss Chinook had taken. "It's hard to mix competitive checkers and romance," he wrote later. While his wife, Steph, may have already suspected his obsessive tendencies, "she didn't have any idea to what extremes I might pursue my insanity," Schaeffer wrote. "Chinook was like a disease that infected my mind."

In August 1990, Schaeffer arrived at the Trace Motor Inn for the Mississippi State Checkers Championship to find "a dozen senior citizens playing and commenting on each other's games," many of them down to their undershirts to combat the oppressive triple-digit temperatures. The Canadian academic felt like a stranger in a strange land. A frail man in a green suit ambled over, saying, "You look like a checkers player! Can I help you?" Schaeffer thanked him but said he was sorry, he hadn't caught his name.

"My name is Marion Tinsley."

Schaeffer was risking his career and family to write a program to beat Tinsley, and he didn't even know what his nemesis looked like.

COMPETITIVE TOURNAMENT checkers games begin with the drawing of a card from a deck. The familiar game, played in living rooms and school cafeterias, with its initial checkers starting in the traditional formation shown below, is known on the competitive circuit as go-as-you-please, or GAYP. But expert players know this version so well that any game can be effortlessly steered toward a draw.

To combat this, the first three moves of a typical competitive game are determined randomly by drawing a card from a predetermined deck of opening moves. This version of checkers is known as three-move ballot or, simply, "three-move." This variation has been played for the game's most prestigious titles. Checkers openings come with colorful names: the White Doctor, the Octopus, the Skull Cracker, the Rattlesnake, the Rattlesnake II. For example, a ballot drawn before a game begins might read "11–16, 23–19, 16–23," indicating, in checkers notation, the starting square and the destination square of the pieces to be moved, by rule, in the first three moves of the game. (That particular sequence is called the Black Widow and is shown in the diagram below.) Once those three forced moves are made, play continues as usual. After that game, the players swap colors and play the opening's opposite side. Other variations include a two-move ballot or an eleven-man ballot, in which each player removes a checker from the board before the game starts.

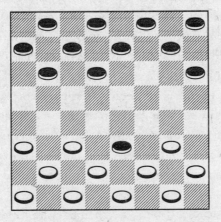

There are 174 possible three-move openings in checkers, but not all of these appear in the deck. Some would simply give too big an advantage to one side or the other, resulting in lopsided and, therefore, uninteresting play. The deck currently sanctioned by the American Checker Federation contains 156 openings, each of which seasons the game with its own unique flavor. Some of them remain bland, typically leading to uneventful draws. But some of them are sharp, bestowing on one side an instant advantage. In those sharp games, it is incumbent upon one player to attack, and upon the other player to fight for his life.

Top players have all of these openings memorized, of course, along with lengthy continuations beyond the third move. This is the sort of thing that Tinsley would have studied in his well-worn checkers bible. Whatever checkers lacks in complexity compared to, say, chess, its top players make up for in *depth*. Elite players can often see some twenty, thirty, or even forty moves ahead. This is what Tinsley meant when he said that playing checkers was like staring down a bottomless well.

Certain rare and powerful moves can sometimes evade the accumulated human knowledge. They haven't appeared in any of the books; they are small blind spots in the literature. When checkers players find them, whether via rote study or divine intervention, they cling to them like loose diamonds. Checkers players call these moves "cooks"—meaning that the opponent's goose is cooked. Something like 80 percent of games between master checkers players are draws. Masters hope to unleash a cook on an unsuspecting opponent now and again to turn a familiar draw into a rare and valuable victory.

Schaeffer set Chinook to work hunting down cooks—tiny cracks in human knowledge that his computer could infiltrate.

THE U.S. NATIONAL CHECKERS championship title has been contested since 1907. The 1990 edition featured forty players in its top division, all of whom descended upon the host city of Tupelo, Mississippi, the birthplace of Elvis Presley, in the middle of August. Tinsley was there, along with his mentor Asa Long and the man who'd brought him back to the competitive game, Don Lafferty. So was Charles Walker, Tinsley's promoter and partner in faith. And so was Chinook. The players took their seats at checkerboards in a "hall that looked like a barn," Schaeffer recalled. There was no air-conditioning.

Tinsley had won this event every time he'd competed since 1950. After the sixth round, Chinook trailed Tinsley by a measly two points. (Checkers tournaments are often played as series of four-game matches. A won match is worth four points and a drawn match two points.) In the seventh round, for the first time in a sanctioned event, the Beast and the Professor would meet across a checkerboard.

Tinsley and Schaeffer shook hands and began to play. The first game of four was drawn. The second game was drawn. The third game was drawn. The fourth game was drawn.

When Schaeffer's computer creation played in human tournaments, Schaeffer (or occasionally one of his colleagues) had to babysit the machine—typing in the opponents' moves, moving the physical pieces on the board after Chinook displayed its move on the screen, hitting the clock that controls the players' allotted time, and monitoring for bugs and errors. Other than those rote tasks, however, during tournament games Schaeffer had a lot of time on his hands. To bide his time, he would compare the current gameplay to the existing human literature, specifically a book called *Basic Checkers* by Richard Fortman, a central component of the game's canon. (Unlike other players, Schaeffer was allowed to consult books during games; he had committed to playing whatever move Chinook told him to make, no matter what.)

Basic Checkers is an opening book. Its seven volumes are divided into chapters, each of which is devoted to a sequence of moves that might begin a game. One is titled "9–14, 22–17, 5–9," another is "10–15, 21–17, 6–10," and so on. Within each chapter, continuations beyond the first three moves are discussed—best checkers practices distilled from decades of human experience and analysis. Certain fourth moves are weak, for example. Certain fifth moves are logical. Certain sixth moves are required, unless you want your game to erode into dust. These required moves are denoted in the book with an asterisk—"star moves."

Herein lies a deep irony about this project. In one sense, Schaeffer rooted for Chinook to make the plays listed in that book. That would mean that its algorithmic reasoning jibed with the finest accumulated human knowledge. But all the top humans knew that book by heart. If Chinook simply aped its moves, it could only ever hope for an endless series of draws. Schaeffer needed Chinook to do something truly *new*. Something nonhuman.

Chinook finished the tournament second, edging out Long, Lafferty, and another silicon rival called Checkers Experimental. Tinsley, the reigning world champion, finished first. (Of course.) By rule, the U.S. national champion earned the right to challenge for the world championship. Tinsley couldn't challenge himself. So, by default, in the summer of 1990, Chinook, a computer program, won the right to challenge Tinsley for the world checkers championship.

Schaeffer tried to call his spiritual predecessor and AI pioneer Arthur Samuel to tell him the news. But Samuel had died two weeks earlier. Schaeffer realized he was fighting humanity on two fronts: its intuition and its mortality. The truest test of his checkers program was the great Marion Tinsley. And Tinsley was growing old.

But Chinook energized the aging master. For decades, no human had challenged him like Chinook. After tough draws against the machine in the 1990 tournament, he had cheered loudly and looked to the heavens—"Thank you, Lord." He felt like a teenager again, at least over the checkerboard. Rather than distance himself from a seemingly losing battle with the machine, Tinsley embraced it. Perhaps he would have preferred to put it this way: "Iron sharpeneth iron; so a man sharpeneth the countenance of his friend."

Thanks to the vagaries of competitive checkers' scheduling and logistics, a world championship match would still be two years away, leaving ample time for further analysis, testing, and improvement. In 1991, a former student of Schaeffer's heard about Chinook and offered to help. The alumnus worked at Lawrence Livermore National Laboratory, fifty miles east of San Francisco. The lab owned a BBN TC2000, a gleaming black monolithic supercomputer that was used by the laboratory's scientists to study things such as cold matter Monte Carlo photonics, mixed-zone Eulerian hydrodynamics, and plasma simulations for fusion energy devices, according to an internal lab paper. For decades, the focus of Lawrence Livermore has been nuclear weapons, and this expensive machine furthered that pursuit. The paper did not mention, however, the computer's next task: it would contribute to the utter destruction of checkers.

Schaeffer and his team were granted access to the machine when it was idle, via a network connection from Edmonton. An hour on the supercomputer was an invaluable resource. "Instead of a bicycle," Schaeffer recalled, "I now had access to a Lamborghini." And it was a resource that Schaeffer exploited to frightening effect. In the spring of 1992, Schaeffer received startling word from a university computer administrator: an investigation had been opened into possible criminal activity on the school's network. Fully 80 percent of all the western internet traffic between Canada and the United States was coming through Schaeffer's office. But that was just Schaeffer and his Chinook team, sending checkers positions between the University of Alberta and the nuclear weapons research lab in California.

Schaeffer had to be "wrestled away" from his work with the Lawrence Livermore supercomputer to take his wife, Steph, to the hospital. She was in labor; their daughter was being born. Weeks later, Schaeffer left his wife and their newborn alone once again. Charles Walker, the Mississippi checkers booster, had arranged a match.

Schaeffer held the unorthodox view that his computer program ought to be able simply to compete for the human world title. "You can't discriminate based on race, religion, or sex," he wrote. "You shouldn't discriminate based on a computational model." In his view, Tinsley's natural abilities were every bit as human as Schaeffer's skill at designing a tool to match them. Walker, the secretary of the American Checker Federation, disagreed. After extensive lobbying, the ACF agreed to sanction four separate world titles: man versus man, woman versus woman, machine versus machine, and human versus machine. A $10,000 prize fund was arranged, and terms were agreed on. Tinsley hadn't lost a single game of checkers in six years. He'd lost only three times since 1950. The match with Chinook would begin in one year.

By the summer of 1992, Chinook was equipped with all of the endgames up to seven pieces, along with a big chunk of the eight-piece database—tens of billions of checkers positions in total, in all of which it was guaranteed to play perfectly. (Fixing a single error in the seven-piece database had cost the project more than a month.) It also had an opening library of thousands of moves culled from the best of the published human literature by Norman Treloar. After hardware upgrades, it was running in parallel on eight processors in a refrigerator-sized machine.

Tinsley, now sixty-five years old, naturally opted for more human preparation. Before the match, he invited Don Lafferty, his one true disciple and the man who had promised to quit drinking if he returned to competitive checkers, to stay at his home for intensive study and practice. Lafferty, fifty-nine, brought along his checkers library, its books' margins filled with years of handwritten analysis. Lafferty would wake in the middle of the night, wander the house, and find Tinsley still up, working in his bed with the books and his miniature checkerboard.

The world championship match would last forty games and take place at the same Park Lane Hotel in London where Chinook had successfully debuted against silicon competition three years earlier. As Schaeffer put it: "For the first time in history in an intellectual domain, man must defend his supremacy against the challenge of a computer."

The British press was out in force, fascinated by the born-again American professor in the green suit and colorful Jesus tie pin defending the species against the machine, like Saint George against the dragon. To the *Guardian*, Tinsley said, "I have a better programmer than Chinook. His was Jonathan, mine was the Lord." To the *Independent*, he added, "I don't want to let my programmer down, and I'm sure I won't." And while he preferred more evangelistic congregations, Tinsley spent the morning before the first game "reprogramming" himself at an Anglican chapel not far from the playing venue.

The first game was a tense draw over five and a half hours of play; to confirm the draw, Chinook peered nineteen moves into the future to arrive safely at a conclusion in its endgame database. In the second game, Chinook played one of its "cooks," a move criticized by human experts in the audience as "ugly." Despite the aesthetics, Tinsley defended accurately—another draw. Game Three was a "peaceful" draw. Game Four was another draw.

Treloar operated Chinook for the fifth game as Schaeffer broke for tea. Something slipped in the opening; Chinook erred and went down the computational equivalent of nearly half a checker. The program managed to fight back and equalize the game. At one point, it had a choice of two moves in a complex middle game. One led to a draw and the other to a sure loss, but at the time Chinook evaluated them as equal. It was programmed to decide arbitrarily between two equal moves. Chinook chose wrong. Tinsley won. With five more minutes of computation, the machine would have found the right answer, and the game would have been a draw.

Tinsley had drawn blood from the dragon. As was revealed in the game's postmortem analysis, the problem wasn't in Chinook's programming but in its database. There were mistakes in Fortman's *Basic Checkers*. These errors were known by certain players, but the book hadn't sold enough copies to warrant a second, corrected edition. One needed to search more than twenty moves deep into the game to find the weakness. Just as human ingenuity had built Chinook, so human errors had infected it.

Game Six was a draw. In Game Seven, Tinsley finally erred, allowing a would-be victory to descend into yet another draw. Tinsley hadn't been sleeping well, he wrote in his notes on the match, admitting, "The resulting mental fatigue really began to hit me." Chinook won Game Eight, and the match was tied. On his twenty-sixth move of that game, Tinsley, playing the white pieces in the position pictured, resigned and extended his hand in congratulations. A Tinsley loss was so rare—this was the first in seven years—that the crowd assumed the players were agreeing to a draw.* The Chinook team's ostensibly celebratory dinner took on the cast of a funeral. They had gotten what they wished for and the regret that came along with it. They had defeated the great old man. Schaeffer recalled being interviewed afterward by a journalist from a Christian newspaper: "Are you the devil?" the reporter asked.

The next five games were drawn. Chinook won the fourteenth, taking the lead in the match. For the first time, Schaeffer recalled,

---

* If white moves to create a king on d8, for example, black wins with the following line: c7 to b6, a5 jumps to c7, c3 jumps to a5, c5 to d6, a5 to b6, a3 to b4, b6 to a5, b4 to c5, and finally a5 to b6, trapping a piece. That's a trip down the checkers well for you.

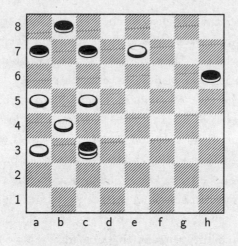

Tinsley looked old. "In contrast to the other team members, I felt a little sad that Chinook had been that successful because he was a god to serious checkers players like me," Treloar told me. "One win against Marion might be hoped for, but two wins was something of a shock." The next three games were drawn.

The Park Lane Hotel staff had been instructed, after each August day's play, to turn the lights off and leave the air-conditioning on. The night before the eighteenth game, they'd done the opposite. Play was delayed that morning as desperate attempts were made to cool what had become a very hot hall in which Chinook's hardware had been sitting overnight, baking. On the seventeenth move of the eighteenth game, Chinook's all-seeing eye recognized the position in its archive—Tinsley had played it before. Not only that, the program thought it held the advantage. It considered how best to proceed. It searched fifteen moves ahead and then seventeen moves and then tried for nineteen, for which it gave itself some extra time. It then displayed a message on Schaeffer's screen: "Time up but search unstable!"

It continued to search the tree and refused to make a move. It displayed that same message again and again as a wave of nausea overcame its operator. Schaeffer and his colleagues tried to reboot the program, but it kept on searching, lost somewhere deep in the bottomless well. The Chinook team had no choice but to resign the game. The match was tied again, and the problem never entirely diagnosed—the heat or, perhaps, simple program bugs. "Divine retribution has also been suggested," reported the *Independent*. The problem eventually disappeared. The next six games were draws.

A refreshed Tinsley, who'd spent his off days in prayer, was now playing the toughest checkers of his life across the table from an unshaven, unwashed computer science professor. Tinsley won the twenty-fifth game. The next thirteen games would be draws. When ten games of the forty remained in the world championship, Schaeffer's wife, Steph, and nine-month-old daughter, Rebecca, arrived in London to cheer him on. Schaeffer couldn't even pick them up from the airport. He had to tend to Chinook.

Tinsley won yet again in the thirty-ninth game, and it was over: four wins for the human, two wins for the machine, and thirty-three draws. Despite fatigue and a blistering technological assault, this was surely some of the finest checkers ever played by a human. "Three cheers for human beings," Tinsley shouted in triumph over the applause as Chinook resigned the decisive game. "And that includes Jonathan."

The loser's share of the championship's prize fund was $4,000, all but $400 of which had been spent on travel, lodging, food, and other essentials. Treloar thought the rest of the money should be his. Much of his early and important work on Chinook had been unpaid; Schaeffer had sent him only "the occasional $1,000." There was an ugly argument in which "tempers flared and common sense was forgotten," Schaeffer recalled.

Their real conflict may have been philosophical. Treloar, like Samuel before him, was less interested in winning than in learning. What good was Chinook as an AI if all it did was look up keyed-in human openings and precalculated endgames—if it didn't think for itself? "You will of course reply that beating Tinsley would prove something to the world," Treloar wrote in an email to Schaeffer. "Only I am not sure what that is."

Treloar also feared for checkers itself. "I worried that AI systems like Chinook might lower interest in the game," he told me. "No matter how good a human player is, she will realize that winning against the machine is impossible." Treloar left the project.

Schaeffer, now without his research partner, took a semester sabbatical at the University of Limburg (now the University of Maastricht), leaving his family behind as well. In the Netherlands, Schaeffer found an academic Eden of gaming AI. He was surrounded by experts in chess, international checkers, even Connect Four.

"In Maastricht I could work for hours on end at night, alone in my office, without fear of distraction," Schaeffer wrote. Like a sort of chimeric Rocky before a fight with Apollo Creed, Schaeffer and Chinook trained together in the Netherlands. Schaeffer exercised and lost weight. By the summer, more than two hundred computers, at universities in the Netherlands, Switzerland, and Canada, as well as a nuclear weapons lab in California, were working on Chinook— on its opening book, its middle-game search and evaluation, and its endgame database. Awaiting this behemoth was a lonesome sexagenarian professor from Ohio in a green suit and glasses.

While on sabbatical, Schaeffer received another letter from Charles Walker. Walker wrote that Tinsley sent his regards and, by the way, "Have you taken the time to investigate Jesus Christ yet? I believe you will find it more interesting than your records with Chinook."

Schaeffer returned home to Canada shortly before the planned rematch with Tinsley. But domestic life brought no respite from his crusade. "You're thinking about him again, aren't you?" his wife would lament as the two lay in bed. Inevitably, he was.

The Man-Machine World Championship rematch began in the summer of 1994, at the Computer Museum in Boston. The Chinook team rode into the Bay State with its saddlebags overflowing with fresh "cooks," which they had categorized by strength: more than forty silver, eight gold, and one plutonium. Chinook's weaponry was upgraded, too, as Silicon Graphics had flown in a new machine special for the match. Tinsley also arrived ready to fight. He had prepared about a dozen moves, he said, "to get the computer into trouble."

Monday, August 15. On the morning before the first game, Schaeffer met Tinsley, and the two walked the fifteen-minute route to the venue together, like two enemy gunslingers walking peaceably together toward the saloon. They chatted. Tinsley told Schaeffer what had happened to him the night before.

"I had a dream last night," Tinsley said. "In it, God told me that he loves you, too."

Schaeffer didn't know what to say and was silent.

"I know," Tinsley said. "I found it very disturbing."

They arrived at the museum and made their way to the playing hall, which was mostly empty, save for a small smattering of journalists and other onlookers. They took their seats in office chairs across a small table abutting an exposed brick wall. Silicon Graphics–branded banners framed the playing area: WORLD CHECKERS CHAMPIONSHIP. The computer monitor Schaeffer was working from loomed large over the table. Play began, but the golden cooks remained holstered. Games One and Two were draws. Games Three and Four were "easy draws." Game Five was a "boring draw." Game Six was a draw. One day done and no blood drawn.

The next playing day was Wednesday, August 17. The Chinook project had been running for nearly five and a half years. Tinsley took his seat again in his office chair across the small table and looked over to Schaeffer but not exactly *at* him. Tinsley's stomach was upset, he said. He wondered aloud if someone might take his place for the remainder of the match. Schaeffer, surprised, wondered why a stomachache ought to disrupt the championship. He suggested that they go see a doctor. They ended up at Massachusetts General Hospital. If anything should go wrong—you know, really *wrong*—Tinsley said, would Schaeffer please contact his twin sister, Mary, who he'd once worried was their parents' favored child. Tinsley added that he was "ready to go." The doctor gave him Maalox and Tylenol and asked him to take an X-ray. The results would be ready in the morning.

Thursday, August 18. Schaeffer awoke early and called Tinsley to see if they might head to the checkers venue together again. And, by the way, how was his stomach?

"I resign the match and the title to Chinook," Tinsley responded. Schaeffer put his head in his hotel pillow and began to cry.

Tinsley's X-ray had revealed a lump on his pancreas. A few days later, a biopsy showed that it was cancerous. He left Boston to begin chemotherapy treatment. Chinook stayed and completed the match against Tinsley's ad hoc replacement, Don Lafferty. On August 25, 1994, before a crowd of fewer than twenty people, Schaeffer and the Chinook team accepted their trophy as the machine victors of the Man-Machine World Championship.

Tinsley died on April 3, 1995. He is buried in Columbus, Ohio, and a checkerboard is etched into his gravestone, showing a position from a game against Chinook. Also etched into it is "Hebrews 13:1." That Bible verse reads, "Let brotherly love continue."

After Tinsley's death, Schaeffer lost his passion for the tournament scene. His wife, Steph, operated Chinook for its final competitive game, in November 1996. She was getting Rebecca ready for school, sending moves at seven-thirty in the morning from her Edmonton home via a network connection to a checkers tournament in Virginia.

"SOLVING" HAS A PARTICULAR meaning when it comes to the mathematics of games. It means, essentially, that you can play like God. It means that you know, and can prove mathematically that you know, the optimal moves, and the optimal responses to those moves, and the optimal responses to *those* moves, and so on to the end of the game. A by-product of this knowledge is that if you solve a game, you also know, to a mathematical certainty, how any particular match will end.

Tic-tac-toe, for example, is solved. One can set up any possible tic-tac-toe board and prove, fairly easily, that a certain move is the best move. With optimal play, tic-tac-toe, of course, is a guaranteed draw. Connect Four was solved by two researchers independently in 1988, one of whom worked down the hall from Schaeffer in Maastricht. With optimal play, Connect Four is a guaranteed win for the player who goes first. That is, you could beat God in Connect Four if you went first. Awari, a game in the mancala family, and nine-men's morris, an ancient strategy game also known as mill, are also solved games—both are guaranteed draws.

Chess, however, is not solved. While the best chess programs today are light-years better than the best humans, even a top program could not guarantee a win or even a draw against God. Therefore, we don't know the outcome of a perfectly played game of chess, though many suspect it would be a draw. Getting the better of God is a difficult proposition. A mathematician named Hans-Joachim Bremermann, writing in 1967, argued that "no computer, however constructed, will ever be able to examine the entire tree of possible move sequences of the game of chess."

With Tinsley dead, Schaeffer might have abandoned competitive play, but he let his machines continue to run, seeking the ultimate solution to checkers. He'd solved chunks of the game already—that's what the endgame databases were all about. If eight checkers or fewer were on the board, Chinook always knew to a mathematical certainty what the best moves were and how the game would end. But extending those databases by brute force—to nine, ten, and eventually the initial twenty-four pieces—wasn't feasible. Schaeffer estimated that with optimistic levels of data compression, a fully solved database of every position in checkers would require one billion gigabytes. That sort of storage space would've cost more than $1 billion at the time. (Even today, with hardware advances, it'd likely cost some $20 million.)

Instead, solving checkers would require a few strokes of relatively inexpensive human ingenuity, creative shortcuts to cut down on the raw data required. Imagine the game of checkers—that is, *every possible* game of checkers—as a giant ice cream cone. At the bottom is a single point, the number of possible positions when there are zero checkers on the board: one. At the top is a wide mouth, the number of possible positions when there are twelve checkers a side on the board: 500 billion billion. Some of the work at the bottom of the cone was already done by the endgame databases. Therefore, what remained to be proved was that a player could, with a certain sequence of moves, force a winning—or, at the worst, drawing—path from the top of the cone down through its unknown middle and into its well-known endgames at the bottom. All day, every day, Chinook searched for such a path.

THE UNIVERSITY OF ALBERTA'S Department of Computing Science, Schaeffer's professional home, is an unassuming powerhouse. Despite the obvious difficulties in recruiting scientists to its frigid Edmonton campus during the discipline's traditional January–February job market window, it is ranked among the best AI programs in the world. The program's graduate students are consulted by professional poker players. More than one professor works on a complicated chess-Go hybrid called Amazons. Others consult for video game companies. Another is developing an artificial intelligence system for the sport of curling, which in Canada qualifies as work of high national importance.

I arrived on campus on a recent snowy, late-winter day. One professor's office shelves were lined with Rubik's Cubes of various sizes. Down the hall, another office was littered with paraphernalia for the board game Hex, a favorite of John Nash, a founding father of game theory.* Schaeffer, who at age sixty-three could now plausibly be mistaken for either Mel Brooks or Noam Chomsky, sat in his office amid the typical academic detritus of papers, coffee cups, boxes, and books—including the worn collection of Tinsley's games that he had maimed with his pocketknife decades earlier. There were the large rolls of magnetic tape, now obsolete, that held Chinook's early databases. There were also, stuffed in a large blue vinyl bag in the corner, two trophies from Man-Machine World Championships past, in bad need of a polish. One said: "Runner-up." The other, in letters twice as large: "Champion."

There was also a stack of copies of Schaeffer's own book—his take on the history of the project. The second edition of the programming memoir is dedicated to "Steph and Rebecca for their patience and love throughout. It's finally over. Really!" But the couple divorced—a human relationship lost to checkers and AI.

In Edmonton, the computer scientists cautioned me against anthropomorphizing AI programs, or granting them undue agency, or forgetting that there are always *humans* who created them. But as we sat amid the memorabilia and scholarly rubble, Schaeffer recalled the early years of Chinook, when both of his offspring were young. "I created something biological with my wife, and now I was creating something digital largely by myself," he said. "What's unfortunate is that I was playing with two creations—my daughter and my

---

*An early copy of Hex was regularly obsessed over in a Princeton grad student common room, where the game was known as "John" or "Nash."

program—and for whatever deep psychological reasons that maybe only therapy can figure out, I chose to spend most of my time with my digital creation rather than with my biological creation. Why that is so I do not know. The answer to that question may be something I don't *want* to know." (Steph Schaeffer declined an interview request for this book. "I'm not sure you want a lot of family stuff in a book about games," she said.)

Schaeffer and Tinsley devoted their lives to a game played with another person, but they were both often alone. In Tinsley's case, this seems to have been by choice; in Schaeffer's, it was through fault. For his part, Schaeffer is now forthcoming about the strife his checkers project caused. "I'm not trying to paint myself as an asshole," he said. "But if you tell a story and you only tell the good side and you don't touch on the reality, then you're deceiving people. To be an obsessive-compulsive scientist, it takes a lot of effort, and you get blinded by science. It's like people get blinded by religion or people get blinded by money. It takes a personal toll."

Schaeffer is also now desperate for his checkers project to be remembered. "In terms of the field of artificial intelligence, it's almost an invisible footnote," he said of Chinook. Perhaps his fear of a vanishing legacy is because other things have already disappeared. "It's easy to take family for granted, just because they're always there," he said. "But then one day maybe they're not there. And you say, 'Holy shit, what have I done?'"

THERE IS AN ODD, semi-tragic postscript to the Marion Tinsley story. When Charles Walker founded the International Checker Hall of Fame in 1979, he incorporated the museum into the so-called Château Walker, a twenty-acre Tudor-style estate in the woods of Petal, Mississippi, population ten thousand. The hall featured a seven-story tower, paintings adorned its walls, and Bibles filled its shelves. The site hosted some of Tinsley's world championship victories and was home to a statue of the legend. Schaeffer showed me old photos of himself in the Crown Room, sitting on its royally appointed bed.

Walker was reportedly a rich insurance tycoon, but in the fall of 2004, according to court documents, Walker twice met with a man, at an airport and in an RV, who gave him thousands of dollars in cash concealed in fabric softener, evidently to thwart the efforts of "dope-sniffing dogs." In exchange, Walker sent the man three checks: one from a personal account, one from the International Christian Church, and one from the International Checker Hall of Fame, in the amount of $20,000. Unbeknownst to Walker, the man was an undercover agent from U.S. Immigration and Customs Enforcement. Walker and he had struck a deal to launder $6 million in proceeds from narcotics trafficking, for which Walker had drafted phony employment papers claiming the man worked as a pilot and a consultant for a fictitious company. In June 2005, Walker was charged with money laundering in federal court. He pleaded guilty and was sentenced to sixty-three months in federal prison.

Walker resigned his positions in the world of checkers and closed the Hall of Fame. In 2007, with Walker incarcerated, the mansion that housed the hall was destroyed in a fire, along with nearly all of its checkers memorabilia, including the largest and second-largest checkerboards in the world. The Walker family reportedly suspected an electrical fire caused by bats in the mansion's tower. Investigators later sorted through some five feet of rubble, but no cause was ever determined, and the fire and police departments have no records of the incident, the Petal city attorney told me. Perhaps it's fitting that this monument to the game fell when it did, given what else happened to the game that same year.

On Sunday, April 29, 2007, at 5:01 p.m., Schaeffer was returning home from a business trip, sitting in an airport lounge in San Francisco eating peanuts with his daughter, Rebecca, whose childhood had unfolded during her father's checkers project. While waiting to board, Schaeffer logged on to his university account to check the progress of his program. Chinook had been silently seeking the solution to checkers all along. Schaeffer was dismayed at what he saw. The logs were empty; the machines on the other end weren't running. Schaeffer slowly realized that the machines weren't running because there was no work left to be done. After eighteen years, he had finished. With perfect play, he'd just proved, the game of checkers is a mathematically guaranteed draw. He'd found the bottom of the well.

Schaeffer had tied with God.

"Checkers is solved," he said softly.

Rebecca smiled and gave him a hug. "Congratulations, Dad."

CHESS

And we shall play a game of chess,
Pressing lidless eyes and waiting for
a knock upon the door.

—T. S. ELIOT, *THE WASTE LAND*

FRIDAY AT DUSK, SPRINGTIME in Manhattan's Greenwich Village. City dwellers and students were wandering through Washington Square Park, making out on its benches, skateboarding in its empty fountain, and pretending to ignore the drug dealers who made the park their office.

"Smoke? Smoke?" they called.

The park's grizzled chess hustlers sat in the misty evening at stone tables in the park's southwest corner. In front of them were thirty-two pieces, half black, half white, standing tall on fields of sixty-four squares. Littering the margins were half-smoked packs of menthols and the remains of cigars, Bic lighters, wads of singles and fives, and empty coffee cups. There were also dual-faced chess clocks, their digits ready to count down the five minutes that define a blitz-paced game.

I approached a table, assessing the countenance of my would-be opponent, a man of about fifty in a beanie and a worn houndstooth jacket who stared at the carnage his previous game had wrought on the board.

"So, you want a game?" he asked.

"What'll it cost me?" I wondered aloud.

"Don't worry, brother, we'll figure that out together."

A strong spine of chess runs through New York City: from the Chess Forum north a few blocks to Washington Square Park, from the Marshall Chess Club to Union Square Park, where they play on old office chairs and upturned milk crates. The chess tables in Washington Square Park have their own musical score: *click, thwack, click, thwack.* Plastic pieces on marble tabletops and quick hands on chess clocks. Bobby Fischer played here as a kid. Stanley Kubrick was a regular. Countless grandmasters have sat down on these benches, often incognito. In the popular perception, chess is a plodding game of deep concentration. Reimagined by street hustlers who eke out livings through the strategic manipulation of little plastic statues, the game is bebop, improvisational and virtuosic.

In 1917, the artist Marcel Duchamp and some friends climbed to the top of the park's grand marble arch to declare the park and its bohemian neighborhood the Free and Independent Republic of Washington Square. They ascended armed with food, liquor, cap guns, and balloons. Soused, they recited poetry, tied the balloons to the parapet, and fired the cap guns into the night. Duchamp had written a declaration for the occasion; it consisted of the single repeated word "Whereas." Once the revolutionaries descended, the authorities locked the door to the arch forever.

Duchamp soon left New York for Buenos Aires and announced he was devoting his life to chess. He meant it. In Argentina, Duchamp crafted his own custom chess pieces, carving them out of wood. Photographs depict art deco monarchs, storybook rooks, and tragic bowing knights. Duchamp was a strong player. He represented France in a handful of Chess Olympiads and played alongside the world champion Alexander Alekhine.

"I have come to the conclusion that while all artists are not chess players, all chess players are artists," Duchamp said.

Other top players see it this way, too. Garry Kasparov, one of the all-time greats, contends that "chess is a unique cognitive nexus, a place where art and science come together in the human mind and are then refined and improved by experience." Some see the game as dialectic. "Chess can never reach its height by following in the path of science," the former world champion José Raúl Capablanca once said. "Let us, therefore, . . . turn the struggle of technique into a battle of ideas." Anatoly Karpov, another former world champion and Kasparov's rival, said that "chess is everything—art, science, and sport."

Others are more technocratic, their views shaped in large part by a quixotic engineering project stretching back to the Enlightenment. Magnus Carlsen, the former wunderkind and now reigning world champion, believes that chess is a science. For art, he said in the midst of his recent title defense, you'd "have to look elsewhere."

THE BEST THEORIES place chess's origins in India around fifteen hundred years ago, where it was called *chaturanga* and had likely been invented as a miniaturized military exercise. The pieces, for example, comport with elements of the actual Indian army of the day: the all-important raja, or king; the chariot, or modern-day rook; and the elephant, or modern-day bishop. While a debate continues to simmer over the game's precise genesis, some researchers contend that chess did not evolve from ancient games over decades and centuries, as many others had; rather, it was invented, at some single moment in time, by some singular genius.

"Arguably the really striking feature in the long development of chess is its subsequent triumph in the Darwinian competitive process which has kept some games alive while driving others into disuse and even obliteration from the records," writes the historian Richard Eales. Chess was the fittest game, in other words, and it survived. By the high Middle Ages, chess was being played all across Eurasia, from China to Scandinavia to Spain, down to northern Africa and up to Iceland. And despite its relatively complex rules, which would seem to make uniform dissemination unlikely, an identical version of the game was in use throughout both Christendom and the Islamic world by the twelfth century. According to legend, a visiting king asked a caliph, "What is chess?" The caliph responded, "What is life?"

In Europe, the game became "a picture of Western feudal society in miniature," the pieces settling into their familiar iconography: king, queen, bishop, knight. The game spread orally in royal courts and through documents circulating among clerics, as well as through secular poetry. A book dated to the early twelfth century, the *Disciplina Clericalis*, lists chess as one of the seven skills required of a good knight.

In the East, chaturanga cleaved into distinct modern games, including *xiangqi*, or Chinese chess, and *shogi*, or Japanese chess. Each of these bears at once obvious similarities to chess and also important differences from it. In xiangqi, for example, there is a piece called the cannon and special areas of the board called the river and the palace. In shogi, nearly every piece, like pawns in Western chess, can be promoted, and captured pieces can be returned to the board by the capturing player.

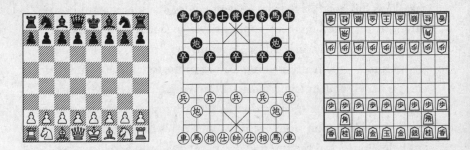

The boards and starting positions for chess, xiangqi, and shogi

Over the centuries, as chess traveled from Indian military exercise to European chivalric refinement, the game became a metaphorical stand-in for any number of human traits: cunning, daring, wisdom, fortitude, perseverance, perceptiveness, strategic planning, and tactical acumen. Chess skill became a rhetorical stand-in for intelligence itself.

"If one could devise a successful chess machine," the computing pioneers Allen Newell, J. C. Shaw, and Herbert Simon wrote in 1958, "one would seem to have penetrated to the core of human intellectual endeavor."

IN THE SPRING OF 1770 in Vienna, in the royal court of Austria-Hungary, an audience including the empress Maria Theresa gathered around a cabinet four feet wide, three feet tall, and two and a half feet deep. This moment of unveiling had been eagerly awaited. Behind the cabinet sat a life-sized figure of a man carved out of wood and dressed in fashionable Ottoman garb, a robe with ermine trim and a turban. On the top of the cabinet sat a chessboard.

Wolfgang von Kempelen, the court scientist and the contraption's creator, announced to the assembled crowd that he had built an automaton chess player, a fully mechanical machine capable of playing the game on its own against a human challenger. Automatons were all the rage in the eighteenth century—there was a famous automaton flute player and an automaton duck that gave the impression of eating, digesting, and defecating. But no inventor had attempted something so explicitly *human*. To demonstrate his device's authenticity, like a magician before an illusion, von Kempelen unlocked and opened a door on the front of the cabinet to reveal "an elaborate mechanism of densely packed wheels, cogs, levers, and clockwork machinery, prominent among which was a large horizontal cylinder with a complex configuration of protruding studs on its surface, similar to that found in a clockwork music box," according to journalist Tom Standage's history of the device. He lit a candle so the onlookers could see into every dark corner.

Removing red and white ivory pieces from a drawer, von Kempelen set the board. A count from the royal audience was selected as the automaton's first opponent. Von Kempelen inserted a key and wound the automaton's clockwork. With a whirr, the machine turned its head, reached out a gloved left hand, and grasped and moved a piece. The count was quickly defeated.

Early witnesses were credulous and impressed. "It seems impossible to obtain a more perfect knowledge of mechanics than this gentleman has done," read a letter in a Paris newspaper. "No one has been able to produce so wonderful a machine . . . an automaton which can play chess with the most skillful players."

The contraption, now known as the Mechanical Turk, or simply the Turk, thanks to its attire, toured the world to great fanfare. It held court at the Café de la Régence, an important nineteenth-century Parisian chess salon frequented by Voltaire and Rousseau. In 1783, it defeated Benjamin Franklin, a chess nut who had just signed the Treaty of Paris. In 1809, it thrice dispensed with Napoleon Bonaparte, the emperor of France—who, it's said, was accustomed to functionaries letting him win. The Turk went up against François-André Danican Philidor, one of the greatest players of the eighteenth century, who won but described the encounter as the most fatiguing game of chess he'd ever played. Philidor believed the machine to be a genuine— and, therefore, terrifying—chess player. But the illusion had already begun to crumble. In the *Journal des Savants*, members of the Academy of Sciences concluded that the Turk ran on a combination of actual mechanical inventiveness and magnetic chicanery.

The Turk was a fraud, of course, though a mechanically impressive one. Over the decades, the device concealed a series of human chess masters inside a small, well-hidden compartment. The machin-

ery did not extend as deeply into the cabinet as it appeared, allowing the secret operator to clamber in and place himself on a sliding
seat. After the exhibitor's ruse appeased the audience, the operator
would light a small candle, the smoke from which vented through
the Turk's turban. The operator held a small chessboard of his own,
which was connected to a sophisticated mechanism that controlled
the movements of the Turk's arm, and a knob, which clenched its
fingers. And there were magnets involved. They sat under the public board connected to metal disks, and the secret operator watched
these to see when and where the Turk's opponent had moved. The
identity of the original secret operator is unknown.

A young Edgar Allan Poe further dissected the ruse. He'd seen
the Turk as the machine toured America—the device had long out-
lived its creator and been sold to new ownership. The inventor of the
detective story was both fascinated and suspicious. In a lengthy article in 1836, he argued that a human had to be hidden within its inner
workings. This essay is regarded as a schematic for the author's later
mysteries. Poe perceived that the Turk was nothing like the early
mechanical calculating machines of the day, which could add, sub-
tract, and multiply. Chess wasn't deterministic—like, say, the solution to a quadratic equation. Chess depended on the moves of one's
opponent, and the matter of the best move was subject to human
reasoning and opinion. "It is quite certain that the operations of the
Automaton are regulated by *mind*, and by nothing else," Poe wrote.
Chess, he argued, was the unique domain of human intelligence,
irreplicable by a machine.

But the fraud precipitated genuine effects. Around 1800, when
he was eight years old, a boy named Charles Babbage visited a
museum in London that specialized in automatons. Babbage was
especially taken by an automaton dancing woman with a bird on
her finger—"Her eyes were full of imagination, and irresistible." In
1819, Babbage saw the Turk and was impressed by its play, though

suspicious of its authenticity. The next year, he saw it again, played against it, and lost. He was convinced that it was being operated by a human, but he began to wonder if an authentic chess-playing machine could actually be built.

Babbage would go on to conceive of the first digital programmable computer, known as the Analytical Engine. Its predecessor, the Difference Engine, composed entirely of mechanical components, could compute data such as actuarial, astronomical, logarithmic, and tide tables. He became the father of computing. At a party in 1833, he met Ada Lovelace. She was entranced by a demonstration of the Analytical Engine. She realized that it "might act upon other things besides numbers . . . the Engine might compose elaborate and scientific pieces of music of any degree of complexity or extent." Lovelace became the first computer programmer and the mother of computing. "In other words," Standage writes, "as a result of Babbage's visit to Merlin's Mechanical Museum, the subjects of chess, intelligence, and computing were well on their way to becoming inextricably intertwined."

The Turk burned in a fire in Philadelphia in 1854. But in 1912, almost a century and a half after the Turk's first royal audience in Vienna, a Spanish civil engineer and inventor named Leonardo Torres y Quevedo, influenced by Babbage, created the first real and functional chess machine. It was called El Ajedrecista—the Chess Player. And while it could play only a small slice of the game—endgames of a king and a rook versus a king—the device is considered the first computer game of any sort. It could win with the rook in fewer than fifty moves, regardless of the defense its human opponent employed.

"CAN MACHINES THINK?" That was the question Alan Turing considered in a paper published in 1950. Turing, a Cambridge- and Princeton-trained English mathematician and computer scientist, had already helped the Allies win the war by cracking the code of the Nazis' Enigma machine; one estimate credits this work with saving millions of lives. Chess was the young Turing's most social activity, and at Bletchley Park, where he did his wartime cryptography in secret, chess was something he could safely discuss when off duty. "As a practical model for mechanical 'thinking' it fascinated Alan to the point of obsession," writes Andrew Hodges, his biographer.

That same year, Claude Shannon, another giant of his field, published a paper. Shannon was an applied mathematician at Bell Labs; two years earlier he'd published "A Mathematical Theory of Communication" in the lab's in-house journal. With that single revolutionary document, which introduced the term "bit," he founded a branch of science known as information theory, which straddles computer science, probability, statistics, and electrical engineering and makes nearly every aspect of the contemporary world possible. At the office, Shannon was a colorful figure. He unicycled down its hallways, sometimes while juggling. Either that or he hopped about on a pogo stick. And he set up camp in the office common areas, where he would take on all comers in chess. In a life of many, varied, and sometimes fleeting interests, chess was a constant for Shannon. He was good enough to give the world champion Mikhail Botvinnik a run for his money. Word of Shannon's talent spread, attracting new challengers to the lounge at Bell Labs. "At least one supervisor became somewhat worried" about the effect of all this play on office productivity, write Jimmy Soni and Rob Goodman, his biographers.

Chess was the subject of the article Shannon published in 1950. "This paper is concerned with the problem of constructing a computing routine or 'program' for a modern general purpose computer which will enable it to play chess," he wrote. "Although perhaps of no practical importance, the question is of theoretical interest, and it is hoped that a satisfactory solution of this problem will act as a wedge in attacking other problems of a similar nature and of greater significance." Shannon's précis articulates the importance of chess to AI:

> The chess machine is an ideal one to start with, since: (1) the problem is sharply defined both in allowed operations (the moves) and in the ultimate goal (checkmate); (2) it is neither so simple as to be trivial nor too difficult for satisfactory solution; (3) chess is generally considered to require "thinking" for skillful play; a solution of this problem will force us either to admit the possibility of mechanized thinking or to further restrict our concept of "thinking"; (4) the discrete structure of chess fits well into the digital nature of modern computers.

The rest of the paper lays out the basic mathematics that would make a real chess machine tick. As he had with information theory, with a single publication Shannon had erected a scaffolding onto which countless others would build; according to Google Scholar, the article has been cited more than sixteen hundred times.

Turing was another early proponent of computer chess. By 1952, he had written code for a chess-playing program. But the computers of the day had neither the speed nor the storage to execute it. So Turing executed it himself, leafing with every move through his scattered sheets of typewriter paper and performing the voluminous calculations they prescribed by hand. For example, the first step of many was to "count the square root of the number of moves the piece can make from the position, counting a capture as two moves, and not forgetting that the king must not be left in check." As the Turk was a human in the guise of a machine, so Turing was a machine in the guise of a human. An initial test of his program against a student opponent took hours. The game was filled with lengthy silences of longhand arithmetic punctuated by Turing's "hoots and growls" of disappointment as he debated intervening when he saw his program missing obviously better positions. The human won after twenty-nine painstaking moves. Nevertheless, this contest, in Turing's bare office in Manchester, was the first full game of chess a human ever played against a program.

Other early pioneers thought the rest would come easy. "Within ten years a digital computer will be the world's chess champion, unless the rules bar it from competition," predicted AI trailblazers Herbert Simon and Allen Newell in 1958. This prediction was wrong for two reasons. First, it was off by about thirty years. Second, they supposed that computers would "use processes that are closely parallel to human problem-solving processes." Nothing would be further from the truth.

Shannon's paper described two strategies for programming a computer to play chess. Type A programs employed brute-force search and evaluation, analyzing every possible move, and all possible subsequent moves, no matter how unpromising they might look to a human observer. In other words, they exploited the computer's chief strength: sheer calculation. Shannon, however, thought such a player would be "both slow and weak." Type B programs were more selective, examining only certain small yet promising branches on chess's enormous tree. In other words, they exploited something like human intuition. Early computer scientists thought the successful players would be Type B, but with the rapid expansion of computing power, computer scientists were lured into pursuing Type A. It's hardly the only time technology has strayed from its biological inspiration; just because a bird flaps its wings doesn't mean an airplane ought to.

In the mid-1950s, scientists at Los Alamos National Laboratory, the birthplace of the atomic bomb, built an early game of computer chess. But their machines were only strong enough for an abridged version of the game on a six-by-six board, sans bishops. Around the same time, IBM recruited programmers with an ad describing the newfangled job as perfect for "those who enjoy playing chess." In the 1970s, Ken Thompson, the designer of the Unix operating system, created Belle, the first master-level chess program. Thompson realized that *speed* was king; the more positions a program searched, he found, the better it played. In other words: "Search is knowledge." In the late 1970s and early '80s, Kathleen and Dan Spracklen dominated the early microcomputer years with their program Sargon. In high school, Kathleen had chanced upon a book describing Claude Shannon's work. At a major tournament, her microcomputer defeated a $6 million mainframe. The 1980s saw the first grandmasters fall to machines. Researchers began aiming for the world's best human.

"Ridiculous!" that human, Garry Kasparov, said in 1989. "A machine will always remain a machine, that is to say a tool to help the player work and prepare. Never shall I be beaten by a machine! Never will a program be invented which surpasses human intelligence."

MURRAY CAMPBELL LOOKED every bit the IBM man. On a recent visit to the corporate research campus, I found him sitting at his desk, clean-shaven and balding, his light blue dress shirt tucked neatly into his pleated khakis. His company ID badge, worn and faded, was neatly clipped to his breast pocket. Campbell's desk was strewn with crusty computers and keyboards, and the shelves of his office groaned under the weight of books, among them *A History of Chess* and *The MIT Encyclopedia of the Cognitive Sciences*. In one corner was a stack of chessboards, and in another was a large wooden trophy shaped like a knight. On a wall he'd pinned an old *New Yorker* cartoon, in which a man faces off over the board against a toaster. "I remember when you could only lose a chess game to a supercomputer," its caption read.* Campbell was a central member of the team that created Deep Blue, the supercomputer that defeated Kasparov. More than twenty years after his technological triumph, we discussed his legacy, and that of his supercomputer creation.

Campbell was trained in computer science at Carnegie Mellon University, in Pittsburgh. In the late eighties at Carnegie Mellon, two computer chess projects ran in parallel. One, Hitech, was overseen by the famous professor Hans Berliner. Berliner was a grandmaster and world champion in correspondence chess, a lumbering game played through the mail. The other project, ChipTest, according to team member Feng-hsiung Hsu, was the domain of "a group of free-willed, mostly unsupervised graduate students." These self-described troublemakers scrounged hardware parts from the department and cadged time on valuable workstations. Initially, Campbell had a foot in both camps. But he recognized that the ChipTest approach could scale faster. It was built, above all, for speed. *Search is knowledge.* At the 1989 World Computer Chess Championships, the troublemakers beat the tenured professor. Claude Shannon, the father of information theory, handed them the winner's trophy.

Between 1985 and 1989, ChipTest became Deep Thought became Deep Blue. ChipTest had been so named because it was just that—a tester of computer chips for chess. Deep Thought was named after the supercomputer in *The Hitchhiker's Guide to the Galaxy*. In the novel, a race of hyperintelligent aliens create the computer to answer the "Ultimate Question of Life, the Universe, and Everything." After millions of years of calculation, the computer answers "42," but by that point no one remembers the question. Hsu and Campbell joined IBM in 1989. Deep Blue was a play on IBM's

---

* Another cartoon from the magazine features a man talking to his microwave: "No, I don't want to play chess. I just want you to reheat the lasagna."

nickname, Big Blue, chosen via a contest run by the corporation's communications department.

"A chess machine has three main components," Hsu explains in his account of the creation of Deep Blue. "The *move generator* which finds the chess moves, the *evaluation function* which assesses the quality of the positions reached when the chess machine looks ahead, and the *search control* which guides analysis of move sequences examined by the chess machine." In addition to searching very fast, Deep Blue was guided by human knowledge, fine-tuned parameters based on human ideas about the game, and an extensive "opening book." IBM also had a top grandmaster on the payroll. Today this combination of speedy calculation within human-defined parameters is sometimes called "good old-fashioned AI," or GOFAI.

In 1988, Garry Kasparov was asked if a computer would beat a grandmaster by the year 2000. "No way," he replied, "and if any grandmaster has difficulties playing computers, I would be happy to provide my advice." Kasparov did have experience playing machines. Three years prior, he had played against thirty-two different computers at once in a simultaneous exhibition; eight of the computers were named after him. He won every game.

Within a decade, in May 1997, Campbell and Hsu's machine would humble the great Kasparov in an event that is today seen as a watershed in the long marriage of computers and games. When the event began, in a postmodern skyscraper in midtown Manhattan, Kasparov had reigned as world champion for twelve years. He had achieved the highest rating in history and was at that point likely the greatest player who had ever lived. The match in New York was actually the second time Kasparov and Deep Blue played. They had first met a year earlier in Philadelphia, where Kasparov held off the machine over six games, four to two. It wasn't easy, though. After one particularly grueling game, according to the grandmaster's computer consultant, Kasparov "went back to his hotel room, stripped to his underpants, and stared at the ceiling for a long time." In postgame comments in Philadelphia, Kasparov said of the machine, "In certain kinds of positions, it sees so deeply that it plays like God."

"To some extent, this is a defense of the whole human race," Kasparov said. "Computers play such a huge role in society. They're everywhere. But there is a frontier that they must not cross. They must not cross into the area of human creativity."

Working in a room at IBM called the "Chess Lab," Campbell and Hsu and their colleagues had developed not just a piece of software but, rather, a purpose-built supercomputer, an IBM RISC System/6000 packed with nearly five hundred custom chess chips. It looked like a very large black refrigerator and weighed 1.4 tons. The beast could analyze some two hundred million chess positions per second, with a theoretical maximum of one billion. Kasparov could analyze maybe three. Another machine using this IBM architecture would briefly become the fastest supercomputer in the world and was used by the Department of Energy to simulate nuclear weapons tests.

In New York, the 1997 rematch would be the best of six games, with wins worth one point, draws a half point for each player. Team Deep Blue set up camp in a closet on the thirty-fifth floor of the Equitable Center, an area that the supercomputer made uncomfortably warm even for someone in a T-shirt and shorts, Hsu recalled. Kasparov had a private room with plenty of bananas and bottled water.

The games themselves took place elsewhere on the same floor in a studio staged like an upper-middle-class suburban study. Reproductions of gauzy paintings in gold frames hung on the walls. Stage left was a bookshelf holding not one wooden duck decoy but three, alongside the embossed spines of thick prop books. Stage right was a shelf with more books and a large model of a sailing ship. Behind each player was a houseplant. Governing the pace of play was an enormous clock from the luxury maker Audemars Piguet. One supposes that this set dressing was to soften the blow, as it were. To reassure the viewing public that even if "we" lost, we'd still be able to relax beneath our leather volumes and sailing ships. No glowing red robot eyes here. On the Deep Blue operator's side of the board, the table had been extended at an angle to fit an expensive IBM monitor, a keyboard, a mouse, and a telephone.

A separate viewing hall held a few hundred spectators and, for dramatic effect, a scale wooden model of Deep Blue. Outside on Seventh Avenue, scalpers sold $25 tickets for $500. Grandmasters and international masters were surveyed, and the consensus was a Kasparov victory. Vegas bookmakers agreed.

True to predicted form, Kasparov won Game One in forty-five moves, with the white pieces employing a system known as the King's Indian Attack.* But something funny happened along the way. By the forty-fourth move of this game, Kasparov was far ahead and victory was all but guaranteed. Then Deep Blue moved its rook from the center of the board to the bottom; it was a seemingly useless move—and, indeed, it *was* a useless move. (A more standard play might be moving the rook to f5, putting white in check.) In this position, my present-day laptop, searching about two million positions a second, finds a guaranteed checkmate for Kasparov within seventeen moves. But in the heat of battle Kasparov imbued this useless move with deep meaning, as is our human wont. He didn't understand it, so he took it as a sign that Deep Blue was operating on a higher plane. Despite the fact that the computer resigned a move later, this notion lingered.

It turned out, however, that this move was simply the result of a computer bug; not even Deep Blue was immune to these irritations.

---

* 1.Nf3 d5 2.g3

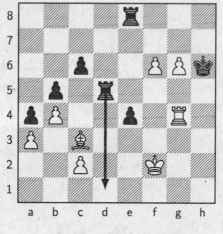

44 . . . Rd1, Deep Blue's strange move

The computer's code had hit a snag, and it had a built-in fail-safe whereby it would make a random legal move if its calculations ate up too much of its time. Rook to d1 was that random legal move. But in this random glitch a human observer saw "human" intent. Kasparov and his team "were not *exactly* sure what was going on," the journalist and statistician Nate Silver wrote in 2012, "but what had seemed to casual observers like a random and inexplicable blunder instead seemed to them to reveal great wisdom." It was the last time Kasparov would beat Deep Blue.

In Game Two, Kasparov controlled the black pieces; the black side is at a nominal disadvantage in chess, because it moves second. Murray Campbell sat among the houseplants and controlled the white pieces on behalf of Deep Blue. The game began with the Ruy Lopez opening,* named for the priest who analyzed it 450 years ago in the hills of western Spain. The position evolved into a complex

---

* 1. e4 e5 2. Nf3 Nc6 3. Bb5

traffic jam—even after nineteen moves, no pieces had been captured by either side. After subtle jousting and threats of attack, twenty moves later Deep Blue was able to fully invade Kasparov's territory along the left side of the board. Kasparov resigned shortly thereafter, with his king exposed and under fire from the computer's queen and rook. Some experts believe he might still have had a chance. But the champion had conceded. The match was now tied, 1–1.

In his postgame comments, Kasparov angrily maintained that "Deep Blue hasn't won a single game." Maurice Ashley, a grandmaster and match commentator, asked if Kasparov suspected "human intervention."

Kasparov replied, "It reminds me of the famous goal that Maradona scored against England in '86. He said it was the hand of God."

Kasparov's meaning was clear enough: he was accusing the Deep Blue team of cheating, just as Diego Maradona had cheated in the World Cup when he'd redirected the ball into the back of the net with his fist rather than with his head.

"Maybe [Kasparov] should come to grips with the fact that Deep Blue can do a lot of things that he did not think were possible," retorted Joel Benjamin, an American grandmaster who consulted for IBM. Kasparov demanded to see the computer's logs. The Deep Blue team refused but agreed to place them in escrow with a neutral arbiter until the match was complete.

Games Three, Four, and Five were draws. In Game Three, Kasparov opened with a pawn to d3, sliding his queen's pawn forward one square. This irregular play is known as the Mieses Opening and is almost never seen in high-level games, for the simple reason that it's not a very good move. But it was a meta-gambit by Kasparov, something known as anti-computer chess. The idea was that by playing something esoteric, a human could kick the computer out of its opening book—its extensive baked-in knowledge of opening theory—and thereby gain an advantage. Kasparov would do something similar in Game Four, avoiding his typical lines of play. Games Four and Five saw Kasparov with occasional attacking initiatives, yet nothing to show for them. Many commentators noted the absence of Kasparov's usual bravado in these games. He was being careful. He was playing, perhaps for the first time in his career, like an underdog.

Game Six began with the score level, 2.5–2.5, and the match hanging in the balance. Kasparov arrived at the Equitable Center in a dark mood. He controlled the black pieces and opened with the Caro-Kann Defense.* The book *Modern Chess Openings* explains that "this modest defense has gained great respectability in recent years." Indeed, it has had its great exponents, world champions who frequently deployed it in competition—Capablanca, Botvinnik, Karpov—but Kasparov was never among them.

Perhaps it was his relative inexperience with Caro-Kann that led him to make questionable decisions on his seventh, eighth, and eleventh moves of the game. On its eighth move, Deep Blue sacrificed a knight to launch an attack on Kasparov's king, one that would never abate. By the twelfth move, no time at all in high-level chess, the game was effectively over. "It is practically impossible to defend such an open position with an insecure king against a powerful calculating machine that acts like a shark that smells blood," wrote international master Karsten Müller. The game continued for just a few more moves.

Kasparov sat staring at the position with his head in his hand. In violation of chess decorum, he began speaking in Russian to his mother, who was sitting in the room. Even after examination of the match footage, it's not clear what was said. Perhaps that he'd realized the inevitable, and that he *would* be beaten by a machine. Eventually,

---

* 1. e4 c6

he reached out his hand and offered his resignation. Then Kasparov abruptly stood and stormed from the board, toward the television camera, with his arms extended in a gesture of disbelief, shaking his head and disappearing into the shadows.

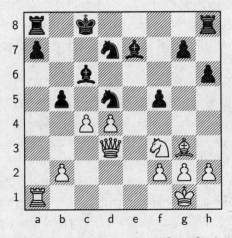

The position in which Kasparov, black, resigned Game Six, losing the match

The Deep Blue team was asked by the corporate PR division to dress well and not smile during the closing ceremony—in deference, apparently, to the human race. The day after the match, IBM's stock price soared to a ten-year high.

The best photograph of the match was taken by Peter Morgan for Reuters. It was captured in the spectators' viewing hall during the final game and has a composition worthy of a Renaissance painting. In the near foreground are two monitors. The one on the left shows the chessboard itself, around move ten as the machine's attack unfolds. The one on the right shows Kasparov, his elbows on the table and his face invisible, buried deeply in his hands. Behind the monitors, maybe a hundred spectators fill the frame. The central figure, a middle-aged man in a gray T-shirt, looks up with his mouth agape as if he is witnessing the ascension of Christ. A woman to his left touches a hand to her chest in a universal symbol of woe. Two men over his left shoulder smile as if in mid-chuckle. A woman over his right shoulder looks as if she is about to cry, while her companion covers his mouth in what appears to be horror. An insouciant man farther to the left simply picks something out of his teeth.

Such was the range of human response to Deep Blue's victory. Some took the side of the species: "One day in the far future, we will be up against machines—not just in chess but in life—that are not only monstrously intelligent but utterly unfeeling," wrote the political columnist Charles Krauthammer. "Whom do you think that gives the edge to? Ask Garry Kasparov." And some that of the machine: It "would represent yet another assault on humanity's arrogant belief in its own supremacy," an observer told the *Washington Post*. Nate Silver wrote, "It was like the moment when, exactly thirteen seconds into 'Love Will Tear Us Apart,' the synthesizer overpowers the guitar riff, leaving rock and roll in its dust."

"My God, I used to think chess required thought," the author and scholar Douglas Hofstadter said in response to Deep Blue. "Now I realize it doesn't. It doesn't mean Kasparov isn't a deep thinker, just that you can bypass deep thinking in playing chess."

The victory was in many ways a realization of von Kempelen's fantasy of an intelligent chess-playing machine. But there had been promise implicit in Deep Blue: that it would do something in the "real world," that it would act, as Shannon supposed, as a "wedge" to attack real problems. For Murray Campbell, the luster of that promise has faded.

It was quiet in his office at the IBM Research headquarters. "In the past few years, I've started thinking differently about games like Go and chess and certainly checkers," Campbell told me, amid memorabilia from his career in games. "As hard as they are for people to play, they are, in hindsight, not that interesting for AI. There are methods for dealing with games like that which don't seem particularly generalizable, in the sense that they allow us to do other things better. When people play chess, they might say, 'Well, what do I learn from playing chess? Well, I become more disciplined, more systematic about how I think about the options in my life, more willing to look ahead a few steps and think about consequences, better able to take losses.' All of those things—Deep Blue wouldn't learn any of that. . . . It would learn: This kind of pawn structure is really good for this kind of piece play. I guess the question is 'Are two-player zero-sum games of perfect information the best domains for continued AI research?' I think not."

He continued: "If you ask me what code that we took from Deep Blue and applied to other problems, there wasn't anything."

Leaving IBM, I realized that the familiar story—of computers surpassing humanity in the moment of Kasparov's concession—was a red herring. Computers had done no such thing. Newell, Shaw, and Simon had been wrong. Rather than "penetrate to the core of human intellectual endeavor," humans had simply built a working Mechanical Turk. But that building *was* human intellectual endeavor. And it penetrated toward the core of chess itself.

I STILL REMEMBER the first board on which I ever played chess. It was an irregular and heavy slab of walnut, maybe fourteen inches on a side, onto which green squares of felt had been carefully glued by hand. It was a homemade Christmas gift from my mother's siblings to their father, my grandfather Jack. The felt had curled up at its corners after hosting decades of battle in a small farmhouse in eastern Iowa. The pieces, purchased by my grandparents on their honeymoon to Mexico in 1949, were slender, made of ebony and ivory. By the time I arrived, one of the knights had lost its head. The other knights, I thought, had a look of terror in their eyes. I remember the sharp spikes on the rims of the queens' crowns and the neat, crenellated battlements of the rooks. I remember the clunk of the dense pieces on wood.

As a child, I spent every summer on that farm, jumping on hay bales and swimming and playing game after game of chess in the late-afternoon light. Grandpa Jack was a strong player, the wielder of a conservative and positional style. And as a matter of strict principle, he never let kids win. Therefore, every chess player in my family has a cherished memory of their first victory. When I finally beat Grandpa Jack, around age nine, I remember running into the kitchen to tell Grandma Shirley, who hugged me and who was, to borrow her word, tickled.

At first, I saw the game like a machine, not unlike the Turk, its parts moving and interacting according to complex yet intuitive principles. I took chess apart like a child disassembling a motor—curious and eager but mostly hapless and messy. Occasionally, the reassembled machine ran smoothly, and I won. More often, it sputtered out, and I lost. I was, to use my favorite chess insult, a woodpusher, curious about how the pieces worked. Experimentation was enough for me.

As I grew older, I grew fascinated with chess theory and studied diagrams of the intricate machine picked apart by countless tinkerers over hundreds of years. I would fall asleep reading the heavy reference book *Modern Chess Openings*, comforted and delighted by the fine-grained taxonomy and analysis of just the first few possible moves in a game, and the names they'd acquired—the Halloween Gambit, the Maróczy Bind, the Accelerated Dragon, the Hedgehog Defense.

Today I enjoy chess on an aesthetic level. My competitive career never amounted to much; my fourth-grade Greenwood Elementary championship remains its only highlight. I lacked skill, and, just as important, I lacked the obsession to internalize—to actualize—all those volumes of theory. But even if I've never stretched a canvas, I can still appreciate Rothko and de Kooning—appreciate the beauty in the picture. And one can appreciate beauty in a game of chess; it *is* art, with due respect to the views of the current world champion. Lengthy tactical combinations, complex and previously unseen, can, like music, unfold as if they were ordained. Essences of gnarly complex positions can, like painting, be distilled and altered and presented in pure form.

If Grandpa Jack's chessboard has Proustian resonance for me, one of the more recent boards on which I played chess was entirely forgettable, except for the setting. It was one of many arranged in a conference room in the headquarters of the United Nations, on the East Side of Manhattan. The pieces were chunky plastic and the board a rollable vinyl. Along its edges was the logo of Play Magnus, the mobile app touted by Norway's Magnus Carlsen, the strongest player in the world today.

It was a few months before Carlsen would play for yet another world title. Fifteen of us sat at identical boards along the outside of an enormous horseshoe table: the mayor of Oslo, the Afghan ambassador to the U.N., a legal adviser with the Maldives mission, other dignitaries, and, for some reason, me. We'd been invited here mysteriously, like children to Willy Wonka's factory, for a simultaneous chess exhibition. Carlsen, the exhibitor, darted from board to board, rarely taking more than a couple of seconds to make his move against each of us challengers, while we sat contemplating our own futility. Trembling, I channeled the simple homegrown lessons of Grandpa Jack: develop your pieces, defend your pieces.

Were this poker or backgammon or Scrabble, subject to the randomness of the draw or the dice, I might have clung to a sliver of hope. But this was chess; I was going to lose. I wrote at the time that Carlsen was about to do to my psyche what Mike Tyson would've done to my face. There was no escape.

We began in the Queen's Gambit Declined, Exchange Variation.* Before I even got my bearings in the position, Carlsen's rook and bishop were aggressively harassing my kingside. By the twelfth move, however, I'd managed to advance a pawn just two squares from the far end of the board, where it could be promoted to a queen. Not only that, on the next move, that little pawn defended my queen, which flew the length of the board and put Carlsen's bare king in check. *I put Magnus Carlsen in check.* I remember thinking, despite myself, "I am going to fucking win."

I didn't, of course. Carlsen simply slid his king over one square to safety. He parried my attack with ease, launching a frontal assault led by his bishop and rook, with his queen providing covering fire. I was dead meat within a handful of moves.

I asked Carlsen if he considered his game against me to be part of his official world championship preparation.

"Um, no," he said.

Carlsen, twenty-seven at the time, went on to win that world championship in late 2018, his fourth. And over the year that followed, his competitive rating, which already placed him at No. 1 in the world, would climb higher than any human had ever before achieved, thanks to another sort of preparation altogether.

TO QUANTIFY SKILL, chess associations use a statistical rating system called Elo, named after the Hungarian-American physicist and chess master Arpad Elo. The higher your rating relative to your opponent's, the likelier you are to win. A rank novice might be rated around 1000; a middling player like me around 1500; a master around 2300; a grandmaster around 2500 (there are about seven-

---

*1. d4 d5 2. c4 e6 3. Nc3 Nf6 4. cxd5

teen hundred of them); and the top human in the world just below 2900. The current best computer engines are rated around 3500 and climbing. According to the Computer Chess Rating Lists, there are currently about ninety different engines rated higher than the world's best human. A top pro could play a hundred games against a top program and be happy to draw one. The technology has developed to the point where no human would stand a chance against a free app running on your smartphone.

A program called Stockfish is the handcrafted chess engine ne plus ultra and one of the strongest programs available today. The program, which debuted in 2008, is open-source, meaning you can easily browse through its source code yourself. There you will find things like "polynomial material imbalance parameters," followed by lists of numbers typed in with care by a human. Anyone in the world can submit a potential improvement to the code via a system called Fishtest. That potential improvement is then tested against the old version over tens of thousands of games on volunteers' computers. If the tweak does indeed improve Stockfish in a statistically significant way, it is officially implemented, and the program grows stronger still. Stockfish is, therefore, not only handcrafted but crowdsourced—a sort of meritocratic populist technocracy of chess. Like the pyramids, Stockfish is a masterpiece of group effort.

The program has become a ubiquitous and trusted tool for human players, including the world's top grandmasters. It's not typically a sparring partner (it's too good) but, rather, tends to serve as an analyzer. The key to elite chess is preparation, which Stockfish facilitates. It helps players hone and deepen their opening repertoires, shedding light on traps either to spring or to avoid. It's a sort of digital canary in a coal mine, allowing for safe and reliable analysis of potentially treacherous tactical territory. And players like me can use it after the fact to find, and hopefully rectify, their (many) blunders. To play against it competitively, though, is to abandon all hope. While it's governed only by relatively simple calculations, it is unblinking, and seems to favor a stodgy, clean, materialistic style.

Recently Stockfish has been confronted by an altogether different approach. DeepMind, an artificial intelligence company founded in 2010 and acquired by Google in 2014 for a reported $650 million, was cofounded by a former chess prodigy. Its stated goal is not modest: "solve intelligence." The company became a household name in 2016 when its computer system AlphaGo defeated a world champion in the ancient and impossibly complex game of Go.

In 2017, DeepMind decided to try its hand at chess. It pitted its AlphaZero system, a generalized offshoot of AlphaGo, against Stockfish. DeepMind first presented the results in a paper published on arXiv, a repository for scientific preprints. The computer scientists set the programs against each other for a series of a hundred games, of which AlphaZero won twenty-eight, drew seventy-two, and lost *zero*. The results indicated that a new sort of program, with a new sort of approach, was now the best chess-playing entity in the universe. AlphaZero has no fine-tuning; its parameters have not been fiddled with by human hands. It is given nothing beyond its learning algorithm and the rules of the game—and some heavy-duty custom Google hardware. It learned solely by playing itself, tabula rasa, forty-four million times. DeepMind claimed that after just four hours of training, AlphaZero outperformed Stockfish.

In the middle of that research paper is a breathtaking chart called Table 2. It shows the sequences of opening moves AlphaZero played during its hours of training. Unaided by humans, it discovered, one by one, the fruits of centuries of human experimentation, including those I had read about as a child: the English Opening, the Queen's Gambit, the Sicilian Defense, the Ruy Lopez.

AlphaZero plays with a certain sort of terrifying panache. Consider an example from one of the games published by DeepMind.

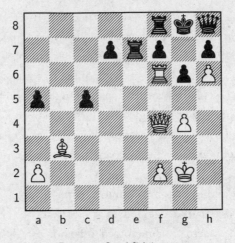

AlphaZero puts Stockfish in *zugzwang*.

On paper, the old-guard Stockfish, marshaling the black pieces, is far ahead. Poised to move, it's up two pawns, and its extra rook is more powerful than white's bishop. But consider its position, its strategic options. They are nonexistent. Stockfish here is said to be in *zugzwang*, German for "forced move," an exotic situation rarely observed outside of theoretical chess books. Anything Stockfish does makes it worse off. It would rather not move at all. But it must, to its demise.

The Stockfish developer Tord Romstad objected to the match results published by DeepMind, calling them a comparison of "apples to orangutans." But pro players were paying close attention. In interviews with Chess.com, one top grandmaster said he'd pay "maybe $100,000" for access to AlphaZero, and another said it was worth "at least seven figures."

Regardless of the specific result, this game was not only a clash between two strong computer chess players. It was a clash between the two competing approaches to artificial intelligence. Playing the black pieces was a "good old-fashioned AI" program. Stockfish came preloaded with the sum total of human knowledge about the game, and then it searched through possibilities very, very fast. Playing the white pieces was a representative of the new-school deep-learning programs, unpolluted by human knowledge, deciphering the world of chess on its own. And while its training process is incredibly costly, computationally speaking, it breezes through the game itself: AlphaZero searches only about eighty thousand positions per second, compared to Stockfish's seventy million.

In 2018, DeepMind's researchers published an expanded version of the paper, this time in *Science*. Now they reported the results of a thousand-game match against Stockfish. Of those, AlphaZero won 155, lost six, and drew the rest. The earliest computer-chess thinkers believed that computers ought to emulate humans. The next generation sought to exploit the strengths of computers. And with AlphaZero, yet a new sort of chess player emerged. It didn't play like a human, with a human's intuitive grasp of strategy. Nor did it play like a computer, with a machine's cold mastery of tactics and its deep calculation. Rather, it played the chess of some other species entirely. Demis Hassabis, a former chess prodigy and one of DeepMind's cofounders, says it plays in a way that is "almost alien."

But there's a problem: we don't speak alien. Regardless of the strange beauty of AlphaZero's games and the astronomical strength of its play, it cannot explain itself. As long ago as 1991, Tim Krabbé, a Dutch journalist, wrote about certain endgame positions where computers had found guaranteed checkmates hundreds of moves into the future:

> The moves are beyond comprehension. A grandmaster wouldn't be better at these endgames than someone who had learned chess yesterday. It's a sort of chess that has nothing to

do with chess, a chess that we could never have imagined without computers. The moves are awesome, almost scary, because you know they are the truth, God's algorithm—it's like being revealed the Meaning of Life, but you don't understand a word.

Magnus Carlsen wants to understand.

CARLSEN, THE UNINTERRUPTED world No. 1 since 2011, went into the 2018 world championship against his American challenger, Fabiano Caruana, with an Elo rating higher than that of any human being in history. To help me understand Carlsen's strength, and to quantify the history of artificial chess intelligence, Murray Campbell sent me data on the relative rankings of humans and computer chess players since 1980:

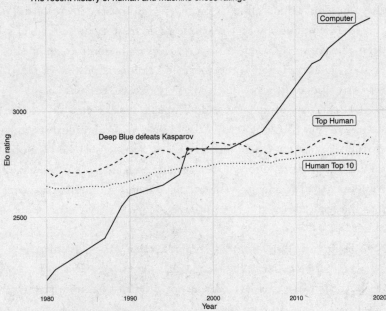

The recent history of human and machine chess ratings

The chart tells a few stories. The first, and most obvious, is the steep rise of computer chess performance, vaulting in forty years from OK to *otherworldly*. Second, there is during much of this time a large gap between the top human and the average of the top ten humans. From 1984 to 2005, that top human was Garry Kasparov.

Far removed from his despondence following his 1997 defeat, Kasparov now calls himself "a lucky man to be part of this great experiment." He has recognized his loss as a human victory of another kind and views AI with a rosy optimism, its development being what he has referred to as "the wonderful human process of making our machines and our lives better." As for machines and chess, Kasparov has famously promoted the idea of "advanced chess": that a computer and a human sitting side by side, a cyborg playing the pieces together, is stronger than any machine on its own.

A certain sort of centaur chess, a close coupling of human and machine, may also help explain a third trend visible in Campbell's data: the sharp increase in the late 2010s in the performance of the new top human, in this case Magnus Carlsen. Kasparov was right that computers would be tools for chess players. They're tools the way weapons in an arms race are tools. The other guy has them, so if you want to compete, you must have them. And the world's best player has embraced a new, powerful tool.

Such arms-race tensions led to a moment of off-the-board drama between Carlsen and Caruana in 2018. A promotional clip created by the Saint Louis Chess Club—Caruana's de facto office—had been posted to and then deleted from YouTube. The video appeared to show Caruana's pre-match training sessions, and interested viewers fixed on a few frames of the video in which the screen of Caruana's laptop was visible. The screen showed a number of ideas related to chess openings, variations with names such as the Fianchetto Grünfeld, the Queen's Gambit Declined, and the Petroff. Given the importance of computers to the modern game, glimpsing Caruana's laptop screen was like looking inside his brain.

Something else curious happened at that 2018 world championship: every single game was a draw, an unprecedented twelve in a row. The championship had to go to speedier tie-breaker games to determine a winner. The computer is partly responsible for this. The arms race it fosters, like its nuclear counterpart, often leads to bloodless tension.

"It's like you're playing against a phantom," said Judit Polgár, a top grandmaster providing official match commentary. In fact, it's like two phantoms playing against each other.

Some famous human players have resisted, even fought, the lure of software. In 1996, an overweight Bobby Fischer, the elusive and troubled American former world champion, appeared in Buenos Aires touting "Fischerandom," a chess variant in which the white pieces on the back row of the board are randomized and the black pieces are set up to mirror them. (It is also called Chess960, after the number of possible starting positions.)

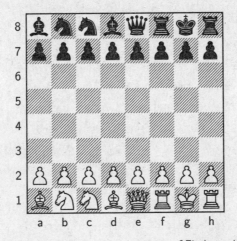

An example starting position in a game of Fischerandom

For Fischer, chess had become a once-rich mine stripped bare. He claimed that more and more top players wore glasses, thanks to the hours they spent staring at their computer screens. The *Washington Post* called Fischerandom "the grandmaster's effort to save chess from the computer-mad players who have turned it into a bore," and noted that it ensured that nearly every game would be different, and that meticulous computer preparation and analysis would be rendered moot.

Most players, however, continue on the centaur's path. Since the 2018 championship, Carlsen has only improved. He has studied the games of AlphaZero, trying to make sense of its alien language. Murray Campbell, a strong player himself and the four-time defending champion of the IBM Research company chess tournament, said of Carlsen, "It seems like over the past year he has been playing significantly better than he had the year before."

Carlsen said he'd read a book called *Game Changer*, a collection of the program's games by Matthew Sadler and Natasha Regan, which he called "inspirational." In another interview he called AlphaZero one of his "heroes," remarking that it helped instill confidence and aggression in his game. "In essence, I've become a very different player in terms of style than I was a bit earlier," Carlsen said.

Recently, the *Guardian*'s chess column compared Carlsen's peculiar use of his queen to that of AlphaZero. "The queen was a long-distance general for his attack," the columnist wrote, calling Carlsen's technique a stroke of originality akin to the maneuvering of the neural network program. Campbell concurred: "He's been willing to play a little more in the style of AlphaZero, which means caring less about material and more about long-term pressure and positional trumps that just don't go away."

In stark ways, the prevalence of superhuman chess machines in the world of professional chess is a glimpse into our own civilian future, when AI technologies will seep into our personal and professional lives, and where the only way to make a living in many fields will be to work side by side with an artificially intelligent machine. In chess, that future is here. The computers have "increased pure understanding of the game at the expense of creativity, mystery, and dynamism," writer Yoni Wilkenfeld put it in a recent essay titled "Can Chess Survive Artificial Intelligence?" Gone is Capablanca's swashbuckling "battle of ideas." The computer will tell you, within seconds, if your ideas are right or wrong. The sole source of originality in chess is now the machine, and humans struggle to channel it, or at least to mimic it.

The pros aren't the only ones the machines affect. For the viewer, the amateur chess *fan* (me very much included), modern chess is experienced through the eyes of a computer. Abutting the image of the professionals' board on match broadcasters such as Chess.com, Chess24, and Lichess is a simple diagram, a sort of thermometer, filled to some extent with white and to some extent with black. This represents a powerful computer's evaluation of the position measured in the equivalents of a pawn. A reading like +2.3 means white is clearly ahead; something like −0.5 means perhaps black has a small edge.

This has democratized chess fandom. Without a computer, I don't have much hope of understanding the intricate lines in a game between two grandmasters, or the exact implications of this move versus that move. With a computer, I have a quantitative lens through which to view the game. I can see exactly what threats are looming and whom the computer deems to be winning. I can watch the thermometer twitch up or down with each move and pass some quasi-informed judgement on the pros. But this understanding is often hollow. Take the computer and its thermometer away, and I risk being more lost than I ever was.

I'm still inclined to Karpov's view that "chess is everything—art, science, and sport." My own appreciation of the game has progressed from the mechanical to the theoretical to the aesthetic. By coincidence, my progression mirrors how we taught our computers, too. The earliest programs, gawkish code running on ungainly mainframes or without any computer at all, were woodpushers, capable of playing chess technically but not well. Their successors, running on sleeker supercomputers or speedier modern desktops, had mastered theory—openings and endgames, as well as the sophisticated tactics of the middle game—and now played better than any human. And *their* successors, the latest evolution, ungodly chess beings sprung from the secretive labs of trillion-dollar companies, play a hyper-advanced alien chess, exotic and beautiful, something no human is capable of fully understanding, let alone replicating, but so full of awesome style.

I INVITE YOU to navigate your web browser to tcec-chess.com, home to an online arena called the Top Chess Engine Championship. Twenty-four hours a day, seven days a week, elite computer chess programs—with names such as Ethereal, Fire, Fizbo, Komodo, Laser, Winter, and Xiphos—play against each other there, and you can watch them live. The engines each run on four high-end Intel Xeon processors with eighty-eight cores, analyzing tens of millions of positions per second. You can watch them consider lines dozens of moves into the future and evaluate positions to the hundredth of a pawn. They constantly produce some of the best chess ever played. You can even, if you are so inclined, watch an insolent human commentariat chat about the programs' games in real time:

> "ez draw."
> "it blundered away a good position."
> "pathetic play."

But the machines don't care, and they never stop playing.
One imagines a not-too-distant future, after the temperatures

and oceans have risen and the coastal cities of the world have flooded and emptied, after the human population has migrated inland, after crops have died during droughts and species have gone extinct, after famine and economic collapse, where on a long-abandoned server, as long as the power holds out, the highest expression of our human culture, our last art, is created in chess games played in silence with no one watching.

IN THE EVENING MIST, the man in Washington Square Park with the houndstooth jacket moved first. The game started innocently enough. Our kings' pawns met in the middle of the board, and our knights quickly backed them up. Houndstooth moved his bishop into attack formation, while I brought out my second knight. He advanced his knight farther onto the flank, into my territory, and I countered with a pawn of my own in the center. We traded pawn captures and then he leapt his knight yet again, capturing a pawn near my king. He'd sacrificed the knight, but my king was now exposed. He put it in check with his queen, and my king was forced into an even more precarious position near the center of the board. I don't remember the precise sequence of moves that ensued after this; suffice to say that my king got a good workout, and I was eventually caught in Houndstooth's net and checkmated.

Houndstooth's opening has a name that described how I felt: the Fried Liver Attack.[*] Its earliest known use was more than five hundred years ago by an Italian player who belonged to the royal household of a duke and authored codices on the game. I pulled out another five-dollar bill, and we set the pieces up again.

---

[*] 1. e4 e5 2. Nf3 Nc6 3. Bc4 Nf6 4. Ng5 d5 5. exd5 Nxd5 6. Nxf7 Kxf7

GO

Go is to Western chess what philosophy is to double-entry accounting.

—TREVANIAN, *SHIBUMI*

THE MASTER DELIBERATED ON his next move for an hour and forty-six minutes as a thunderstorm gathered outside. Every play at this point, the intricate middle game, was difficult. His opponent's previous move had been a diabolical masterstroke, a black stone wedged between two of the Master's white stones, like the "flash of a dagger," threatening to wrench away his control of the board. It was the sort of ferocious move Honinbo Shusai had come to expect from his young challenger. After an hour and forty-six minutes, the Master placed a white stone just so, fortifying his position. It was a brilliant response, a precise defensive move.

But now the storm had come. Its violence in the gardens outside only intensified the stillness in the room. The doors were pulled shut. The Master, though he sat in what resembled a priestly throne, looked drawn and anguished. His cheeks and eyelids were swollen, and he had pains in his chest; he had recently been hospitalized for a heart condition. He sipped strong tea.

Shusai the Master was the twenty-first and final head of the house of Honinbo, the strongest of the four Go houses, rarefied schools of the game established by the Japanese warlords in the seventeenth century, in the early days of the Tokugawa shogunate. The house was named for a monastic pavilion in a Buddhist temple in Kyoto. The Master was a Go player of the ninth rank, the exalted pinnacle of a rating system similar to the degrees of karate black belts. But the Master loved all games. Between his Go games, he would challenge bystanders to shogi, renju, mah-jongg, or billiards.

The contest unfolding in the downpour was the Master's retirement game—his farewell exhibition—and one of only two official games of Go he'd play in the last ten years of his life. He was sixty-four years old. The game lasted more than five months, from late June to early December of 1938. The players toured a number of towns in Japan, making only a few moves each day, followed closely by reporters, whose dispatches were serialized in the biggest newspapers.

"A thunderstorm? A tempest?" said his opponent, a young prodigy of the seventh rank named Otaké. The heavy rains caused boulders to crash down into a river near the playing venue; the noise made it difficult to play.

By now, around the eightieth move, likely near the game's halfway point, both players had built long walls of stones along the west side of the board, and a skirmish was fanning out from the north side. The Master looked thinner every day. Play was limited to two hours in the morning. For lunch, he ate porridge and salted plums.

By tradition, great deference had always been paid to the more senior player. The elder combatant would normally decide when to adjourn a day's play, for example, providing himself a chance to spend the night pondering his next move, or perhaps even quietly consulting with other members of his house, though that was against the rules. But modern reforms had begun to creep into the ancient game. Otaké threatened not to play unless certain changes were implemented. In this match, play was adjourned according to a strict schedule, and each day's final move was sealed in an envelope, to be revealed the next morning. The Master begrudgingly agreed, but the reforms rankled. Even the path up the vaunted rankings ladder was now governed by a fastidious points system, whereas the Master had inherited his title under the legacy house system, as had his predecessors dating back to 1612. A game once governed by custom and respect was now controlled by what traditionalists considered "fussy rules" and "modern rationalism."

"Everything had become science and regulation," wrote Yasunari Kawabata, one of the newspaper reporters. "One conducted the battle only to win, and there was no margin for remembering the dignity and the fragrance of Go as an art." Honinbo Shusai, he continued, was probably "the last of the true masters revered in the tradition of Go as a way of life and art," and he "stood at the boundary between the old and the new." No method had been established to determine his successor as Master, a title that, in any case, was bound to be degraded into a commercial asset, a label of strength and nothing else, the old ideals now feudal relics.

At the sluggish pace of play, after just a few dozen moves the seasons had changed, and it was cold outside. The Master was running a fever; he wore an overcoat and a muffler at the board, while water boiled on a brazier nearby.

"Might we call it a wintry gale, or are we still too early?" wondered the young prodigy.

Like his body, the Master's position at the board was deteriorating. Shusai, who had earlier dyed his white hair black, had by now shaved it off. But with the 130th move of the game, the Master showed his own diabolical side, counterattacking a black group on the east side of the board.

"A fine thing," the young prodigy muttered. "Earthshattering."

And while it looked fine at first, the 130th move would be the

Master's undoing. He had tried to turn the tide—of the game, of its modernization—yet his counterattack had failed. What was once promising would fall apart. That became clear over the next hundred moves as his position unraveled and the result became unavoidable. The Master lost by five points. "Yes, five points," he muttered as the score was counted, nearly six months after the game began. His young challenger was "the representative of a new day" being "carried by the currents of history." The Master would play some practice games afterward, with friends, but the stones would slip from his fingers. A year later he was dead.

The account above, and the commentary on this changing tide, unfolds in Yasunari Kawabata's *The Master of Go*, his 1954 "chronicle-novel" based on his reporting for the newspaper *Mainichi*.* Kawabata, who later won the Nobel Prize in Literature, concluded, "One may say that in the end the match took the Master's life."

Go is often touted as the most complex board game played by humans. As a matter of sheer calculation, that may be true. But in another sense, it is the simplest. The rules of Go are few, elemental, and pure. You can learn them in a minute or two. It's the *expression* of those rules that generates intricacy. In his Nobel lecture, Kawabata reflected on Zen and Japanese poetry. "My own works have been described as works of emptiness, but it is not to be taken for the nihilism of the West," he said. Go, too, is a game of emptiness but not of meaninglessness—it begins with a single stone placed on an empty board. And then another and then another. *The Master of Go* is a sparse book, though the account it contains is not.

Honinbo Shusai, the Master, died in January 1940. In April 1972, Kawabata was found dead in the office where he wrote with a

---

* Minor fictional liberties are taken in the book. The Master's challenger's real name, for example, was Minoru Kitani, and Kawabata also gives himself a pseudonym.

gas hose in his mouth and an empty whiskey bottle nearby. He left behind no further explanation.

"I WANT TO APOLOGIZE for being so powerless."

These were the words of Lee Sedol, the eighteen-time international Go champion and a nine-*dan* professional, upon his defeat in March 2016 at the hands of a computer program.

Lee is a thin man with the haircut of a Beatle and a whisper of a mustache. He was born on a tiny island in southwest South Korea, a place known for its sea salt, in 1983. The Western press often compares him to Roger Federer—a dominant and era-defining competitor, the possessor of a classic sportsman's style. Like Garry Kasparov two decades earlier, Lee had been selected by a giant corporation as a test subject in a grand experiment of artificial intelligence. Like Kasparov, Lee was favored to win. Unlike Kasparov, Lee was favored to win easily. His game hadn't been under the blistering assault that chess had. Go demanded, it was said, not brute-force calculation but human intuition. When a Go master is asked why he moved where he moved, he will often say that it "felt right." A meaningful computer victory in Go was perpetually seen, even in 2016, as "decades away."

Perhaps the oddsmakers hadn't been paying close enough attention. In 2015, DeepMind had invited Fan Hui, the European champion, into its offices to test its program, AlphaGo. When Fan received the invitation, sent by a former chess prodigy and DeepMind cofounder, he wondered if the company might want to put him in a special room, stick wires in his head, and scan his brain while he played Go—maybe they'd learn something. Instead, the executives told him that they had a strong program and wanted to play him.

"Oh, it's just a program, it's so easy," Fan says he thought, laughing, in a scene captured in a documentary about AlphaGo. The program beat him five games to zero. It was the first time a professional had lost to a machine on level terms.

"I feel something very strange," Fan said afterward. "I lose with the program and I don't understand myself anymore."

THE RULES OF GO—called *weiqi* in Chinese, *igo* in Japanese, and *baduk* in Korean—are stark and elegant, as if they were discovered rather than invented. A Go board, or goban, is a nineteen-by-nineteen grid of lines. There is only one type of piece, and there is only one type of move. As the game begins, to one player's side is a bowl of black stones; to the other player's side is a bowl of white stones. The players alternate placing these stones on one of the grid's intersections. Once placed, the stones are fixed.

Checkers and chess are games of destruction: players capture their opponents' pieces in a war of attrition. The players' armies start on opposite ends of the board and march toward each other, with many pieces moving in only one direction. A polar gravity reigns. The image of the final position of a chess game is typically uninteresting: a few surviving pieces—a king, a few pawns, and maybe the odd rook—survey an emptied battlefield. Go, however, is a game of creation and effervescence. The stones create their own radiant gravity, rippling in every direction across the space-time of the board. The final position of a game of Go is the stuff of rich narrative, of production, of achievement.

Here is an orienting visual aid. On the left is the empty board before the game begins; on the right is a completed professional game—in fact, the final game of Honinbo Shusai, the Master.

Unlike the games of destruction, which involve defending certain squares for passing moments in the contest, Go is entirely a game of controlling territory; its Chinese name means "surrounding game." The base goal is to surround more empty intersections on

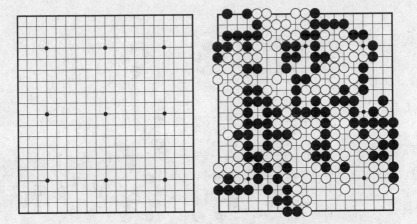

the grid—called points—with your stones than your opponent does. In the game above, for example, black has staked out territories in the northeast and southwest, while white controls swaths in the west and southeast. The center is a more contested battleground.

Stones are placed on the board in an effort to lay claim to this territory. Their proper placement is crucial because their positions are fixed. The only time stones move is if they are *captured* and removed from the board entirely. Stones are captured if they themselves are completely surrounded by the enemy. Friendly adjacent stones, connected horizontally or vertically, work together as a unit. Any empty points adjacent to such a unit are called *liberties*. A liberty is breathing room; any stones with liberties stay on the board. Any stones without liberties suffocate and are immediately removed. Below are four illustrative examples of how capturing works. All of the white groups below have just one liberty, putting them at risk of capture—they are said to be in *atari*, sort of like being in check in chess. When they become completely surrounded after the highlighted black move, they are captured and removed from the board.

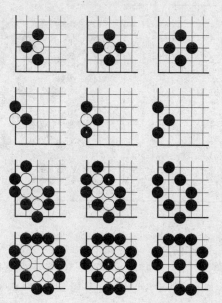

Four examples of, from left to right, the process of black capturing white stones

A player may pass her turn if she wishes, and the game ends if both players pass consecutively. A player's final score is equal to the number of empty points she has surrounded plus the number of prisoner stones she has captured.* In this simple miniature example game, the final position of which is shown below, white controls twenty-seven points of territory and black controls twenty-eight, and no prisoners have been taken, so black wins by one point.

---

* This is called territory scoring, or Japanese rules. In area scoring, or Chinese rules, your score is the number of empty points you have surrounded plus the number of your own stones on the board. The net result under these two systems is typically the same. Black goes first; to offset the advantage this confers, white is often given handicap points, called *komi*.

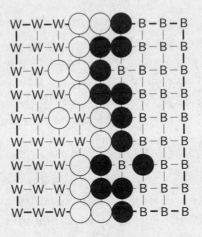

Black ekes out a victory.

Although the rules of Go can be almost completely explained in a couple of pages, the game contains a universe of possibilities. The Song dynasty poet Huang Tingjian, working around the year 1100, wrote that when playing Go "our minds are like spider threads roaming the empyrean"—strands between the stars. Even Confucius begrudgingly agreed that playing Go was better than sitting idle.

Go is many orders of magnitude more complex than chess, mathematically speaking, due in large part to its *branching factor*—the number of different paths a game can take with each successive turn and, therefore, the number of possible futures a human or machine may have to consider. In chess, each turn presents, on average, about thirty-five possible moves; in Go, that number is about 250. Multiply thirty-five by itself four times to calculate the number of possible four-move chess sequences, say, and you've got some 1.5 million. Multiply 250 by itself four times and you've got nearly four *billion*. The gulf only widens from there. Compounding the complexity, the average chess game lasts about forty moves per player; the average Go game lasts about a hundred. Even just the *number* of possible

Go positions wasn't precisely calculated until 2016, and obtaining that result required a serious server and a few months of computation time. It's roughly two times ten to the 170th power, or a number with 171 digits. The number of atoms in the universe has only about eighty digits. We could run every single computer on earth all day every day for a million years and it wouldn't be enough computing power to analyze all of them.

THE STANDARD-ISSUE HISTORY of Go comes from the legend of a mythical emperor named Yao who ruled for ninety-nine years in the twenty-fourth and twenty-third centuries B.C. He is said to have invented Go in order to teach his unruly son, Dan Zhu. The legend is the genesis of the oft-quoted statistic that Go is four thousand years old. The extant archaeological evidence, however, is more modest. A stone board, the oldest one known, resides in a museum in Beijing. It dates to around A.D. 200.

The literary evidence, the modern-day Go historian John Fairbairn explains, pushes Go's likely origins a bit earlier. Yin Xi, a legendary philosopher, writing around the third century B.C., recognized the depth of the game: "Take the accomplishments of archery, chariot-driving, playing the zither, and Go: in none of these it is ultimately possible to stop learning."

Ban Gu, a historian, laid out the game's symbolism in the first century A.D.: "The board must be square and represents the laws of the earth. The lines must be straight like the divine virtues. There are black and white stones, divided like yin and yang. Their arrangements on a board is like a model of the heavens."

And the poet Ma Rong, in the second century A.D., penned the following, called the *Go Rhapsody*:

In brief envisioned, the game of Go
Is modeled on our art of war.

For on that board, just three-foot square,
Is where a battle royal proceeds. . . .
Inherent laws lie deep in Go—
I pray your leave to tell you how.

The poem goes on to detail technical strategies and Go idioms that are still in use today—"attack instead where he is weak," "covet captures with greed," "if dykes are breached, the floods ne'er cease." This poem was written, Fairbairn points out, "at a time when other cultures were barely above the level of games of chance."

By the eighth century, the Chinese considered the game one of the four noble arts to which gentlepeople ought to aspire—alongside calligraphy, painting, and the zither. One of a beautiful series of four hanging scrolls dedicated to these arts, dated to the sixteenth century and now in the National Palace Museum in Taipei, depicts two Ming dynasty Go players at the beginning of a game. The players are much larger than their enraptured onlookers, one reaching his hand into a bowl of stones.

By this point, the game had spread to Korea and Japan, where it was popular with the upper classes and in the imperial court. Aesthetes determined that Nachiguro slate, mined deep in the mountains of Kumano, in the south of Japan, made the finest black Go stones. Clamshells, gathered from a small beach in Hyuga, on the island of Kyushu, made the best white ones. Other refinements emerged. The white stones were made smaller than the black ones to account for the optical illusion that makes white stones appear larger. Though the grid's dimensions are square, the boards became rectangular, about an inch longer than wide, to account for foreshortening when viewed from the standard seated playing positions. Board makers would use a sword to cut the grid lines on their preferred kaya wood, taken from the Japanese nutmeg yew—a tree that might live to be five hundred years old but flourished on only one hill southwest of Tokyo. By the seventeenth century, the ruling shoguns had begun hosting prestigious tournaments in their castles. They also established the four Go schools, including Honinbo, home of Shusai the Master.

THE COMMON ROOM in the math building at Princeton University is a legendary game-playing venue. Not as distinguished, of course, as the great Go houses of Japan, but nevertheless a reverential space at the university, which has been central to modern game theory. Players there have explored backgammon, poker, bridge, and Kriegspiel, a complex wargame variant also called blind chess that requires three chessboards and an arbiter. It's boasted that Fine Hall "could produce a champion in any game that was played sitting down," according to the school's alumni magazine. Ralph Fox, a mathematician and pioneer in knot theory, introduced Go here in the 1940s. He called it "the most interesting game in the world." Fox's passion soon spread to the nearby Institute for Advanced Study. The game-theory genius John Nash played it. So did Albert Einstein. The story goes that Einstein befriended a chess master and Go enthusiast named Edward Lasker. At Princeton, Lasker gifted Einstein a signed copy of a book he'd written on Go, and Einstein gave Lasker a signed copy of one of his papers on relativity. A signed copy of the Go book was later found in a used bookstore. Someone told Lasker, who said, "That's all right. I left his relativity paper on the subway."

Inspired by Go and the tiles on a bathroom floor, Nash invented the fascinating and mathematically important game known then as "John" or "Nash" and known today as Hex. Using a Go board and stones, John Horton Conway, the great games mathematician, invented philosopher's football.* By accident, while studying end-

---

* Conway described that game thus: "Every time you take your turn you get this horrible feeling in the pit of your stomach. Because every move is bad. . . . You

games in Go, Conway also came up with the concept of surreal numbers—a class containing all the real numbers along with infinite and infinitesimal numbers. "Numbers *are* games," he said.

Across the Atlantic, Alan Turing played—he'd known the game since at least the 1930s. Turing taught it to Jack Good, a mathematician and his colleague in wartime cryptography at Bletchley Park. Good was a famous enthusiast of artificial intelligence. He hypothesized an "intelligence explosion"—the phenomenon wherein a superintelligent machine designs an even *more* superintelligent machine, which designs an even *more* . . . and so on, situating advanced AI as "the last invention that man need ever make." He later recanted his enthusiasm and became an adviser to filmmaker Stanley Kubrick on *2001: A Space Odyssey*, which featured the famously inhumane chess-playing computer HAL 9000.

Back in 1965, however, Good could find only a handful of books in English about Go. He helped spread the word in Europe with an article in *New Scientist* titled "The Mystery of Go." In the article, he speculated on the relative challenges of teaching a computer to play the game. "The principles are more qualitative and mysterious than in chess, and depend more on judgment," he said, concluding that it would require humans to "design a learning programme."

Good saw in Go an elegance that might make it intriguing and pleasurable to any kind of intelligence—artificial or otherwise. He wrote, "The rules are basically so simple that perhaps a game very much like Go is played in many extra-terrestrial places, even within our own galaxy."

Good wasn't the only one to hypothesize this way. Lasker, the man who taught the game to Einstein, commented, "While the baroque rules of chess could only have been created by humans,

_____

make any move and immediately feel you shouldn't have done it, and you think to yourself, 'Oh God, what have I done?'"

the rules of Go are so elegant, organic, and rigorously logical that if intelligent life forms exist elsewhere in the universe, they almost certainly play Go."

An underpinning of Go's haunting beauty is a concept called *emergence*—the idea that from simple elements can emerge complex systems, that the whole is more than the sum of its parts. From dry molecular chemistry emerges *life*. From lumps of gray matter emerges *consciousness*. From individual humans emerges society: culture, science, politics, and war.

Everything interesting about Go is the result of emergent behavior. Consider, as an example, this group of black stones. It has five liberties around its edge and two liberties in its interior, including one at the board's corner. These inner liberties are called *eyes*. To capture this group, white would have to occupy all the liberties around the edge and both of those in the interior. But any white stone placed in the interior would *itself* have no liberties and immediately be captured by black. Therefore, this little group of black stones can never be captured. It will live forever.

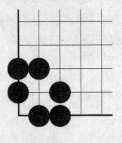

Live stones

There is nothing explicit in the rules of Go that says a group of stones with two eyes can't be captured. Rather, that fact arises solely from subtle interactions of the game's atomic parts. It's no accident, therefore, that *life* and *death* are themselves core concepts in the game. Stones are said to be alive when they can never be captured, like those above. Stones are said to be dead when they cannot avoid capture. It's not always easy to tell what's alive and what's dead. In fact, this is a subject of deep study.

The importance of emergence poses a deep cognitive challenge to the player of Go: the game's strategies and tactics aren't simply performed; they are *discovered*. Go is like a kind of intellectual chemistry, its atomic rules being combined into molecular forms and added, over the centuries, to the game's periodic table.

"It is intensely contemplative," said Frank Lantz, director of the NYU Game Center, in Greg Kohs's recent documentary on the game. "It is almost hypnotic. It's like you're putting your hand on the third rail of the universe. Go is putting you in a place where you're always at the edge of your capacity. There's a reason people have been playing Go for thousands and thousands of years. It's not just that they want to understand Go. It's that they want to understand what *understanding* is. Maybe that's truly what it means to be a human."

What does it mean, then, when a computer understands this game better than any of us?

ON A BITTERLY COLD Canadian afternoon, Martin Müller and I sat across from each other at a large conference table in the computer science department at the University of Alberta. The office of Jonathan Schaeffer, the man who solved checkers, was just down the hall. The department's aura and institutional history are defined by its faculty's monklike devotion to artificial intelligence and games. Müller, a giant and friendly Austrian with a large face and glasses, has studied Hex (John Nash's game), Amazons (a sort of chess-Go hybrid), and clobber (a game played on a rectangular checkerboard), and he has worked on Go for decades.

We discussed the lengthy, fraught, and largely failed effort to craft a strong computer Go player. The game simply did not yield to the trusty methods of AI. The first PhD on computer Go was completed in 1970 by a student at the University of Wisconsin. "That program apparently could *sometimes* beat a complete beginner," Müller told me, laughing. "That was about the level." Progress was slow. In the 1980s and early '90s, computers were losing to youth players at enormous fifteen- and even seventeen-stone handicaps. In 1992, the computer champion was a program named Go Intellect, which took on schoolchildren after winning its silicon-based title. "The computer took forever to think, and then came up with stupid moves," an eleven-year-old from Taiwan told the Associated Press. In 1998, Martin Müller himself beat a program called the Many Faces of Go, even after spotting the machine a gargantuan twenty-nine-stone handicap.

The onerous pursuit of a superhuman player wasn't for lack of incentive. Ing Chang-ki, a Taiwanese industrialist and Go obsessive, sought to put his own stamp on the game, including hawking his own set of rules, the Ing Rules, and advocating changing its name to "Goe," so as to avoid confusion with the English verb "go." Beginning in 1985, he financed a schedule of prizes, to be awarded during the Ing Cup, which was held, according to the repository computer-go.info, "on the eleventh day of the eleventh month, for numerological reasons favoured by Mr. Ing": $100,000 (in Taiwanese dollars) for a computer beating a pro in training at a seventeen-stone handicap, with increasing purses up to TWD$40 million (about US$1.3 million today) for no handicap at all. The prizes expired in 2000, and only those up to eleven-stone handicaps were ever claimed.

Müller, however, got into the Go business not for money but because he, too, wanted to understand what understanding is. He is a strong player, but even strong players struggle to explain how they do what they do—how they recognize intricate patterns on the

board and how they toggle between the local and the global battles, which simultaneously and uniquely define Go. Müller hoped
the computer could help explain things. At first, he said, "we tried
to program the rules." Programming the rules was the bedrock of
games AI. It's what Jonathan Schaeffer was doing when he sliced
apart the collected checkers games of Marion Tinsley and what
IBM did when it hired a grandmaster to advise the Deep Blue team.
The "rules" Müller referred to are how humans internalize and
express Go's complicated and abstract ideas. The game, for example, is famous for its proverbs, sayings such as "Big dragons never
die," "A rich man should not pick quarrels," "Sacrifice plums for
peaches," and "Don't go fishing while your house is on fire." Early
Go programmers tried to encode these maxims into their machines,
a process the *New Yorker* once called "computational exegesis." And
indeed, as Fan Hui thought might happen to him at DeepMind,
scientists *have* stuck Go professionals into brain scanners to see what
makes them tick, finding, in one case documented in the journal
Cognitive Brain Research, "enhanced activations . . . in many cortical
areas, such as dorsal prefrontal, parietal, occipital, posterior temporal, and primary somatosensory and motor areas." Scientists have
also found that Go, unlike chess, lights up a player's Broca's area, a
part of the brain associated with language. But what humans tend to
be good at computers do not, and vice versa, an observation known
as Moravec's paradox,* and Müller's goal of *understanding understanding* remained unfulfilled.

  Philosophers and epistemologists, with a few exceptions, don't
think explicitly about games much, but they have implicitly recognized their importance since the middle of the twentieth century,

---

* Its eponym, the Carnegie Mellon roboticist Hans Moravec, also predicted in 1998
that the "general intellectual performance of the human brain" would be matched
by machines in the 2020s.

largely via artificial intelligence. "The history of AI reveals a long-standing acknowledgment, on the part of philosophers, of the epistemic significance of games," Jenny Judge, a philosopher at NYU, told me.

Philosophers are hardly all in agreement about the importance of artificial intelligence. Some believe that AI could indeed become a legitimate manifestation of human understanding, in the sense of intelligence or cognition; these are advocates of "strong AI." Others balk at this notion but do defend "weak AI," the idea that AI may mimic limited aspects of human understanding. Others still reject both ideas, arguing that AI could never become a legitimate manifestation of human understanding at all.

AI developers have largely stood with the "strong AI" camp and believe that AI's success in games will help prove their point. "This design decision trades on the assumption that the playing of games of particular kinds is a clear manifestation of human understanding," Judge said. "This being the case, if you can get AIs to play the right kind of games, you'll have successfully reverse-engineered human understanding and, it is often assumed, come to understand its nature in the process." This was Müller's project and his struggle.

This argument, that games are useful media for understanding understanding, could be extended not just to academics but to games' rank-and-file players, too. "One could argue that the playing of games offers the perceptive player the opportunity to witness one's own intelligence at work with a clarity that one is rarely afforded in everyday contexts," Judge said. This is the art of games: a distilled, crystallized experience of human agency. To play Go is to witness one's intelligence hard at work indeed.

But the computer player that saw the game of Go with anything resembling clarity remained elusive. In 1997, shortly after Deep Blue defeated Garry Kasparov, the *New York Times* quoted an astrophysicist and Go player at the Institute for Advanced Study as saying, "It

may be a hundred years before a computer beats humans at Go—
maybe even longer."

LITTLE PROGRESS WAS MADE on the problem of Go, its tree largely
unclimbable by digital ants, until Rémi Coulom, a former computer
science professor at the University of Lille, in France, reached a breakthrough. Drawing on his background in computer chess, he built a
program called Crazy Stone, which debuted in 2005. It was among
the first to successfully deploy an algorithm called *Monte Carlo tree
search*, a term Coulom coined. The effect seemed miraculous.

Broadly speaking, the Monte Carlo method, named after the
famous casino in Monaco, uses the results of random events to solve
deterministic problems—that is, problems where there is a fixed,
true answer. The modern version of the idea was developed as part
of the Manhattan Project. The method is often useful when the
calculation would be tedious. Say, for example, you want to estimate the number π. One way to do so would be to measure very
carefully the circumference and diameter of a perfect circle, if you
can find one, and calculate their ratio. Another, more fun method
would be to spill a box of matches on a hardwood floor. Each match
represents the diameter of an imaginary circle. The probability that
one of these circles crosses any of the lines between floorboards is
a figure that contains π.* The more matchsticks you drop, and the
more times you run the experiment, the better your estimate for π
will be. Elegance emerges from the randomness.

Monte Carlo tree search, or MCTS, leverages randomness to
create a powerful shortcut. In most chess programs, an algorithm
searches through copious possible positions and evaluates the quality
of each potential move by, in large part, counting the pieces on each

---

* Specifically, the probability that a randomly dropped matchstick overlaps a line is
$(2/\pi)(l/w)$, where l is the length of a stick and w is the width of the floorboards.

side.* In Go, counting pieces is largely pointless. Each player has roughly the same number of pieces on the board, and all the pieces are the same. It's like trying to compare two Rothko paintings by counting the number of brushstrokes. Furthermore, the entire board is in play. Small disputes can become full-scale battles, and a stone is one corner can affect another stone in another corner a hundred moves down the road. Feng-hsiung Hsu, the Deep Blue scientist, put it this way in an article in 2007: "In a typical [Go] game, we may easily have more than ten such problems on the board at the same time, and the status of one group can affect that of its neighbors— like a cowboy who points a revolver at another cowboy only to find himself covered by a rifleman on a roof."

In other words, a chess program starts at the base of the tree trunk and frantically assesses branches and twigs until it has found a promising route to the canopy. In Go, where the "tree" is obscenely complicated, MCTS skips this tedious climbing and just scans a random bunch of whole trees. It plays the game to the end many times using *random* moves and maps the results. Some of these random moves will have led to more victories. Those moves are probably good, and the program weighs them more heavily when it randomly simulates the game the next time. After doing this over and over, MCTS produces a map of good and bad moves without ever playing the game in the traditional way. Indeed, Go is so complicated that it is easier for a computer to play it by accident than to attempt a traditional search-and-evaluation approach. It's as surprising and beautiful as finding π in a mess of matchsticks.

Armed to the teeth with brainpower and hardware, DeepMind

---

* In a traditional formula, pawns are worth one point, knights and bishops three, rooks five, and queens nine. To get a finer idea, researchers can assign bonus points for passed pawns and well-protected kings and so on. The king itself, of course, is invaluable.

and AlphaGo stretched MCTS to superhuman levels. They took deep-learning algorithms, like those trained to recognize human faces, and programmed them to recognize strong Go moves. Faster than anyone expected, Go programs went from bad to otherworldly.

Müller had spent his career studying Go. His academic department had devoted countless hours to the problem. Besides a recondite paper or two out of DeepMind, there had been no warning of what was developing. And then all of a sudden Go was done. Did it come as a surprise?

"Oh, yeah," Müller said, nodding solemnly. "Oh yeah, oh yeah."

As his research agenda was usurped by one of the biggest tech companies in the world, Müller pivoted to studying the thinking of deep-learning systems like AlphaGo, and how we might learn from them—a field known as explainability. AlphaGo can win at Go, but it can't explain why it played the way it played. It can do, but it can't *teach*. And maybe that's fine for a Go player. But consider a structural engineer or a medical doctor, say, on the receiving end of some advice from a machine-learning system. It's reasonable for them to want some proof—some *why*—from the system. Müller, therefore, has evolved from someone who studied human thinking through computer models to someone who studies computer thinking for human models.

"We won't run out of interesting research projects—that's the good news," he said. We departed the conference room for a tour of the department and to play a few games. Back in his office, Müller's enormous computer monitor lit up with the black and white of stones, the dull yellow of a digitally simulated wooden board, and the garish greens and reds of a deep neural network's analysis of the position in front of us.

"It's very early in a revolution," he said. "The revolution just happened, so there's high uncertainty."

———

THE ALPHAGO-LEE SEDOL match, officially billed as the Google DeepMind Challenge Match, was held at the Four Seasons in Seoul, South Korea. It began on March 9, 2016, and was to be the best of five games. It was broadcast to an estimated eighty million people worldwide and was shown on little screens in Go clubs across the country and giant screens outside the Seoul Finance Center. As the match began, commentators online were imploring Lee to "save the world."

"Is it strange that your dad is fighting against a machine?" a reporter asked Lee's daughter, Hye-lim, a young child in a sparkly sweatshirt.

"I'd like it if the machine didn't beat a human in Go yet," she said.

She wasn't alone. Experts and fans of the game predicted a Lee victory, and most foresaw a 5–0 rout in his favor. Lee himself was confident in winning 5–0. "I believe that human intuition is still too advanced for AI to have caught up," he said in a pre-match press conference. "I'm going to do my best to protect human intelligence." Minutes later, Lee stood outside the small playing room, accompanied by men in red ties and Secret Service–like earpieces, and closed his eyes, as if meditating.

Game One saw fighting from the very beginning, and the quick and surprised consensus among experts was that AlphaGo played "like a human." But then, just as quick, the consensus was that it played nothing like a human at all. Sentiment would pendulum between these feelings over the course of the next week. With echoes of the Kasparov match, the Korean commentators sensed self-doubt in Lee. Out of habit, Lee kept glancing at AlphaGo's operator, who, of course, revealed nothing. In the absence of human emotional cues, Lee could only look inward.

On move 102, AlphaGo unleashed its attack, invading one of Lee's black encampments from its thick vertical wall of white stones. Lee stared at the stone, mouth agape.

"Look at his face, look at his face!" said David Silver, the AlphaGo project leader, watching on television from DeepMind's war room elsewhere in the hotel, another moment captured in the documentary *AlphaGo*.

"He's pretty horrified by that," said Demis Hassabis, one of DeepMind's cofounders.

Fan Hui, providing official annotation on the games for Deep-Mind, wrote, "Black must have felt the sharp pain of the incision at White 102." Indeed, some eighty moves after the invasion, Lee, who was playing the black stones, placed a white stone on the board, a gesture of resignation. The commentators could only laugh—letting out that sort of involuntary laugh that overcomes you when you're overwhelmed, when there's no other response, when you can't cry.

At various points in the match, Google cofounder Sergey Brin and executive chairman Eric Schmidt mingled in the DeepMind war room, inquiring as to the machine's winning chances. It was almost all good news.

Lee slowed his pace of play dramatically during Game Two, having been chastened by the machine. Staffers brought him coffees on silver platters. The man and the algorithm traded jabs early on, playing out a traditional *joseki* opening, jockeying for position in the corners of the board. Because Lee is a smoker, a private terrace with security guards had been arranged so that he could take breaks during games. While he was on the terrace pacing and having a cigarette, staring off toward the mountain peaks, AlphaGo played move 37.

At first, everyone thought it was a mistake. Perhaps the stone had been placed on the wrong point accidentally. You simply do not make a shoulder hit on the fifth line, went the collective wisdom.

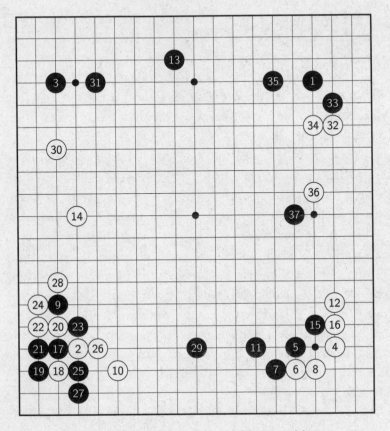

The position after AlphaGo's move 37, center right,
the stone heard 'round the world

It's just a bad idea. The move was "surprising" and "unthinkable,"
declared the commentariat.

Lee returned to the playing room to see the new black stone on
the board, placed there without emotion by AlphaGo's lead programmer and operator, Aja Huang. Within a matter of seconds,
Lee's face contorted from a tragically pained grimace to a knowing
smile to a good impression of Rodin's *Thinker*. Though it flouted
established human Go doctrine, move 37 wasn't bad. It was great. It

recognized the subtle influence that each part of the Go board has on every other. As more and more moves were played, the move 37 stone connected the other black stones perfectly, helping them form a beautiful network, strands between the stars.

AlphaGo was made up of three main parts. There is the policy network, which was trained on tens of thousands of high-level games downloaded from the internet to imitate those elite players; the value network, which evaluates the position and delivers the probability of winning; and the tree search, which tries to divine the future of the game. Each of these is just computer code, mathematics. But as creative beauty emerges from the simple rules of Go, so too does it arise from the collaboration of these parts.

"I thought AlphaGo was based on probability calculation and it was merely a machine," Lee said after the game. "But when I saw this move, I changed my mind. Surely AlphaGo is creative. This move was really creative and beautiful." He said that the move made him see Go in a new light. He resigned after the 211th move. That night, he assembled some of his professional Go-playing friends and analyzed the game into the wee hours.

Lee's hands were shaking as he placed the stones early in Game Three. He opened with the High Chinese *fuseki*—a whole-board opening—indicating that he was there to fight. But as early as the eighteenth move, his position was already being torn apart. Lee's face began to turn red, and he took to sighing. He stepped outside for another smoke break after the thirty-third move, but it was no help. By the seventy-seventh move, the game was seemingly out of reach. Lee resorted to a last-ditch "zombie" style, flailing recklessly around the board in an effort to catch the machine off guard. He wouldn't. A distraught Lee resigned on the 176th move; the match was over.

One professional commented that "playing with AlphaGo can feel distressingly like euthanasia: by the time we feel what is going on, we are already dead."

———

ON A BLUSTERY AUTUMN DAY, in a small glass room inside Harvard Medical School, I met Mohammed AlQuraishi, a research fellow in systems pharmacology. AlQuraishi is the owner of a lengthy and impressive résumé, which lists roles as a geneticist, biophysicist, programmer, digital artist, and dot-com entrepreneur. We sat at a small table, AlQuraishi a slender, balding figure in sneakers, blue jeans, and an orange sweater. On one wall of the room was a whiteboard, dense with multicolored mathematical scribblings—layers of graphs, diagrams, and equations, the oldest of which remained faint on the surface, not quite fully erased. On the other wall was a colorful abstract painting, garish and bright.

In late 2018, in the wake of AlphaGo's victory, DeepMind entered another one of its computer systems—this one called AlphaFold—into a different sort of competition. Every two years since 1994, there has been a contest called the Critical Assessment of protein Structure Prediction, or CASP. It is a contest about predicting how proteins will fold. Proteins are the fundamental molecules of life, and protein folding is the intricate process by which chains of amino acids contort themselves, like microscopic origami, into highly specific three-dimensional shapes. These shapes allow the proteins to do useful things, such as deliver messages or transport ions. Understanding this folding process is a basic scientific pursuit and can spur the discovery of drugs—for example, small-molecule drugs, which bind to proteins to activate them, inhibit them, or otherwise alter their behavior. The mathematics of protein folding dwarf even those of Go; a protein with a hundred amino acids could take on a huge number of different structures—a number, in fact, that has something like three hundred digits.

"This is a lighthouse project, our first major investment in terms of people and resources into a fundamental, very important, real-world scientific problem," Hassabis, the DeepMind cofounder, told the *Guardian*.

At CASP13, in December 2018, tens of thousands of models were submitted by about a hundred research groups around the world with the goal of predicting just how certain proteins will fold into three dimensions. DeepMind's AlphaFold won in a rout. It predicted the most accurate structure for twenty-five out of the forty-three proteins it was presented with; the second-place team predicted three. I learned about AlQuraishi's work in the wake of the competition, when he published a wide-eyed blog post subtitled "What Just Happened?"

AlQuraishi's post presented an indictment of both academic science (because of its failure to adequately address a vital problem) and the pharmaceutical industry (with its failure to outperform an outside lab that knew nothing about pharmaceuticals). An outsider to the field, armed not with hard-won knowledge but with high technology, had put them all to shame. "There was, in many ways, a broad sense of existential angst felt by most academic researchers at CASP13, including myself," he wrote. "For academic scientists, especially the more junior among us, we will have to contend with whether it's strategically sound for our careers to continue working on structure prediction." He sounded a lot like Martin Müller in Alberta after AlphaGo debuted.

"This is not Go, which had a handful of researchers working on the problem, and which had no direct applications beyond the core problem itself," AlQuraishi continued. "Protein folding is a central problem of biochemistry, with profound implications for the biological and chemical sciences."

But I wondered if these two projects weren't more closely connected than it appeared, and if Go was being too quickly dismissed as just a game. After all, the response to AlphaGo was the same as AlQuraishi's response to AlphaFold: *What just happened?* In both cases there was a sense of stupefaction and also of loss—that some hard-won scaffolding, man-made and climbable, had been toppled and replaced with an inscrutable monolith. Had experiences from the world of games—that is, the obliteration of very hard, very human problems—repeated themselves now in the "real world"?

"A lot of people lament that the *art* of the science is getting lost," AlQuraishi told me. "There are people who have prided themselves on reasoning about these biological systems and trying to come up with models that capture something about the underlying phenomenon, that require some degree of human reasoning and some degree of experimentation." But, he continued, "there has been this shift to: collect data, take an off-the-shelf machine learning model, apply it on that data, and see what comes out. Taking the fun out of science is maybe too harsh, but I think it's taken a little bit of the art out of science."

This, too, sounded familiar. In 1954, Yasunari Kawabata had written that Go had succumbed to science and regulation. That one "conducted the battle only to win, and there was no margin for remembering the dignity and the fragrance of Go as an art." In 2018, the Harvard biologist Marc Kirschner said, "I believe that science, at its most creative, is more akin to a hunter-gatherer society than it is to a highly regimented industrial activity, more like a play group than a corporation." Perhaps certain sorts of scientific research are games, as they're conceived in Bernard Suits's definition: the voluntary attempt (developing theories) to overcome unnecessary obstacles (concordance with some specific set of empirical observations). Perhaps the ludic attitude of a games player, and the creativity and ingenuity that comes with it, is a boon for a scientist. Nevertheless, this play-group ethos has started to be abandoned. "In the last three or four years, there has been this *revolution* where all these hand-engineered models are getting swept away by machine-learning models," AlQuraishi said.

Even games as complex as Go are infinitely tidy compared to the mess of the real world. But some of these differences may disappear as technology improves, drawing games and the real world closer together still.

"One thing that's made AlphaGo possible is the fact that it plays games, and games are simulatable," he said. "You can generate data by compute—you can turn compute into data," meaning that the computer can play itself many times and study the results. "In some aspects of science, that's where there's a fundamental break. You can't do medical trials on the computer. You can't simulate humans—yet. However, there are areas of science which may lend themselves to exactly that type of exercise. Quantum computers could in fact be very good chemical simulators. If that were to happen, then you have a situation in which compute can be turned into data for some applications. That would be very, very exciting. Then you'd have a situation which would be directly analogous to AlphaGo, which you don't really have right now."

BY THE MORNING of March 13, 2016, the result of the best-of-five match was mathematically decided, with AlphaGo boasting a 3–0 lead over Lee Sedol. But they'd play on for pride, posterity, and PR. (And money: while the winner's prize was $1 million, which Google said it planned to donate to charity, Lee would still earn $150,000 for completing the match and $20,000 for a win in any individual game.) Lee was calm as Game Four began, his burden of defending his species having now been set aside. The game's official annotator noted that "Lee had finally found the confidence to play his own game, regardless of anyone's approval. This was the Lee Sedol I knew: the wolf that, starving in the winter winds, still waited for his prey to come closer."

As the game progressed, a crowd gathered outside. The rumor was spreading that Lee would soon resign. But Lee did not resign.

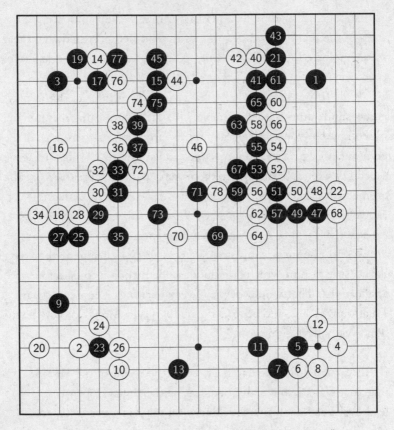

White 78, just northeast of the center, Lee's "divine move"

Traditionally, Go stones are placed on the board in a particular way. They are grasped not between the thumb and index finger, as seems natural at first, but, rather, with the index finger and middle finger pincering the stone from the bottom and top; then they are gently snapped down onto the board, all the better to place a precise stone in the midst of a crowded battle. The maneuver even has a name in Japanese: *tetsuki*, as in "beautiful *tetsuki*" or "clumsy *tetsuki*." Lee grasped a stone and snapped it onto the wooden surface.

"Like an earthquake, the wedge at seventy-eight"—shown above, near the center of the board—"tore apart the cracks in Black's fortress!" It was Lee's divine move, and it sent AlphaGo reeling. The computer flailed, trying to save stones that were already dead, committing blunder after blunder. For the next twenty-five moves, it appeared to have gone insane. The commentators and the audience began laughing at the machine. AlphaGo resigned on the 180th move. From his chair in the playing room, Lee could hear people outside shouting for joy.

The engineers later looked under the hood of their system, trying to diagnose what had gone wrong. They discovered, for one thing, that AlphaGo didn't place move seventy-eight among the top five moves in the position. In fact, it thought that only one in ten thousand players would have played it. Lee was that player.

"At the point in the game, move seventy-eight was the only move I could see," he said.

Lee had never been congratulated so much for winning a single game, and he entered the press room to thunderous applause. Perhaps it was a small fluke in the machine's defenses—like Achilles' heel or the Death Star's exhaust port—but the win mattered.

"Winning this one time, it felt like it was enough," he said. "One time was enough."

Before Game Five, Lee and AlphaGo were meant to draw lots to see who would play with which color stones. But Lee asked Hassabis and Silver if he could play black. In other words, he was asking for the toughest possible challenge. (Late in his career, given the deference paid to him, the Master hadn't played black in more than thirty years.) They agreed.

Early on, it seemed as if AlphaGo may still have been deluded, and experts gave the edge to Lee. AlphaGo had chosen to attack a small group of Lee's stones, letting a large group of its own stones die in the process—which appeared to be a blunder. This appearance was an illusion. Instead, it seems, we humans simply didn't understand Go well enough to judge what the machine was up to. As Fan Hui commented, "Of course, from the human perspective of seeking the best moves, AlphaGo's choice was a foolish one. From a global perspective, however, white is by no means behind." The program's "mistakes" weren't mistakes at all. In fact, they might influence the way Go is played for centuries to come. They revealed how much there is that we didn't know, and how much there is that we didn't know we didn't know. The final game took 280 moves, the longest game of the match, but Lee lost again.

The final score was four games to one. South Korea's Go association awarded AlphaGo the honorary rank of nine *dan*, the same as Lee Sedol and Honinbo Shusai. The program was a runner-up in *Science*'s 2016 breakthroughs of the year, second only to the discovery of ripples in the very fabric of space-time caused by the collision of two black holes a million light-years away.

AlphaGo is not something you or I can access. We can't buy the proprietary software or get destroyed by it or learn lessons from it in the comfort of our own homes. But one hobbyist and a legion of amateur followers, over a year or so of spare computer time, unlocked its powerful abilities and released them to the world. They liberated AlphaGo.

I spoke with Gian-Carlo Pascutto from his home in Belgium. Pascutto's background is in computer chess, but a lucky confluence of events, culminating with the 2008 Computer Olympiad in Beijing, brought him to Go. "I thought, 'OK, if we're going to China, we might as well play in the Go tournament,'" he told me. His program, named Leela, finished a respectable third.

A few years later, though, the field was upended. "Like everyone, I heard the news that DeepMind had created a new Go-playing program that was way stronger than anything before it and any human player," Pascutto said. "Of course, this was intriguing."

When the news was first announced, the press releases from DeepMind were light on technical details. Later, DeepMind revealed that it had been using not only over-the-counter CPUs or GPUs, like you might find in your own computer, but also hardware called TPUs—tensor processing units, Google's custom-built chips designed specifically for machine learning.* DeepMind used five thousand of these chips for its computer player. Pascutto sat down and ran the numbers: He calculated that it would take him and his personal computer seventeen hundred years to replicate DeepMind's research. He needed help.

"It did occur to me that the majority of this calculation, the part that was done on those five thousand special-purpose chips, was perfectly distributable," Pascutto said. "So the idea was born: If we can find enough people on the internet that are interested, we might still have a chance of replicating the results."

Like the famous projects SETI@home (Berkeley's search for extraterrestrial life) and Folding@home (Stanford's effort to understand protein folding) before him, Pascutto leveraged the power of the internet to surmount an otherwise impossibly daunting task. He put out a call for interested volunteers to donate their own computing resources, the idle time on their machines, chipping away en masse at the enormous training exercise. They started in November 2017. In less than a year, the program was "very, very strong." Leela Zero, now one of the best Go players in the world, is freely available and open-source.

"I've been asking all these people to run their computers for me,

---

* A tensor is a mathematical object, like a multidimensional matrix, used in machine learning to store data.

and now they will actually have something to show for it," Pascutto said. While he essentially freed their superhuman player from its corporate cage, Pascutto says he's had no interaction with Deep-Mind or Google about his project.* But combined, Rémi Coulom's Monte Carlo tree search, AlphaGo, and Leela Zero sparked a revolution in the ancient game.

I had asked Martin Müller if any professionals had used computers to train before AlphaGo and Leela Zero, as they have in chess for decades.

"No, they were too weak," he said flatly.

And now?

"Oh yeah, everyone's using it now. All the young ones use it, and there are a few who are especially technically savvy, and they teach or even sell their services to other professionals."

Within months of AlphaGo's triumph, and inspired by it, unprecedentedly superhuman Go-playing software began to spring from other corporate labs. Tencent, the Chinese multinational con-glomerate, created Fine Art. Thinker Technology, a Chinese AI company, created Golaxy. And NHN Entertainment, a Korean IT company, created HanDol. These days, in the study rooms of Asian Go schools, the modern successors to the famed houses, such as Honinbo, one can find rows of students at laptops, staring at screens, learning from the machine.

IN 1938, HONINBO SHUSAI, the Master of Go, at age sixty-four, lost his retirement game to a young prodigy. He was put off by the modern reforms that had reshaped the game to which he had devoted his life. The match, according to its renowned chronicler,

---

* A similar distributed project, called Leela Chess Zero, or Lc0, was undertaken to replicate DeepMind's chess results, led by a programmer named Gary Linscott. The results were similar, too: Lc0 is now among the strongest chess engines in the world.

claimed the Master's life. As the Japanese novelist Naoki Sanjugo was dying young (Kawabata would write his eulogy), he authored an autobiographical piece reflecting on his interest in the game. "If one chooses to look upon Go as valueless, then absolutely valueless it is," he wrote. "And if one chooses to look upon it as a thing of value, then a thing of absolute value it is."

In late 2019, at the age of thirty-six, Lee Sedol abruptly retired from the game. Like Shusai decades before him, Lee "stood at the boundary between the old and the new," and as it had for the Master, the new spelled his end. "With the debut of AI in Go games, I've realized that I'm not at the top even if I become the number one through frantic efforts," he told a Korean news agency. "Even if I become the number one, there is an entity that cannot be defeated."

The human brain, yours and mine and Lee Sedol's, is unbelievably complex. It's home to some hundred billion neurons that make some hundred trillion connections. The human brain is also remarkably efficient. It operates on about twenty watts of power—barely enough to power a dim lightbulb. AlphaGo, on the other hand, required somewhat more resources.

In recent years, computer scientists such as Carnegie Mellon's Emma Strubell have been studying the environmental impact of training AI models. In a world being warmed by human emissions of greenhouse gases, advanced AI can be ecologically questionable. "Training a state-of-the-art model now requires substantial computational resources which demand considerable energy, along with the associated financial and environmental costs," she and her coauthors write in a 2019 paper. They continue: "We recommend a concerted effort by industry and academia to promote research of more computationally efficient algorithms, as well as hardware that requires less energy."

An applied mathematician named Aidan Rocke estimated that merely training one version of AlphaGo had a footprint of ninety-six metric tons of carbon dioxide—roughly equivalent to a thousand hours of air travel or a year's worth of electricity usage for twenty-three American homes. An engineer named Dan Huang estimated that replicating a certain forty-day experiment by DeepMind to train AlphaGo would cost $35 million. Put another way, it took the equivalent of nearly thirteen thousand human brains running continuously. The machine may have triumphed. But it was never a fair fight.

BACKGAMMON

Luck is not chance—
It's Toil—
Fortune's expensive smile
Is earned—
The Father of the Mine
Is that old-fashioned Coin
We spurned—

—EMILY DICKINSON

NINETY YEARS AGO, a team of archaeologists, surveyors, and dozens of workmen traveled down the Nile on a pair of large sailboats, distinctive and magnificent vessels called dahabeahs, loaded with documents, equipment, and tins of food. It had recently been decided that the massive Aswan Dam, in the southeast of Egypt, was to be heightened—a project that would flood swaths of Lower Nubia. The team raced to excavate and catalog the region's ancient sites before they were engulfed. They embarked during three consecutive winters to avoid the heat. The first two seasons of painstaking work, however, brought disappointingly few discoveries, nothing that would eclipse the earlier archaeological finds to the north. But during the final season, in 1931, the group arrived at the royal cemetery of Qustul.

In an otherwise empty desert, amid only a few scattered palm and acacia trees, they saw a group of earthen mounds, some more than forty feet high. After climbing one, and observing its perfectly circular shape, the team began "to consider the possibility of them being the work of man." Others had gazed upon mounds like these before; none had cataloged what was beneath them. With their funds running low, the team took a calculated gamble. They outlaid the two hundred pounds such work would cost, and they began to dig.

In the side of one mound they lucked upon a passage, just two feet tall, left by grave robbers perhaps a thousand years earlier. They cleared the debris from the ancient robbers' path, crawling on their hands and knees, and, after fifty feet or so, smashed through a wall and into a tomb. It turned out to be one of sixty-one tombs they'd find under the mounds at Qustul, and in this one, the largest of them all, objects filled it "like currants in a cake."

The team found an elaborately embossed leather shield. They found a wood-and-iron spear—"a most formidable weapon." And they found an ivory knife decorated with the image of Bes, the Egyptian god of fertility. Deeper down still, they came upon yet another object, one that at first appeared something like a picture frame. Its elaborate underside was inlaid with ivory, and its corners were bracketed with silver. It was also marked with rows of twelve squares and sported a silver carrying handle. Beneath the object, in a leather pouch, they discovered fifteen ivory pieces, fifteen ebony pieces, and a set of ivory dice.

"The value of the finds buried within the mound spurred our workmen on to greater efforts," wrote Walter Emery, the Egyptologist leading the expedition. But they had to work fast. Two years later, the dam went higher and the reservoir began to rise. Today, Qustul is 250 feet under water.

The game discovered in that Nubian tomb is now known as *duodecim scripta*, or the game of twelve signs, and it is a direct forebear of modern-day backgammon; scholarship dates that specific relic to the fourth century A.D., though its ancestors may be far older. Backgammon has rows of twelve spaces. It has fifteen pieces in each of two colors. And, crucially, it has dice. The unpredictable ricochets of a simple pair of cubes at the beginning of each turn classify backgammon as a game of chance.

As with human genealogy, the subject of game lineage is fraught. The trail goes cold or grows convoluted. Games are invented and reinvented, and games evolve as they spread through the tumult of trade and diplomacy, migration and settlement, war and conquest. We know that the game Emery found at Qustul has Roman origins. The Romans conquered Egypt in 30 B.C., arriving on warships and deposing Cleopatra. This theory holds that the centurions brought their dice. A competing theory traces backgammon to India around the second century B.C. Researcher Micaela Soar writes that "Indian tradition associates it with the notions of regeneration and two-way movement that underlie rebirth, cosmic cycles and royal sacrifices."

Despite the thicket of history, modern researchers have established reliable facts and even full rule sets for a precious handful of other ancient games. All of them (like backgammon) rely on randomness, and all of them (like backgammon) are at their core a *race*—get your pieces to the finish line before the other player. A game called fifty-eight holes, the oldest example of which was found in Azerbaijan and dated to the eighteenth century B.C., features skinny playing pieces shaped like hounds and jackals. A game called nard, another backgammon forebear, hails from Persia around 2000 B.C., and an early reference to it appears in the Babylonian Talmud; it is still played in some countries today. Ancient Egyptians enjoyed senet (played on a grid of thirty squares) and mehen (with a racetrack shaped like a snake god) at least as early as 2600 B.C. King Tutankhamen was buried with a number of senet boards, and Queen Nefertari is shown playing the game in an ancient wall painting. At the same time, Mesopotamians played the Royal Game of Ur, also known as the game of twenty squares, on a board using pyramidal dice. Ur was one of the most popular games in the Near East for two thousand years but seems to have died out in late antiquity. In the 1980s, a philologist at the British Museum unriddled its rules after translating a Babylonian cuneiform tablet.

Given their provenance (we often find them in tombs), ancient games have often been connected to cosmology or religion or fortune-telling. Senet, for example, has been said to symbolize the rituals and obstacles on the path to the afterlife. But the real reason for games' spread and longevity might be more basic. In the ancient world, as the philologist Irving Finkel once told the *New Yorker*, "there were long periods of time when there was bugger all to do."

AN HOUR NORTH of Manhattan, tucked into deep woods and abutting a nature preserve, sits an enormous architectural marvel, unmistakably the work of man. The glass office building, designed by a pioneer of modernism, Eero Saarinen, emerges from the landscape in a wide arc, like a rising moon. IBM Research is the professional home of some fifteen hundred highly skilled employees; researchers shaped large swaths of the modern computer industry inside its walls. Inside the sweeping glass structure, on the third floor, is the cramped and windowless office of Gerald Tesauro, the man who conquered backgammon. A balding fellow of sixty, he sat at his desk in a green gingham shirt and a black fleece vest emblazoned with the IBM logo. I sat in a chair nearby with barely enough room to cross my legs. This was the site of Tesauro's triumph. I had brought my board along and wondered aloud if we might have a game, human against human. I had been studying backgammon strategy very seriously, I warned him, for the past seventy-two hours. He agreed to play after our interview.

"It's sort of an unusual journey to go from a theoretical physicist and turn into a game-player guy," Tesauro told me with a laugh. He was being modest. To any strong backgammon player today, Tesauro is the godfather of the modern game. His AI research project, and the commercial software products it would inspire, became both booster and barometer of human skill and the answer to all of backgammon's complex strategic questions—the game's *I Ching*, its Deep Thought.

Tesauro received his doctorate in physics at Princeton in

1986, with a dissertation on "steady-state dynamics and selection principles in nonequilibrium pattern-forming systems." Tesauro's conversion to computer science—and, therefore, the fate of competitive backgammon—was sealed by a single academic talk given decades ago at Bell Labs by John Hopfield, another Princeton physicist, about an exotic idea from condensed matter physics called spin glass. Spin glasses, roughly speaking, are made up of tiny little magnets, their north and south poles each "spun" to some random orientation, pointing this way or that way. Hopfield had developed a mathematical model whereby you could use this material, and the random tugging influences of its magnets on each other, to store memories.

"I just thought this was coolest thing I'd ever heard in my whole life," Tesauro said. "That was the beginning of starting to think about the brain and about neural networks."

Armed with new inspiration and a fresh field of study, Tesauro began trawling for a subject. At a workshop at the Santa Fe Institute, a nonprofit largely devoted to the study of complex systems, he chanced into Hans Berliner, the Carnegie Mellon computer scientist famous for his work on chess. Berliner had recently taken an interest in backgammon and had a new creation in tow. "He had his little, completely handcrafted backgammon program," Tesauro recalled. "I played two games against it and I beat the computer both times and I said, 'That's it, I'm quitting while I'm up.'"

But Tesauro, who describes himself as a "very, very casual" backgammon player who played in college for quarters, didn't quit the game entirely. Instead, he saw its potential as an application for neural networks. With some games, such as checkers or chess, a computer's main strength is its ability to search deeply into many potential futures, finding and evaluating positions far faster than any human player could. But that approach was ill-suited to backgammon, where one can't plan very far ahead. Each move begins randomly with one of twenty-one possible dice rolls,* any of which could provoke a wildly different state of affairs.

Put another way, backgammon's branching factor—the number of ways in which the game might change from one turn to the next—is much larger than chess's, by a factor of ten. One feels this acutely when playing. When a backgammon player makes a plan, God laughs. Win probabilities and money and world championships swing wildly on random skitters of the dice. Successful players take what the dice provide, then make the best play and move on. This is also a valuable, if difficult, life lesson.

The best backgammon players look for and rely on *patterns*: How are the pieces arranged on the board? What are their weaknesses? What are their strengths? "Neural nets are really, really good at pattern recognition, and that's much like how a human plays backgammon," Tesauro said. "You look at the patterns of the configurations on the board, and based on those patterns you get a sense of which move is going to be better than which other move."

When Tesauro described Berliner's early program as "handcrafted," he meant that it was built with explicit human knowledge, its mathematical dials and knobs specifically turned by a human working off the existing human knowledge of the game. The extent to which a player's pieces are blockaded, the relative safety of those pieces, and the extent to which a player is ahead in the race all earn a certain score, which the program includes in its so-called evaluation function, which eventually spits out a move. Tesauro's goal, beginning in the 1980s, was deeper and more elegant: he wanted the computer to figure out the game on its own.

To teach a neural network how to do something, you need data. One possible source of such data for backgammon could be

---

* There are six times six, or thirty-six, permutations of two dice, but only twenty-one *unique* combinations. E.g., five-two and two-five are operationally the same roll.

the records of expert humans' games. Tesauro pored over backgammon books, but actual complete game records were scant. So he created the training data himself. He played backgammon alone, against himself, hundreds of times, keeping meticulous note of all his plays and the rolls of the dice. He then fed that record into his program, which would come to be known as TD-Gammon.* By 1988, Tesauro had created a program that could beat its creator, the only being it had ever come into contact with. By 1989, he'd won the backgammon section at the Computer Olympiad. This is the hair-raising power of machine learning.

An ensuing version of the program, completed in the early 1990s, didn't even have Tesauro's data set to start from. It trained by playing more than three hundred thousand games against itself over a month of CPU time. After it beat two existing backgammon programs— Sun Microsystems' Gammontool and Tesauro's earlier Neurogammon, 73 and 60 percent of the time, respectively—Tesauro decided it was time to pit the new TD-Gammon against a top human. Tesauro dug up the phone number of Bill Robertie, a two-time world champion and backgammon author who lived in the Boston area. Robertie agreed to come down to New York for a day; in Tesauro's office at IBM Research, the room in which Tesauro and I now sat, he would play a thirty-one-game match against the program.

PEOPLE BORN AFTER the 1970s, the game's heyday, may recognize backgammon only from the inscrutable skinny black and red triangles found on the back of their checkerboard as a kid. Those skinny triangles are called points, and there are twenty-four of them, twelve on a side. Each player starts with fifteen checkers, arranged at the

---

* The "TD" stands for "temporal difference," a type of reinforcement learning where the machine is programmed to maximize some reward—e.g., for winning backgammon games.

start in a particular way on certain of the points. The starting position is shown in the diagram below. The goal is to get all of your checkers off the board. To do this, the players take turns rolling two dice and moving their checkers along a C-shaped track on which the points are station stops. The numbers that come up on the dice are the numbers of points you can move a checker. So, for example, if you roll a five and a two, you move one checker five points and another two points (or a single checker seven total points). Doubles award a bonus: if you roll two fives, say, you get *four* moves of five points apiece.

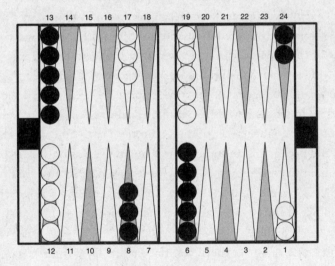

You *cannot*, however, land on a point already occupied by more than one enemy checker—that space is enemy territory. You *can*, however, land on a point occupied by exactly one enemy checker, in which case your checker occupies that point and the enemy checker is sent off the track altogether, and onto a bar in the middle of the board; it has to start over from the beginning, regaining a place on the board before its player can do anything else.

One player moves her checkers clockwise while the other player moves his counterclockwise; one side of the board acts as the finish line. In the diagram, the white checkers move clockwise from the lower right to the upper right (points 1 to 24), while the black checkers move counterclockwise from the upper right to the lower right (points 24 to 1). Once all of your checkers are within your final quadrant of the track, known as your home board, you may begin moving them past the finish line and off the board, according to the rolls of the dice, a practice known as "bearing off." The first player to bear off all her checkers wins.

(If one player wins before the other player has borne off any checkers, that's called a gammon and is worth double stakes. If the other player's checkers are still in their starting quadrant or on the bar, that's called a backgammon and is worth triple stakes.)

Finally, to juice up the gambling action and speed up the play, there is one more piece of equipment, called the doubling cube. It displays on its sides the numbers 2, 4, 8, 16, 32, and 64. It looks like yet another die, but it's not one—it's a counter and a symbol of challenge. On a given turn, before rolling, a player may propose to double the stakes of the current game; the cube is used to keep track of that doubling. Her opponent must then either accept the newly increased stakes ("taking" the cube, which is then turned so that its 2 is faceup) or resign the game immediately at its old stakes ("dropping" it). It's akin to a raise in poker. If the opponent accepts the new stakes, the cube then becomes his and he has the exclusive right to offer to redouble the stakes later on, in which case the right to redouble transfers back to the other player, and so on. No doubling cube was discovered in that tomb in Egypt, and its origins are unknown. The best guess pegs its inventor as an unnamed genius in a New York City gaming club in the 1920s.

The doubling cube is crucial in the modern game and presents the greatest challenge to a player's skills. In one sense, it serves as a basic test of nerves. In another, it serves as a meta-test of a player's ability to assess her own position. We are often predisposed to optimism, or to certain risk-loving behaviors, or to thinking we have a chance to win. It's why we play the lottery; it's why Las Vegas exists. But to be successful at backgammon, one must shed this predisposition. Sometimes, you ought to drop the cube.

BY THE TIME BILL ROBERTIE arrived at IBM in 1991, he had become a fixture on the Giants of Backgammon, a list of top players determined by biennial ballot of world-class competitors. I met Robertie one afternoon in 2019. Heavy snow fell outside his apartment in a tony Boston suburb. One of his backgammon pupils would soon arrive for a pricey lesson. Displayed on a wall nearby was a series of framed vintage magazine advertisements—for Pepsi, *Playboy*, Kahlúa liqueur, and Kent cigarettes—all featuring backgammon in its stylish heyday decades ago. On another wall hung a framed degree from Harvard. Lining broad shelves were books on backgammon, of course, but also on chess and poker, along with a collection of works by Ayn Rand and detective novels and thrillers.

Robertie sat opposite from me across an oversize desk abutting his living room, dressed in a thick brown cardigan and khakis, his wire-rim glasses topped by a wild shock of Einsteinian hair. On the far side of the desk sat a pile of binders, in a rainbow of colors; they contained the completed manuscript of his latest opus: a three-volume treatise on backgammon openings. The first volume is subtitled *A New Way of Thinking*.

"This is going to be revelatory," Robertie told me. "There has never been a book like this."

Robertie's new book, set to be published by the Gammon Press, an outfit headquartered in his apartment, has an unnamed coauthor. In writing it, Robertie relied extensively on an artificial neural network. The book attempts to build a bridge from artificial intelligence to biological intelligence. Robertie has long been an ambassador between these two worlds. He was the first to widely tout TD-Gammon, in a backgammon magazine in 1992, following his match in New York. In 1993, he published *Learning from the Machine*, a transcript of that match with annotations. "Not only is TD-Gammon interesting as a backgammon program, it represents an astonishing achievement for the neural network approach to artificial intelligence," Robertie wrote. "Remember that this program has no human knowledge built into it. Everything it *knows*, it deduced by playing against itself, then modifying its approach after each game." And in 2001, with the publication of *Modern Backgammon*, he continued to explore the lessons humans could learn from the new neural network AIs.

For many aficionados of games, backgammon is a second home—or a second chance. They tend to migrate to backgammon from chess or bridge or gin, attracted by backgammon's money action. Robertie is no exception. He picked up chess when he was around nine years old and later worked at a chess shop in Boston. For a time he ground out a living playing chess tournaments, riding the wave of the Fischer-Spassky boom. Before computers arrived, he had migrated to dice.

"I took up the game in '76," he said. "I can tell you why—it's a funny story. I was still playing chess at the time, but I had reached my peak. I was not going to be a better player, and I wasn't going to make a living at it. I was ready to move on from chess to something else, but I didn't quite know what that was." (Not playing games simply wasn't an option.) "I had a job as a programmer in Cambridge, and one night I had dinner with a friend of mine, a better chess player than I was. He told me that his girlfriend—a weak chess player—came home the other night and was sitting on the bed counting piles of money she'd just won in backgammon at the Cavendish Club in Boston. And I started to put two and two together: weak chess player, piles of money. What if a strong chess player took up that game? So that was my idea. I said, 'OK, I'm gonna learn this game.'"

Robertie bought out the backgammon inventory of every bookstore in the Boston area. He taught his friends at the chess club to play and got a little crew together. He played or studied twenty-five days a month. He stopped working. For a couple of years, backgammon was all he did. He read the old books and then the new books as soon as they came out. He played and played.

But the real meat of his study required a certain kind of manual labor. When Robertie was playing in a club and an especially interesting or tricky position arose, he'd write it down and take that account home. The next day, he'd set up the position on his board and begin to roll the dice. And he'd roll and roll and roll. He'd play the position out, over and over, get a sense of how it tended to evolve, get a sense of what the right moves were, of how it all *felt*. He'd do this, for any given position he wrote down, hundreds of times, performing a process known as rollouts. "It might take two nights of solitary playing," Robertie said. "This sort of homework, month after month after month, gradually made me a better player. And eventually, I got to tournaments where I got to watch other known, top players play, and I realized, 'Hey, they play a lot like I do. This is taking me in the right direction.'" Nowadays, "rollouts" is a standard option in the dropdown menu of any backgammon program. The results, available in milliseconds, undergird the game's theory.

The game solidified in Robertie's mind as resembling "a financial exercise." He explained to me, as he does to his students, "You have a position. You have assets and liabilities. And what you're trying to do, basically, is increase the state of your assets and decrease whatever liabilities you have, to the extent that the dice allow you to do it." After every roll, he said, the player must assess his or her potential moves and ask, "OK, what is this play doing? Am I getting a new asset? Am I taking an old liability and getting rid of it? Am I improving the balance of my pieces in a conceptual way?"

With his training and new mind-set, Robertie soon began making money in the clubs around town. Seven years of work and untold dice rolls later, he won his first world championship. It was 1983, in Monte Carlo. "Throughout the [final] match I had aimed for the most complex positions possible," Robertie recalled. A few years after that, Gerald Tesauro called.

In October 1991, Robertie flew to the office for that thirty-one-game match. They played for most of the day, and Robertie kept meticulous notes on the encounter. TD-Gammon jumped out to an early lead, taking the first two games. Robertie responded with six in a row. The race was on.

A pivotal moment of the match came in the sixteenth game. At that point, Robertie had a fifteen-point advantage. After a flurry of checkers were hit and sent back early in the encounter, the game became a case of offense versus defense; TD-Gammon held a large lead in the race, while Robertie had developed a useful barricade in his home board. On the tenth move, the machine doubled the stakes, and Robertie accepted. The game's edges continued to sharpen. Robertie's barricade was now nearly perfect, yet TD-Gammon was still penning in three of his checkers far from home, and they'd have to find a way to escape. On the twenty-third move, trusting in the integrity of his defense, Robertie doubled, quadrupling the stakes. TD-Gammon accepted. "Computers don't get scared," Robertie wrote in his notes.

Four rolls later, in the position below, on its turn the computer doubled *again*, octupling the stakes, trusting in the speed of its offense. Such a dramatic escalation is rare. Robertie is maneuvering his white checkers clockwise from the lower right around the board to the upper right (and TD-Gammon is doing the reverse with black), and he has to decide whether to accept this massive cube

or forfeit four points. At a glance, it seems nearly hopeless for the
human: the computer is ahead in the race by twenty-nine "pips," or
spaces on the board; three of Robertie's checkers are vulnerable; and
one of those is mired deep in enemy territory.

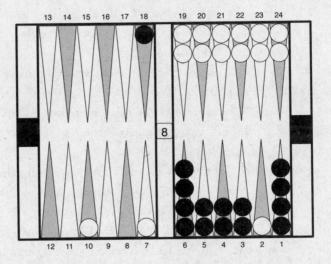

"Scary, but I have plenty of ways to win on the very next roll,"
Robertie wrote. If the computer is unable to run its checker on the
18-point around to safety, Robertie will have a lot of rolls that hit
that checker. And because Robertie's home board is completely pro-
tected, that checker will be unable to reenter, and the computer will
be stuck for a time and will almost surely lose. Robertie accepted
the double. Modern software says this was the right move and gives
Robertie a 40 percent chance to win. In the end, something just
like that did happen. Thanks to an uncharacteristic blunder of calculation, the computer was unable to bear off its checkers safely,
got hit, and got stuck. At this point Robertie doubled again—to
sixteen-fold—and the computer forfeited an eight-point loss. This is

the nature of backgammon. Powerful positions can disintegrate in a roll or two, if they were ever powerful at all.

After thirty-one games, Robertie wound up nineteen points ahead, an average of 0.6 points per game. In his notes he wrote, "On balance, I was lucky." He concluded that he ought to have won around 0.2 points per game, which "would make TD-Gammon the strongest backgammon program ever."

"It was *OK*," Robertie told me recently. "It wasn't as good as the best human players, but it made reasonable moves. It never did anything stupid. That was kind of impressive." He played it again the next year. It had been significantly improved and was now called TD-Gammon 2.0. "This thing was playing world-class backgammon," Robertie said. "I broke even, but if anything, I was lucky. It played really well. I took home a printout of the match, and I actually altered some of my own play, especially in the opening, to conform more to what TD-Gammon was doing."

TD-Gammon never went public, but it inspired some popular, commercially available programs. Two of these, JellyFish and Snowie, which Tesauro called "clones" of his work, reigned in the 1990s and 2000s. Today's machine champion, eXtreme Gammon, known to all serious players as XG, costs $59.95. Though Tesauro appeared to bristle at XG's retail price, and the money its creators must have made, he admitted, "I've seen a little bit of it, and it's frightening. It's just, like, dead perfect."

Many fields resist new technology at first, but in backgammon its adoption was swift. Said Robertie, "There was a hard-core group of good players who didn't want the computer to be better than they were, and you could find reasons, find mistakes it made, and therefore say, 'Well, I don't have to change my play because, look, here it did this stupid thing in some complicated game.' But other players were just trying to copy JellyFish. 'If I can play like this, I'm going to be a good player.' And they were right. They became good players. Twenty years later, the idea of studying backgammon without using XG is ridiculous. My book could not have been written without endless XG rollouts. In every phase of the game, human play has improved."

Our interview ended as Robertie's pupil was arriving. I wondered what Robertie taught his students, considering that XG could provide endless, perfect training. What would be the fruit of the students' labor, both without the computer and with it? How could *they* improve? And what, I wondered, was left for Bill Robertie in this game? Why did he keep playing?

DESPITE ITS ANCIENT and complicated origins, the modern popularity of backgammon was surely the work of one man: Prince Alexis Obolensky, a Russian socialite émigré whose aristocratic family fled during the Russian Revolution. He learned the game as a child, reportedly from his family's Turkish gardener. It became his life's passion project. Once in the United States, he split his time between Manhattan and Florida and he nurtured two things: a playboy reputation and a desire to spread the good word of backgammon. Obolensky was a cofounder and the president of the World Backgammon Club, the author of an early and influential book on the game, and—crucially—the organizer of its first ever world championship, in 1964, a jet-set affair off the coast of Palm Beach.

Backgammon *had* had cultural moments before. The word "backgammon" itself can be traced to the middle of the seventeenth century, found in the letters of a prominent British pamphleteer and novelist named James Howell. Stateside, Thomas Jefferson played, and recorded his gambling wins and losses in a journal dated to the years before the Declaration of Independence.* Charles Darwin and

---

*E.g., July 11, 1770: "Lost at backgammon 1/3." And August 30, 1771: "Won of TMRandolph at Backgammon 1/3."

his wife, Emma, played, keeping meticulous records of their games. In a short story published in 1936, Ernest Hemingway wrote that "the rich were dull and they drank too much or they played too much backgammon."

Obolensky imbued the game with a disco-ball and leisure-suit glitter it sorely lacked. Before Obolensky's arrival, "it was a high-stakes gambling game in fairly exclusive men's clubs," Robertie said. "You go into the Racquet and Tennis Club in New York and you might find people playing there for fifty bucks a point. But they only played each other. There was no tournament scene, no outside scene. Obolensky decided, 'I'm gonna make it popular, I'm gonna run a tournament, I'm gonna invite everybody I know from differ-ent clubs, and go to the Bahamas and have a great time.'"

And he did. Obolensky, along with the Grand Bahama Develop-ment Company, bought 150 backgammon sets from a gaming store in New York and had them shipped to Grand Bahama Island. Forty-eight players competed at the first International Backgammon Tour-nament, assembled beneath a chandelier in the posh Lucayan Beach Hotel. They were barons and counts and princes, Wall Street brokers and Chicago millionaires, Racquet Club members and socialites, and games-playing ringers, all summoned by Obolensky—"Oby" to his friends. The tournament even had its own bookmaker admin-istering thousands of dollars in side action, a "5-foot-6, 267-pound crapshooter" by the name of Jelly, dressed in green pants and a green shirt, who looked "like an avocado salad," according to a *Sports Illustrated* account of the event. "Backgammon is for idiots and rich people," he said. The Chicago millionaire Charles Wacker III took home the championship and its Obolensky Cup. (Years later, he was indicted in what the IRS called a record-setting "multinational scheme to defraud the government of the United States.")

But Obolensky's ambitions weren't limited to this upper crust. Rich people were just the bait. "I made people think they should be doing it, that only the best people were involved," Obolensky once told *Time* magazine. "We brought in snobbism. Only in America can that kind of thing be done in a big way." According to the magazine, Obolensky had a three-phase plan to spread his favorite game. First: ensnare the swells. (Check.) Second: organize lavish tournaments. (Check.) Third: reel in the masses. (Check—at least as far as this author is concerned.)

A simple laundry list of prominent players testifies to Obolensky's success in the decade that followed. Hugh Hefner was a diehard, and the Playboy Mansion hosted all-night backgammon parties; the Playboy bunnies descended on hospitals, distributing backgammon boards and rules. You can sometimes find one of Lucille Ball's many sets for sale in an online auction. The game was a fixture in the lounge at the famed discothèque Studio 54. James Bond himself played it in *Octopussy*: he makes liberal use of the doubling cube, puts up a Fabergé egg as collateral, and rolls double sixes to win. Mick Jagger, Paul Newman, and the band members of Pink Floyd were seen playing. Tina Turner posed for the cover of *Las Vegas Backgammon Magazine*.

Others followed. Over the period from 1969 to 1974, the *New York Times* reported, the number of players in the United States increased tenfold, to two million. One New York manufacturer sold as many backgammon sets in 1973 as it had in the past twenty years combined. The paper called Obolensky a "Russian aristocrat-socialite-huckster," but did give him the lion's share of credit for the boom. The *Times* also pointed out, however, that the chess tsunami Bobby Fischer had triggered had spilled over into another game.

"On the fringes" of the backgammon boom, Robertie said, "there were a lot of very hungry young men with chess backgrounds thinking, 'I'm gonna make some money at this game. I can beat all these clowns.'"

Amid the disco sheen, and the liquor and cigarettes and cocaine and splashy tournaments, a current of despair flows beneath the gameplay. In 1972, near the game's American height, a journalist and backgammon expert wrote in *Harper's*, "I have seen [players] leaning across the board, as if they heard a kind of broken music in the dice. . . . There is a vague sense of promise in the air, a vague presentiment that luck will last, that God is just, that dawn will never come." Backgammon is one of only two things in life, I heard many times during my research, that one never tires of. The *Harper's* contributor, Jon Bradshaw, coauthored an influential backgammon book subtitled *The Cruelest Game*. It's cruel because everything right can always go wrong. It's addictive because everything wrong can always go right. It was Bradshaw's book that roped in Bill Robertie.

Obolensky died in 1986, and the tide he had drawn ebbed around the same time. Some blamed the recession of the 1980s for the decline, saying it dried up the gambling money. But here, too, backgammon's element of chance played an important role. The boom-and-bust cycles of games have a lot to do with how much luck is involved in their play: the more randomness, the longer the cycle—the longer people can keep convincing themselves that they have a chance to win. The chess boom, sparked by Fischer's win in 1972, while fierce, was short, fizzling within a couple of years. In chess, one faces cold, hard truths very quickly. Poker, a game rich with chance and delusion, has enjoyed a prolonged boom sparked by the multimillion-dollar 2003 World Series victory of an unknown accountant named Chris Moneymaker. In terms of the balance between luck and skill, backgammon lies somewhere between chess and poker, and as the '80s rolled on, the popularity of backgammon began to fade.

AROUND THIS SAME TIME, the strong machines began to arrive. The June 1980 issue of *Scientific American* displayed on its cover a garish pixelated backgammon board and pixelated dice. The cover story was written by the Carnegie Mellon computer scientist Hans Berliner, and it describes his backgammon program, BKG 9.8. This program's recent victory in Monte Carlo, he wrote, marked "the first time a computer program had beaten a world champion at any board or card game."

In Monte Carlo, BKG 9.8 took physical form as Gammonoid, a three-and-a-half-foot robot with a screen for a face connected by satellite to a mainframe in Pittsburgh. The world champion at the time was an Italian player named Luigi Villa, and he and Berliner had agreed on a seven-point match with stakes of $5,000, to commence as an added attraction following the actual (human) world championship. During the event's opening ceremonies, an orchestra cued up the *Star Wars* theme and a spotlight shone, ready for Gammonoid's triumphant entrance. The little robot then tangled itself in the stage curtain.

Despite having botched its entrance, Gammonoid was there to play. The match itself began at eleven at night, and a modest crowd was on hand, lounging and sipping champagne. Paul Magriel, a onetime fellow of NYU's famed Courant Institute of Mathematical Sciences and one of the greatest backgammon players of all time, provided commentary. It was Magriel's book, still a bible of the game—and titled simply *Backgammon*—that I'd first read to get my bearings. His expertise was baked into the robot as well.

In the final game, having already built up a solid 5–1 lead and with the doubling cube reading 2, the robot rolled double sixes to bear off its last four checkers and win the match. "Gammonoid the Conqueror," a *Washington Post* headline declared. The paper reported that upon his defeat, a frustrated and then disconsolate Villa "stamped his foot." The newswires also reported that his "disappointment was shared by several fellow Italians, who surrounded him in an indignant and gesticulating mass immediately afterwards and hurled insults at the machine." But by all accounts, BKG 9.8 got lucky. Even the Carnegie Mellon team members had put their own chances of winning at something like 20 percent. Berliner wrote that while "there was no doubt that BKG 9.8 played well . . . Villa played better." Chance was on the robot's side.

It was a version of this program that Berliner would show Tesauro at the Santa Fe Institute, eventually leading to the modern programs that now shape the game. But Tesauro wasn't interested in Berliner's methods. He certainly wasn't interested in lucky victories or in Magriel's human expertise. He wanted a machine that could learn the game for itself. His resulting neural network approach, unlike its gaming predecessors, made TD-Gammon a wedge, as Claude Shannon had put it with regard to chess, to attack other real-world problems.

A neural network is a computing system directly inspired by the human brain, in the hopes of replicating, at least obliquely, the brain's wonders. The brain is made up of billions of interconnected neurons; a neural network is made up of many interconnected mathematical functions. These artificial mathematical neurons are connected to one another in a graph with a series of layers—from an input layer to some hidden layers to an output layer—with varying degrees of numerical strength, like synaptic connections in the real brain. As real neurons transmit chemical signals across synapses, artificial neurons transmit numbers between functions. According to sophisticated algorithms, a neural network's many connections strengthen or weaken as it trains on more and more data, improving its path from input to output. So, as a child eventually learns to say "dog" when she sees a dog, a neural network eventually learns to output "dog" when given a digital image of a dog.

A canonical example of what a neural network can do well is identify handwritten numerals—a task useful for, say, a post office wanting to quickly and accurately route the mail using zip codes. These handwritten numbers—a loopy 2, a slanted 4, a crossed 7—are each presented to the computer as a digital image. From the input layer, the data in the images is filtered through many connections and calculations in the hidden layers, eventually arriving at an output layer of ten neurons, each corresponding to a digit. For the machine to read a handwritten 5 and output a 5, it must learn to recognize patterns. The program will be terrible at first, predicting digits no better than at random. But it can learn and improve through something called back-propagation. Each time the network's synapses fire—passing numbers through the various layers—and the computer outputs the *wrong* digit at the end, it incurs some cost. We tell the program to take pride in its work and do all it can to minimize costs. This is itself a sort of game. The network begins to rejigger its synaptic connections accordingly. The hidden layers may start to take on a kind of meaning beyond the programmer's control. Perhaps one layer begins to detect handwritten loops while another layer identifies diagonal lines. As these connections are altered, so too are the calculations this neural net performs when it sees the next number. Over time, its predictions improve. With enough practice, the neural net will identify the numerals with an amazing degree of accuracy.

It can do much the same when presented with checkers and dice. A neural network like TD-Gammon takes in a backgammon position, performs calculations in its hidden layers, and lights up a "neuron" at the end with, hopefully, the best move. These systems can also operate on human biometrics, foreign languages, and features of a cityscape—these days, neural networks are the "brains" behind facial recognition, machine translation, email spam filtering, self-driving cars, and much of what we today call "artificial intelligence." Tesauro's approach to backgammon held the promise of general application that was missing from the early checkers and chess research.

Tesauro had busied himself publishing his neural net backgammon results in academic journals. By 1994, he'd reported that

TD-Gammon had reached master-level play and that rather than simply making a better and better backgammon bot, perhaps the work should move on. "Other possible applications might include financial trading strategies, military battlefield strategies, and control tasks such as robot motor control, navigation and path planning," he wrote in *Neural Computation*. However: "At this point we are still largely ignorant as to why TD-Gammon is able to learn so well." Much like the human brain, machine-learning systems have a "black box" problem—they might work well, but we don't know exactly *how*. In the years that followed, Tesauro's research covered pricing algorithms, computer virus detection, auctions, and energy consumption in data centers.

In accordance with IBM's corporate policy, Tesauro has never published his backgammon program or its source code. He was willing, however, to hand out records of the games it had played. One world-class player of both backgammon and bridge, Kit Woolsey, came calling. Tesauro gave him a "big stack" of records of TD-Gammon playing against itself. "He went through every single move, and just by looking at what it was doing he could latch on to a new way of thinking about playing backgammon that was better than anything humans were doing before," Tesauro said.

After the TD-Gammon program proved its prowess in its native game, its ideas began to colonize other unexpected domains. At the University of Massachusetts, the approach was used to control elevator traffic. The ability to move checkers off a backgammon board led to an effective simulation of the vertical flow of humans within a tall building. At NASA, it was used for something called job-shop scheduling for the space shuttle. Job-shop scheduling is a classic optimization problem in computer science: you've got a certain number of tasks to perform on a certain number of machines. How do you schedule them so as to minimize the time the entire project takes? Years later, TD-Gammon was used to develop the com-

puter system Watson's aggressive Daily Double wagering strategy on
Jeopardy!—and a similar strategy was used to profound effect by the
professional gambler James Holzhauer during his record-setting run
on the show in 2019.*

In the world of games AI, Tesauro's research led to unprecedented
practical success stories. But during our interview, he occasionally
sounded defensive—worried, I felt, that a layman like me might not
consider his creation to be *intelligent*. He argued, for example, that most
"informed, technical people" would say that TD-Gammon is intelligent, whereas Deep Blue, the chess supercomputer, was not. (One
of Deep Blue's creators kept an office down the hall. Tesauro sheepishly asked the IBM communications employee sitting in the room if
she agreed. She wasn't sure, she said—she is "not a tech person.") For
Tesauro, the difference has to do with elegance. "Elegance is important," he said more than once. Deep Blue was just a big calculator with
tons of handcrafted, ad hoc pieces, carrying the shameful weight of
preprogrammed, freeze-dried human knowledge. TD-Gammon did
it on its own. It taught itself. Isn't that elegant? Isn't that intelligence?

Later that day, Tesauro sent me a clarifying email. He had, he
wrote, been referring to something called the "AI effect"—the idea
that the goalposts for what constitutes "actual intelligence" in a
machine are constantly being moved back. As the author Pamela
McCorduck explains in *Machines Who Think*: "It's part of the field of
artificial intelligence that every time somebody figured out how to
make a computer do something—play good checkers, solve simple
but relatively informal problems—there was a chorus of critics to
say, but that's not thinking." Or as Rodney Brooks, an MIT roboticist, once told *Wired*: "Every time we figure out a piece of it, it stops
being magical; we say, 'Oh, that's just a computation.'"

---

* Holzhauer alone achieved every one of the show's ten richest victories, including
one staggering single-day haul of $131,127, as well as total winnings of $2,462,216.

It stops being magical. Tesauro doesn't want the neural nets that birthed TD-Gammon to stop being magical.

I WANTED TO EXPERIENCE for myself the accuracy with which such a human-made brain can play backgammon. So, curious or masochistic or both, I sat down at my laptop to play against BGBlitz, yet another neural network program descended from Tesauro's and a three-time backgammon champion at Computer Olympiads in the 2000s.

From the actual gameplay, there's not much to report. It was immediately obvious that the program is far better than I am. Better than anyone is. Rationally, I knew this. But the interesting piece of reportage was my own human reaction to losing to the computer over and over—of failing to complete my blockades, of losing bear-off races, of having my checkers hit endlessly. The initial and potent reactions of *H. sapiens* to defeat at the hands of a piece of software in a game of chance are disbelief and distrust: *There is simply no way this thing can be so good—or, specifically, so much better than me. It's lucky. It's cheating!* I fell into backgammon's trap—indeed, into the gambler's trap. I kept playing and playing and playing. And sometimes I won.

So potent is this feeling that the BGBlitz website has an entire section called "Does it cheat?" The answer, of course, is no, but to allay such concerns, the program offers special settings; for example, the dice rolls can be drawn from crisp, clean, unimpeachable streams of chance, such as a random-number cryptography algorithm used by Sun Microsystems or the "quantum randomness of photon arrival times." You can even simply roll your own dice at home and enter the results into the program. "I will pay you $1,000 if you can show that BGBlitz uses unfair dice," the site reads.

Later, an insatiable glutton for punishment, I also bought the mobile version of eXtreme Gammon, the program that has come to define the modern game as played by humans. This way, as I played on the subway or on line at the deli, I could even more frequently be reminded of my brain's inferiority to artificial intelligence in this domain: "eXtreme Gammon thinks you've made a blunder," my phone's screen often read. It could tell me what I ought to have done but not *why*—that part I had to try to figure out for myself. To test the balance of skill versus luck for myself, I decided to play a first-to-a-hundred-points match against the strongest backgammon player in the world over a couple of evenings on my phone in my living room. XG beat me one hundred to sixty-nine. I immediately started another match.

In the end, of course, it was futile. Tesauro, whose research inspired XG, expressed a similar sentiment about human players in light of essentially perfect AI. "They play tournaments and they study very hard," he said. "I just don't see the point."

ON ANOTHER RECENT winter afternoon, in a large hotel on the west bank of the Hudson River, the thirteenth New York Metropolitan Open backgammon tournament, one of the largest on the circuit's calendar, was contested. When I arrived, about a hundred people were sitting in close quarters at tables in the hotel's ballroom, with nearly the entire island of Manhattan visible outside the panoramic windows. But the Statue of Liberty, the World Trade Center, and the Empire State Building were afterthoughts to these people. Probabilities instead filled their heads. They sat in front of large, custom-made tournament boards with merino wool surfaces and inlaid wool points; in their dizzying and garish circus array of colors, sheathed in leather and topped with pearlescent checkers, the boards reminded me of the ivory and silver game found in that tomb in Qustul. These modern custom boards, little coliseums of chance, sell for upwards of a thousand dollars. And to accommodate travel and tournament logistics, the boards fold up into handled objects that look exactly like briefcases, giving a tournament the appearance of a strange business meeting.

But the most noticeable thing about a backgammon tournament is the *noise*. It's as if a distant yet mighty cavalry were approaching over the horizon, countless hooves clapping on the ground. Hundreds of dice being jostled and cast, rattling and skittering, determining with each microscopic tilt and bounce the fates of their players. The dice—specially made so-called precision dice, half an inch or so in width—are placed in small padded cups, with "trip lips" on their rims for maximum randomness and fairness. Then they are shaken—vigorously and at least twice up and down, per federation rules—and rolled, from a height of at least one inch. Alternatively, they can be dropped into the top of a small acrylic tower abutting the playing area, called a baffle box, from which they fall, bouncing through a series of little plastic rods and eventually shooting out the bottom, onto the surface of the board. Similar contraptions were found in that tomb along the Nile.

The second most noticeable thing about a backgammon tournament is the number of *cameras*. Above nearly every board in the room was a small GoPro camera, most of them suspended in midair by a pair of adjustable metal rods. At the boards without video cameras, the players would frequently take cellphone photos of the positions in front of them. Later, the players will plug these visual records into their computers for assessment and analysis. Before GoPro, top players would hire annotators to sit by their sides and record every move of their games by hand.

In the hotel bar down the hall from the tournament, no fewer than six pairs of players were hunched over laptops and iPads, debating positions and consulting their silicon oracle, XG. In the game's heyday, the bar at a backgammon tournament would have been full of money games.

Present at this tournament and fresh off a win in his first match of the day was Masayuki Mochizuki, known in the backgammon community simply as Mochy. He's widely considered to be the best player in the world and has been voted No. 1 on every Giants of Backgammon list since 2013. A slight man with piercing eyes and a wide smile, he was easily recognized because he was wearing the same crisp white shirt as in his Giants of Backgammon photo. He grew up in the game's computer age but also migrated to it from other pursuits. As a young man in Japan, Mochizuki was an enthusiastic and competent player of shogi, also known as Japanese chess. But, like Robertie, he peaked at that game and, as a university student in Tokyo, he was poor. Backgammon, he thought, could solve both of these problems.

Games of no chance, such as chess and shogi, typically offer little gambling action and, therefore, little potential for fast profit—the better player simply wins too often, creating scant opportunity for a betting market to be made. Games of chance, however, such as backgammon and poker, attract gamblers. The worse player *can* win, and by definition sometimes *does* win, and might then misinterpret his good fortune as skill and come back for more. Chance, in other words, is a fertile garden in which human ego and delusion flourish. When the sucker wins, he thinks it's because he's better; when the sucker loses, he thinks it's because his opponent got lucky.

"Now, *that's* an interesting topic," Mochizuki said, perking up as we sat just outside that playing hall in Jersey City, the muffled rattle of dice still audible. I had asked him about the impact of the machines on the game that has become his livelihood. In the view of the best player in the world, that impact was large, undeniable, and twofold.

Impact No. 1: technology has democratized skill. It used to be that humans could learn valuable backgammon lessons only from other humans, in person; now they learn them from the machine.

"Before AI came onto the scene, you really had to go to a good club," Mochizuki said. "If you lived in Japan, you had no chance to be a good player because there's no good players. So you had to go to New York or you had to go to London, where there were big clubs. But now, even if you are born in Iran, you have a chance. That's a good thing." Indeed, every backgammon player I spoke to observed that AI had sparked a dramatic increase in the level of play. Mochizuki had once been the sucker at the table. "If I'm good at this game," Mochizuki thought, "I can make a hundred dollars a day." He recalls, "That was big money for me at the time. But I started to play and I lost, like, every day. I paid every day. I paid the educational cost." Like Robertie, Mochizuki would write down challenging positions from his losing sessions. Unlike Robertie, he could do rapid digital rollouts when he got home. "I put my position into the computer. If I was wrong, then I studied why this is the best play, this is not the best play, and so on." The devotion to the machine worked.

Impact No. 2: the betting well has dried up. "The big downside is it kills action," Mochizuki said with a sigh. "Before bots, everybody believed that they were the best player. 'I know how to play. I'm the best player. Let's play for a hundred dollars a point.' But now, the computer tells you, 'Hey, you suck, you're burning your money.'" As a result, the livelihoods of many elite players have shifted from gambling to teaching. Mochizuki, for example, charges $250 an hour for online lessons and $500 for lessons in person. "The type of people we have now are people who like to study, who enjoy the process of improving their own game."

And Mochizuki, the best in the world, continues to study. Like nearly everyone else, he records his games to video. He then uploads them to YouTube, where he pays a different set of humans to transcribe the raw video into machine-readable game records, ready for XG's analysis. Ancient board games, meet advanced capitalism.

"There's a bunch of people who do transcribing as a profession," he said. They live in developing countries, he told me. "Their income is low. If I pay ten dollars an hour, it's big money. They are nice guys."

In addition to his devotion to the theory of his craft, Mochizuki spent about a hundred days a year traveling, before the pandemic. Over the next few weeks after our meeting, he was due to travel from New York to Florida to Australia to Gibraltar and back to Japan, chasing backgammon tournaments—some thirty thousand miles in pursuit of gaming greatness and prize money.

But I wondered about the toll of a life devoted to dice, to randomness. Mochy took a dispassionate view: that the mathematics are sound and that chance, given a chance, becomes a certainty.

"I always say it this way: it's like playing roulette," he said, comparing himself to the extra numbers on the wheel that give the casino an advantage. "And in roulette, the casino always has an edge, because of 0 and 00. I'm playing roulette, but I have maybe like ten 0's. I have an edge. But, of course, I can lose. A fish can bet this and that, and the fish can win. But in the long run, of course, it's impossible for him to win."

In the long run, there is no luck. In the short run, there is nothing but.

I HAD BROUGHT my backgammon equipment along to IBM Research, and before I headed home Tesauro and I sat down in the company cafeteria to play. After each roll, I maneuvered my checkers gingerly and haltingly, trying to execute the tactics I had learned from the neural nets that derived from Tesauro's research. It was daunting to play the man who had built those godlike machines. I muddled through, avoiding blunders—or at least avoiding disaster. Our checker armies quickly disengaged each other, and the game became a simple race—a dice-rolling contest in which one can appeal only to Lady Luck. I rolled well and managed to advance and then bear off most of my checkers quickly, leaving one two spaces away and another three spaces away as the game reached its climax. Tesauro, meanwhile, had two checkers five spaces away and another two four spaces away. It was his turn to roll. Later, I put the position into my computer. It told me I had just over a 90 percent chance of victory.

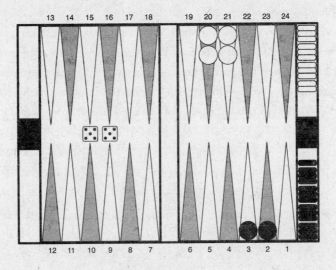

As it happened, Tesauro rolled double fives, bore off all his remaining checkers, and won the game. In the long run, there is no luck. In the short run, there is nothing but.

LONG AFTER MY REPORTING for this chapter was complete, I still couldn't quit. I reread Robertie's books and watched hours of Mochizuki tournament video late into the night. I trawled YouTube for obscure British backgammon documentaries. I priced expensive sets and I taught the game to any friend who would listen. I played nightly on Backgammon Galaxy, a website frequented by many of the best humans in the world. I pored over my XG blunder reports, trying to absorb the AI's lessons. Chance had ensnared me. I don't believe I was deluded; when I faced off against the machine or strong players online, I didn't expect to win. But I *was* improving. I recognized more patterns, moved my checkers more efficiently, and took more of the correct risks. I came to understand that the appeal of this game, like the method used to train its AI players, is not winning but *learning*.

A few weeks after our interview, I saw the world champion Bill Robertie by chance in a bar in Harvard Square. Forty-five years after he'd learned the game, he was there with a small crew playing backgammon. Twenty-dollar bills passed freely across the board as the dice rattled in the beery din of the cold night.

POKER

Mine education, and my learning's such,
As might my self, and others, profit much

—ANNE BRADSTREET,
   "THE FOUR AGES OF MAN"

THERE ARE FIVE OF them, now scattered around the world. One hangs in Paris, in the Musée d'Orsay. Another belongs to the storied collection of the Barnes Foundation in Philadelphia. A third is in the Courtauld in London. A fourth may be somewhere in Doha, having been purchased by the royal family of Qatar for a quarter of a billion dollars. And the fifth hangs in the Metropolitan Museum of Art in New York, where I laid eyes on it one recent afternoon.

The Met's version of Paul Cézanne's *The Card Players* is thought to be the first entry in the series. It's not a big painting—it could almost fit on the back of a large pizza box. Nor is it a joyful painting. The three behatted men playing cards at Cézanne's table cast their doleful gazes down. They are indoors but wear heavy jackets, protecting themselves, it seems, against damp and unseen drafts. Only the man standing behind them, an onlooker with his arms crossed and a tobacco pipe clenched between his teeth, shows interest in the actual card game, carrying just a hint of what could plausibly be interpreted as a smile on his face. The rest play as though driven by solemn obsession. The picture's primary horizontal axis, composed of the card table itself and of the players' hands, is slightly off-kilter, giving the impression of movement—a wobbling clockwise rotation, like a coin or a poker chip spinning down to rest on a countertop.

The picture was flanked, when I saw it in Gallery 826, by a number of other Cézannes, among them *Still Life with Apples and Pears*. A Cézanne apple, it should be said, looks more like an apple than a real apple does, and so a Cézanne card game looks more like a card game than a real card game does. When painting from nature, he once wrote in a letter, an artist should find "the cylinder, the sphere, the cone." A modernist should, in other words, find the subject's true constituent molecules, its elemental geometries.

At a glance, a game of poker is about aces and kings, chips and cash, bets and bluffs. But what it's really about when played at its highest expression—played as though it were a modern art—are the elegant game-theoretic mathematics first formulated by a Nobel Prize–winning genius some seventy years ago. These are the game's cylinders, its cones, its elemental geometries.

Cézanne was a master at uncovering these essences within his subjects. "This process of seeing," wrote the art critic Robert Hughes, "this adding up and weighing of choices, is what Cézanne's peculiar style makes concrete: the broken outlines, strokes of pencil laid side by side, are emblems of scrupulousness in the midst of a welter of doubt."

Scrupulousness in the midst of a welter of doubt. What could be a better description of the game of poker?

As you approach Las Vegas in an airplane from the east, descending through the bright and scorching air, bouldered desert eventually gives way to an endless sea of houses with copper-colored roofs. They look like pennies in a dry wishing well. "Are you here for the poker thing?" were the first words I heard after setting foot on desert land, from my cab driver. Yes, I was there for the poker thing.

A half-size replica of the Eiffel Tower, that French totem of modernism, looms 540 feet in the air above the Paris Las Vegas Hotel. I checked into said hotel on a recent summer afternoon, feeling scrupulous, with $3,000 in my pocket, a portion of what I had been paid in advance to write this book. The appeal of big-time poker for journalists is, it seems to me, obvious. Journalists crave, above all else, *access*. We want to step behind curtains. And poker is essentially democratic. If you get the money together, you can quite literally sit at the table. No press box to peer out of or velvet ropes to lean over or credential around the neck required. It would be far more difficult, say, for a journalist to play in the World Cup or at Wimbledon. But no one can stop us from playing in the World Series of Poker.

Joan Didion once wrote, "Las Vegas is the most extreme and allegorical of American settlements, bizarre and beautiful in its venality and in its devotion to immediate gratification, a place the tone of which is set by mobsters and call girls and ladies' room attendants with amyl nitrite poppers in their uniform pockets." Hunter S. Thompson remarked, "For a loser, Las Vegas is the meanest town on earth." Second only to access, the thing journalists crave most is *color*—vibrant characters and scenes—and Las Vegas is technicolor.

Thousands of poker players, with cash in their pockets and the hunger for more in their eyes, had descended on this desert metropolis for the 2019 World Series of Poker, the fiftieth annual incarnation of the game's richest and most prestigious gathering.

These days, the World Series is held on the outskirts of the Rio All-Suite Hotel and Casino, an enormous and illuminated pink, purple, and blue tower shaped like a whiskey flask across the interstate from the Strip. Or, rather, the World Series *are* held there. The event is not a single enormous tournament but, rather, a sort of perspiratory superfestival of some eighty individual tournaments, many of them enormous, in complex permutations of types and sizes, with buy-ins ranging from $250 to $1 million. There is, for example, the $1,500 H.O.R.S.E.,* the $1,500 Eight Game Mix, the $2,500 Mixed Triple Draw Lowball, the $10,000 Razz Championship, the $1,000/$10,000 Ladies No-Limit Hold 'Em Championship (any men who enter have to pay the $10,000), and the $100,000 High Roller Hold 'Em event. The one you see on television, though, brought to you by the beef jerky and beer companies, is the $10,000 No-Limit Hold 'Em World Championship, also known simply and profoundly as the Main Event.

Certain televisual imagery of the WSOP lingers in the mind. Baseball-capped men in sunglasses and logoed sweatshirts. Teetering piles of gaudily colorful chips. Incantations of the words "all in" accompanied by elbows out, palms in pushing motions. Dealers wearing vests, painstakingly dealing flops, turns, and rivers. And, at the end of it all, a young (they all seem to be young nowadays) victor posing with his or her ruby-and-diamond-encrusted bracelet behind a pile of cash so grotesque that bricks of bills worth roughly the American median household income scatter freely across the baize tabletop.

The actual lived experience of the World Series of Poker, however, comprises five elemental modes: loneliness, boredom, waiting, folding, and, ultimately, devastation. Waiting is the canonical trope of the soldier's memoir. Loneliness, boredom, and devastation similarly have their classic texts. But folding is unique to poker. It's an act of surrender, albeit a necessary part of any successful poker strategy. It's a repeated and voluntary admission of your inadequacy, and it can take a toll. You fold most hands, throwing them into the muck of cards in the center of the large table, unseen by anyone but you. You fold and fold and fold again. Eventually, you get a good hand and you play, hoping to extract enough chips from your tablemates

---

* The acronym stands for Hold 'Em, Omaha Hi-Low, Razz, Seven-Card Stud, and Seven-Card Stud Hi-Low 8-or-Better—a sort of poker pentathlon.

that you can afford to fold some more. During a tournament, as the stakes rise and the pressure for chips builds, you may have to play. You may have to go all in. And more often than not, eventually, you go bust.

It's a mean town for a loser.

LIKE BACKGAMMON, poker has randomness—cards drawn from a shuffled deck rather than rolled dice. This fact has allowed both deceptively simple games to become prominent theaters of gambling. Their adherents are driven by both intellectual curiosity and profit motive. But poker adds another element to vary the rewards for the player while also injecting a deeply human quality: hidden information. In backgammon, you can see all your opponent's checkers and every roll of her dice. In poker, your opponents' cards are hidden and much of the game's betting strategy involves deciphering what's in their hands. In the parlance of game theory, it is a game of *imperfect* information. This, of course, is just like many aspects of the real world, where there is often a whole host of things we would like to know but that we do not: consider courtship, negotiations, warfare.

Decades ago, in the heady days of gun-packing Texas road hustlers like Doyle Brunson and Vegas whiz kids like Stu Ungar, success in the game of poker was all about *exploitation*: identifying and using to your advantage your opponents' tendencies. Reading opponents. Tricking opponents. Intimidating opponents. This may be why, in the popular conception, *tells*—those unconscious physical tics that betray the strength of a player's hand—and bluffing are considered to be such central parts of the game. Poker players still have tells today. And, of course, poker players still bluff. But these are just bergs floating in the large mathematical ocean that now defines the game. Thanks largely to computer analysis, the game has recently turned inward. Rather than exploit, top players leverage the math and try to be unexploitable.

Poker has been an object of serious game-theoretic study since the middle of the twentieth century. In 1951, John Nash, winner of the Nobel Prize and the subject of *A Beautiful Mind*, published a landmark paper titled "Non-Cooperative Games." (Poker is decidedly one of these.) In it, Nash introduces his germinal mathematical idea. "The notion of an equilibrium point is the basic ingredient in our theory," he writes. Such a point is now known as the famous Nash equilibrium. Players in a game are said to be in Nash equilibrium if none of them, even if they knew the strategies of their opponents, want to change their own strategy. For example, suppose we are playing rock, paper, scissors and you've selected rock and I've selected scissors. Knowing that, of course, I want to switch to paper. But knowing that, you'd want to switch to scissors, at which point I'd want to switch to rock, and so on. We're not in equilibrium. The only Nash equilibrium in this game is for each of us to *randomize* over rock, paper, and scissors, playing each with a one-third chance, in which case neither of us has any incentive to change plans. Playing such an equilibrium strategy means that we are *unexploitable*—there is nothing profitable our opponent can do against us, and we are content just to row down our own strategic stream. This line of thinking is also central to modern, high-level poker.

Nash sensed this seventy years ago. After introducing the math in that seminal paper, he turns to the real-world applications of his theory. "Poker is the most obvious target," he writes, before considering an extremely simplified version of the game played by three players. He continues, "The complexity of the mathematical work needed for a complete investigation increases rather rapidly, however, with increasing complexity of the game; so that analysis of a game much more complex than the example given here might only be feasible using approximate computational methods." Nash was right, though it would take these computational methods decades to bear fruit. It wasn't until the late 2000s that computer programs, chief among them one called Polaris, could spar on equal footing with humans.

Poker comes in a number of flavors and structures. The most popular of these flavors today is Texas hold 'em, in which each player is dealt two private cards and five shared community cards are dealt faceup over a series of betting rounds, known as the flop, the turn, and the river. But even hold 'em can be played using a variety of structures, with various restrictions on the number of players and the sizes of bets.

Polaris's specialty was a type of hold 'em called heads-up limit. ("Heads-up" means the game is played one-on-one, and "limit" means that bets and raises are limited to a single, fixed size each round.) In 2015, a man named Michael Bowling and his collaborators *solved* heads-up limit with a bot named Cepheus.* The program is statistically indistinguishable from perfect—it plays like God. It might console humanity to learn that Cepheus, to get as good as it did, played more training hands of poker against itself than the entire human race has played during the entire history of time, times ten.

Cepheus played itself because that's how it learned—but also because no human would have the time or attention to sit through the training. Heads-up limit is a boring game, difficult and slow. It lacks the fireworks that have made no-limit hold 'em so successful. There is no heads-up limit event at the WSOP. AI research soon expanded, though, in two directions: to *no*-limit games and to games with more than two players. In 2017, in a casino in Pittsburgh, a bot named Libratus dispatched a team of expert heads-up no-limit players. In early 2019, *Wired* reported that the technology behind Libratus had been contracted by a Pentagon agency called the Defense Innovation Unit for two years and $10 million. One of

---

*Named for a constellation that contains the star that will succeed Polaris as the North Star around the year 3000.

Libratus's co-creators, Tuomas Sandholm, had long been touting his machine's applications to warfare, including war games and simulations used to perfect military strategy and planning. "I think AI's going to make the world a much safer place," Sandholm told the magazine.

Michael Bowling, the computer scientist who solved heads-up limit, keeps a tidy office at the University of Alberta. Unlike many of his pioneering games colleagues, whose spaces overflow with game detritus, Bowling's only clutter is the dense, inscrutable formulae and graphs scrawled with technicolor markers on a wall-sized whiteboard. One can understand the need for all the mathematics, as Bowling is trying to make sense of a very complex world.

"Even the smallest variant of poker has a billion billion decision points," Bowling, a small man with a softly commanding presence, told me.

The Computer Poker Research Group at the university was formed in 1996, and heavy emphasis was put on the game following Garry Kasparov's chess matches with IBM's Deep Blue. Poker's mathematical complexity rivals that of chess—or exceeds it, depending on the variant—and poker adds randomness and hidden information, hewing it more closely to the "real world" that AI researchers so badly want to influence. The researchers in the poker group aren't interested in conquering the game per se. They see it as "a test bed for doing good science." But in their scientific wake, they have upended, and perhaps destroyed, swaths of the poker world. The poker pros beaten in Pittsburgh by Libratus worried that AI would kill their game. They were right to do so. Bowling explained the threat artificial intelligence posed to poker.

"Poker is a pyramid scheme," he told me. "Online poker is a big pyramid scheme. You need all those people sitting at the bottom that are feeding money to the people who then go win money and walk up to the next level." Getting more specific, he continued: "The size of the pyramid will determine how high the stakes can go up to. If there's a big, long range of skill levels, then you can have people at the one-to-two-dollar level that feed into the five-to-ten-dollar level that feed into the ten-to-twenty-dollar level, all the way up to one to two thousand dollars."

Diversity of skills leads a thriving poker economy. But the computers, as they did with backgammon, democratize skill. They improve the collective wisdom about how the game should be played, and they accelerate the diffusion of that wisdom. More and more players get better, and they do so much faster than they did when the only way to improve was to go to Vegas and play a ton of hands. In a game like chess, this is OK—quality at the highest levels improves and the human game is made healthier, more competitive, and more exciting. But in a game like poker, a big pool of equally excellent players could lead to economic collapse.

"When the skill levels narrow, the pyramid doesn't narrow from the bottom up," Bowling said. "It doesn't mean the one-to-two-dollar level disappears and everyone's just playing one hundred dollars to two hundred dollars up to a thousand dollars to two thousand. It goes the other way."

Given the amount of poker that's been played online over the last couple of decades, I wondered if the damage might be explained by the rise of bots, programs unleashed into the wild by rogue academics or profiteering coders that destroyed the ecosystem like an invasive species.

"I think there's an element of that," Bowling said. "But I think the stronger thing that happened was that *people* started using bots to figure out how to play. I regularly get contacted by poker pros asking if I can help them with something. I would say every one of the top ten pros in the world is paying a poker programmer to do something."

In addition to scouring his academic papers, poker pros began poaching Bowling's talent. "The pros caught wind of what we were doing," Richard Gibson, a former doctoral student of Bowling's, told me. Gibson's dissertation was titled "Regret Minimization in Games and the Development of Champion Multiplayer Computer Poker-Playing Agents." Regret is a formalized mathematical concept when it comes to making decisions in an uncertain environment—it's the difference between an optimal decision and an actual decision. Minimizing regret is an important ingredient in many modern poker-playing algorithms. "It seemed like it was worth a lot to them," Gibson said. "They were paying me pretty good money."

The high price a good poker program can command is an emblem of a dramatically altered game. Computer programs have operationalized John Nash's game theory. In our rock, paper, scissors example, playing each move at random with a one-third chance makes it impossible for your opponent to guess your pattern and beat you. Being unpredictable makes you unexploitable. In poker, this can be accomplished with hand ranges and mixed strategies. If I only ever raise $100 pre-flop in the small blind with a pair of aces, that is a fact that can be exploited. So instead, I bundle my hands into ranges—I raise $100 with aces, kings, and queens, say. Moreover, I shouldn't always do the same thing with the same range of hands—I should mix my strategy and randomize. Maybe two-thirds of the time I raise, and a third of the time I call. Typical output from an advanced commercial poker program is a large and colorful grid, showing all 169 possible starting hands and what to do with them what percentage of the time. Some poker players have even been known to use the second hand on their watch as a randomization device.

Poker players today call this style of play "GTO"—game-theory optimal. Its practitioners are free to cocoon themselves beneath hoodies and big headphones because if you embrace these tenets fully, you can all but ignore the other players at your table. Their specific identities and quirks are immaterial. All that matters is that eventually they will err, and you will profit. And that's why GTO players hire the programmers, to tweak these ranges and percentages, to find and eliminate their games' every exploitable sliver.

In the summer of 2019, Bowling granted me access to his computer program DeepStack, which leverages advanced AI techniques such as "continual re-solving," "intuitive local search," and something called "sparse lookahead trees." The program was developed by Bowling alongside the Computer Poker Research Group and teams at Charles University and Czech Technical University in the Czech Republic. Its creators claim that it is the first computer program to outplay professional humans at heads-up no-limit.

In my Brooklyn apartment, I sat down with my laptop on a sunny afternoon to play DeepStack, leveraging nothing more than my three pounds of mammal brain and a carafe of high-test coffee. The computer and I each started with twenty thousand chips, and the blinds started at fifty and a hundred chips and increased every ten hands, maxing out at fifteen hundred and three thousand if the match went one hundred hands or more. Whenever one player won all the chips, he (or it) tallied a point and the process started again.

Over a few days, DeepStack exhibited a peculiar style of play. It was ferociously aggressive pre-flop, when the only cards a player can see are the two in his own private hand. It raised and re-raised early with just about anything, and sometimes launched early and enormous all-in bets; it almost never folded in the small blind. But after the flop, it calmed considerably, as if having taken a digital Xanax, and played what seemed to me like a passive game. I did what I could to exploit what I saw as the program's tendencies, as was my mammalian instinct, but this was a machine specifically designed and trained *not* to be exploited—to abide by the mathematical maxims found in game theory and the game's elemental geometries. "The main goal of DeepStack is to approximate Nash equilibrium play, i.e., minimize exploitability," reads the academic paper describing the program.

To my surprise, I managed to grind out some wins. Exercising authorial discretion, I stopped the match when I had a lead of fifteen to fourteen games. Much like Kasparov did after playing Deep Blue for the first time in 1996, I stared at the ceiling for a long time after the match, relieved that I had beaten the machine.

The feeling didn't last. Shortly after the end of our match, Bowling sent me an email, debriefing my performance against his creation by analyzing which parts of my success came from skill and which parts had emerged from the thick fog of randomness inherent in no-limit poker. He wrote, "You should expect to win 42% (margin of error of 5%) of your matches against DeepStack. While you won 15 and lost 14, your play (after removing luck) suggests you should have won 12 matches and lost 17." Well, shit.

After removing luck. Luck, good or bad, is essential to the game. And while luck dissipates in the long run, it dominates in the short run. For example, during the World Series I competed in, a magnitude 7.1 earthquake struck near the desert town of Ridgecrest, California. Its tremors reached Las Vegas, where they disrupted the Main Event. A player named Andy Frankenberger was dealt pocket sixes in the small blind before evacuating the cardroom in mid-hand with a couple hundred others. Frankenberger returned soon after to see that his hand had been folded, that the board had come ace-six-five, and that his opponent, who had kept playing during the temblor, held pocket fives.

SOME THIRTY MILLION DECKS of cards were distributed to troops during the Second World War. My grandfather, like millions of other GIs, had a deck and played poker with his fellow soldiers. He never spoke about his experience in combat, but years later, having returned to his farm in Iowa, he'd play five-card draw on riverboats

floating on the Mississippi River. Years later still, around the farmhouse table, he taught the game to me, the eldest son of his youngest daughter. I was six years old. The stakes were distributed from a
jar of change that otherwise sat on a high shelf. On summer nights
there were root beer floats. Whatever nickels and quarters I won, I
could keep. I was hooked.

Like many other aspiring poker players of my generation, I was
inspired by the 1998 film *Rounders* and the improbable victory at the
2003 World Series of Poker of the amateur player and accountant
Chris Moneymaker, who won $2.5 million on an initial invest-
ment of $86. Those events sparked an online poker boom—a Big
Bang, really—the ignition point of which coincided precisely with
my first year of college. With my school's reliable and fast internet
connection, I played thousands of small, low-stakes tournaments
on the website PartyPoker, which was detrimental to my studies
of Aeschylus and linear algebra but was enough to keep me in beer
and takeout.

The poker boom inspired wanton gambling on the part of
the blindly hopeful but also significant study by the mathematically and financially inclined. The economy—from the guppies
to the midsized fish to the whales—began to crystallize. David
Sklansky's *The Theory of Poker* soon sat on as many dorm-room
shelves as Adam Smith's *The Wealth of Nations*, which at the University of Chicago was saying something. Among a certain set,
poker glory mattered more than investment bank job interviews
or elite law school spots. There were rumors of the kid in the
dorm next door having won two hundred grand online. The kid
who bought a Range Rover. The kid who was dropping out and
moving to Vegas. The kid who was playing in the World Series of
Poker. I wasn't any of those kids—I had neither the bankroll nor
the skills—but I wanted to be.

More than a decade out of college, not as a pro poker player but as a reporter, I arrived in Vegas at the World Series of Poker at last. In honor of my computer foe DeepStack, I entered the tournament with some of the deepest stacks available—the $1,500 Monster Stack No-Limit Hold 'Em event. It is so called because players start the event with a hefty fifty thousand tournament chips, allowing, at least in theory, more poker bang for one's tournament buck. The blinds, the forced bets that get the action going in each hand, start small, at one hundred chips, and increase slowly—stepwise every hour for five days, like the razor-sharp torture device slowly descending in Edgar Allan Poe's "The Pit and the Pendulum." This continues until the field is eliminated and a single winner is crowned. Exactly 6,035 people were entered, creating a prize pool of $8,147,250. (Because 7 percent of the buy-in is withheld as an entry fee, and 3 percent is taken to pay the dealers and other staffers.) The winner would become a millionaire.

As I turned the corner to enter the poker room at the Bellagio for a bit of low-stakes practice on the night before the Monster Stack began, Doyle Brunson, the author of the poker bible *Super System* and a two-time winner of the Main Event (1976 and '77), was in my way. Or vice versa. "Excuse me, sir," I said as we nearly collided. He looked up from atop his mobility scooter and beneath his cowboy hat and grumbled something I couldn't understand. Imagine strolling into Fenway Park some idle afternoon during batting practice and running into Ted Williams on the dugout steps. But the legend had aged. The erstwhile face of the game was weathered.

A TAXI DRIVER NAMED Stanley drove me from my hotel to day one of the tournament. He was broke, he told me. He'd just paid for the open-heart surgery of a woman in his trailer park. "She's gonna put me in the poorhouse," he said as he logged our ride neatly into a ledger. I told him where I was going and promised him that if I won, I'd find him and give him the money.

"You poker players sure are kindhearted," Stanley said. "I wish I had time to play poker."

I told him that I wasn't sure that I was representative of poker players as a class, and that I was dreading the coming encounter with the bloodsucking pros. As I left the car and entered the summer heat, Stanley gave me some advice.

"Just hope on that river," he said.

One enters the World Series of Poker through a shopping mall–style bank of doors behind the main Rio casino. The portal is surrounded by an enormous parking lot that was shimmering in the morning light when I arrived. Indoors, many players had donned sweatshirts to protect against the punishing air-conditioning. This was pre-pandemic, and a vibrant economy surrounded the WSOP. Massages for ten dollars per five minutes. Gel seat cushions for twenty dollars. Portable phone chargers for $99. Custom poker tables. The "world's finest playing cards." Wireless headphones. Souvenir photos taken in front of a green screen with bricks of faux hundred-dollar bills. Poker tax specialists. Bracelets promising to "enhance your life" through the removal of harmful toxins. Short-term international phone plans for the visiting international players. A small library's worth of poker instruction books. Sunglasses said to be "proven for poker." And any number of promotions offering a chance to win a seat at the $10,000 Main Event.

This economy extends inside the cardrooms as well, in a series of commercial endeavors with troubling gender and class undertones. A platoon of masseuses, armed with various oils, lotions, and hand sanitizers, prowl the tables, offering their services to players. (The correlation between the number of massages being given and the stakes of the event is positive and strong.) A popular food truck offers direct-to-seat delivery performed exclusively by attractive women. (Twenty-five dollars for a burger. But it was delicious.) A squadron of waiters take drink orders: lots of coffees and waters early on, with requests for alcohol increasing toward day's end. ("Last-level beers," imbibed during the day's final level of blinds, are a time-honored Series tradition.) Las Vegas casinos in general and the World Series of Poker in particular are liquid places in more ways than one. Rolex Submariners dangle from seemingly every other wrist, and rolls of hundred-dollar bills bulge from pant legs. I watched a man pull fifty thousand dollars from the left pocket of his dingy khakis—five thick slabs of bills bound with those paper currency straps I'd only seen in movies. This sight seemed to interest no one but me.

Speaking of currency and images of American statesmen, Warren Harding is said to have lost a set of White House china playing poker—he played so often that his advisers were known as the Poker Cabinet. The name of Franklin Roosevelt's New Deal was derived from poker argot, as was Harry Truman's "the buck stops here." Truman played cards with Winston Churchill on the eve of the Briton's Iron Curtain speech. Dwight Eisenhower played while in the army, winning enough to buy an engagement ring for the future first lady. Richard Nixon funded his first congressional campaign on the back of his poker success. Barack Obama is said to be a good player, and as a senator he hosted a low-stakes, bipartisan home game. When touting his Atlantic City casino, Donald Trump once described his life as "a poker match" to a journalist but, when pressed, said, "I've never had time to play seriously."

I entered a dimly lit cashiers' room and counted out fifteen Ben Franklins, which were promptly whisked away behind cage bars by an efficient woman on the other side. In exchange for a month's rent, I received two white slips of paper. They displayed my location for the day—Table 120, one of 227 tables in the Pavilion Ballroom and one of 523 tables in the massive poker complex in which the Series is held. I navigated the thick matrix of tables arranged on the football field–size floor, eventually finding the one with the "120" sign hanging above it. I handed one of the slips to the dealer, who checked it against my driver's license and invited me to sit down. In front of me on the green baize I found fifty thousand in chips in a variety of denominations and a garish rainbow of colors—black-and-white 100s, pink-and-black 500s, yellow-and-black 1,000s, orange-and-gray 5,000s, and a single red-and-yellow 25,000. These were both my strategic and tactical weaponry and the proof of my continued existence in the tournament. It's amazing how tiny a stack of fifty thousand in chips can look.

A poker tournament is different from a cash game you might play for twenty bucks at the kitchen table. Tournament chips have no monetary value—you can't exchange them at the cashier. Rather, you play until all your chips are gone and you are eliminated or until you possess all the chips in the room. Every hour, the blinds and antes increase, putting mounting pressure on players to engage rather than fold until the right cards arrive. The final 15 percent or so of the field in a tournament wins at least some money, and the prizes increase exponentially as the field approaches the last person standing. In the Monster Stack, there were 6,035 total entrants, so 907th place and worse would take home zero dollars, 906th place would take home $2,249, and the amounts would increase from there, with first place taking home $1,008,850. By the end of the first day, half the field would be gone.

I was in Seat 2, which means I sat two chairs to the dealer's left. The other players at my table, in clockwise order: a woman from Texas who revealed, ironically, that she was concealing a handgun; an Italian who spent the day listening to Radiohead; a teenage-looking Oregonian who wore both a wicked smile and a Wild Turkey bourbon T-shirt, which he later covered with a black sweatshirt bearing the logo of the pistol manufacturer Glock; a man from Staten Island who spent most of the day laughing, presumably at whatever he was watching on his phone but possibly also at the general absurdities of life; a Californian who had adopted with great fidelity all the sartorial elements of the Unabomber; an Australian with strong views on Australian liquor tax laws; a rumored prodigy in a Nike hat and red shirt à la Tiger Woods; a silent Italian with whom I'd often make inadvertent and awkward eye contact; and a shaggy Brazilian who spoke no English other than the numbers he announced for the sizes of his frequently large raises.

In the scheme of things, this was a tame table. On the first day of the World Series of Poker Main Event, a man from Pittsburgh named Ken Strauss went all in, without having looked at his cards, on the very first hand of the tournament. While the other players were considering this unorthodox action, Strauss dropped his pants, took off his shoes, and threw one of them at the dealer. He was ejected. A few weeks later, he was charged by authorities in Clark County with making "terroristic threats" against a Las Vegas casino called the Venetian. The website *PocketFives* reported that his bail was set at $150,000.

It was important, of course, not to get too attached to any of my tablemates, either as characters in some would-be narrative or as just other humans in my life; the field would dwindle and these people would disappear—or I would. The Texan was quickly replaced by a dapper, elderly European with expensive-looking sunglasses. The Australian busted, and his seat was filled by a young gun from China. I myself knocked out the Tiger Woods kid when my pair of tens held up against his ace-seven after the flop delivered him a four-five-six. (It was the worst I'd feel all week.) A German wearing red, white, and blue sat briefly before busting and being replaced with a neo-hippie from San Luis Obispo. Not long after, I crippled the chip stack of the Unabomber, when the flop came jack-seven-four—I held two other jacks, he held two other fours. "Good hand," he said. (Maybe Stanley was right about us kind cardplayers.) I can't remember who took his place.

But despite the inherently ephemeral nature of tournament

participants, and the fact that a certain kind of empathy was probably antithetical to playing good poker, I couldn't help myself. All
I knew, for example, about the young Oregonian Glock enthusiast was his first name. That was enough, after a bit of investigation, to later uncover some basic personal details. He was actually
twenty-one and had been playing in casinos since he was eighteen.
He'd won a total of $10,864 in live poker tournaments. He lived
in Salem and had learned the game from his father. He hadn't
attended college, worked testing backflow in irrigation systems,
and was studying somewhat unenthusiastically to get his real estate
license. He had a dog named Buster. He loved to fish and hunt. He
made goofy YouTube poker videos that garnered about a hundred
views apiece. "I'm a little bit odd, I'm not gonna lie to you guys,"
he says in one.

The human appeal of poker is strong. The equipment is min-
imal; all a player holds are two little pieces of cardboard. The rest
is raw human interaction, on both a macro and a micro scale. Rare
in the world of sports or games is the competitive event with thousands of concurrent competitors. At the WSOP, any one of these
competitors can end your tournament. Any one of them can double your stack and put you in the money; any one of them can send
you home. As such, a player can take an interest in the collective of
humanity surrounding him and in the individuals at his table—at
once his enemies and his compatriots. He may even learn, perhaps,
about a dog named Buster. An old poker adage, indeed one quoted
in *Rounders*, is that "the key to the game is playing the man, not the
cards." This is the old-school attitude, the stance of exploitation.

But computer poker, the unexploitable game, is not interested in
the peculiarities of human players. To be unexploitable, to play the
GTO game of the computer, is to turn inward. It is lonely. There is
no longer a question of whether computers are better than humans
at the game—clearly they are. The salient question is what happens

when every player onboards computer thinking and poker becomes a world of flattened skill and alienation.

The hand against the Unabomber was the only big pot I took down during the fourteen hours of play on day one, but the thing about tournament poker is that one big pot can be plenty. When play officially ended around midnight, I had about double the amount I'd started with. The dealers distributed special clear plastic bags to the surviving players, into which we dumped our chips, labeling the bags with our names and sealing them with adhesive security strips. The bags would be waiting at our new seats in the morning. We'd tear them open, stack our chips in front of us, and begin to play once more.

THAT EVENING, I DROVE ten minutes northwest to a rental house, situated conveniently near a Ferrari dealership, a Popeyes chicken, and a Church of Jesus Christ of Latter-day Saints. This was the temporary WSOP home, a moneyed frat house, of a foursome of brilliant poker-playing friends.

Grant Denison, Mitchell Towner, and Robert Brewer roomed together at various times at Lewis & Clark College in Portland, Oregon, in the mid-2000s. The fourth, Jonathan Levy, later joined the group through Portland's poker scene. They cohabitate each year for the seven weeks of the Series to "grind tournaments," as they put it, playing in as many events as they can, from the $500 Big Fifty to the $10,000 Main Event. They root for each other during the World Series not only because they are friends but also because, thanks to an agreed-upon financial arrangement, they share in each other's action.

Denison and Levy talk about poker for a living and are known online as the Poker Guys—they host a podcast and a vlog featuring in-depth breakdowns of the strategic and tactical minutiae of interesting high-stakes poker hands. Their incisive shows reveal just how complex a game poker is, and just how difficult it is to play it well. The last time I'd seen Towner, who's now a professor, was in the living room of my tiny grad school apartment. He was studying finance; I was studying economics. We sat on folding chairs at a folding table, drinking Lone Star beers, lost somewhere in a twenty-dollar poker game. Years later, in 2016, Towner won the same World Series event that I was currently playing in—he bested a field of nearly seven thousand others, taking home $1 million and a gold bracelet.

The Poker Guys had recently analyzed a televised hand featuring Doyle Brunson, into whom I had nearly collided at the Bellagio, and the great Canadian player Daniel Negreanu, a.k.a. Kid Poker—a hand that threw the difference between old-school and new-school poker into sharp relief. Brunson, in his trademark cowboy hat and a gold bracelet, is dealt a pair of aces, while Negreanu, with bleached blond hair and an earring, is dealt seven-four of clubs. After Brunson re-raises a third player and Negreanu calls, they are the only two players to see the flop. The flop comes ten-ten-seven, giving Negreanu a pair of sevens. Brunson is the first to act, and into a $15,600 pot he bets $18,000. ("That is wild and crazy, especially from a 2020 lens," Levy says in his analysis. What he means is that the bet is way too big. The reason it's "wild and crazy" is that Brunson is still sure to get called by better hands, like those containing a ten, but he might also scare away those weaker hands that would enrich the pot.) Negreanu calls. There's $51,600 in the pot now, and the turn is a five—no help.

"I guess I just got enough for one bet," Brunson drawls, and he pushes his stack to the center of the table, going all in with $86,100. ("This just seems like a game-theory disaster that Doyle's making," Denison says. Again, it seems like Brunson will only get called by hands that beat him and that worse hands will quickly run away. But it doesn't happen that way.)

"Something smells about this hand," Negreanu says in response to the monster bet. "Everything leads me to believe that I should never fold here, for some stupid reason." Indeed, Negreanu doesn't fold. He calls, the river is a queen, and Brunson's aces hold up and win him the $223,800 pot.

The Poker Guys chose this hand because it was such an outlier. Its victor goes against everything we currently understand about poker theory, but the theoretical faux pas nets the master nearly a quarter of a million dollars. The Guys offered some semblance of logic for Negreanu's own thought-theoretical process, flawed though it was, which they hypothesized might run something like this: "Wouldn't Doyle be afraid of a ten? Aren't I the guy who could have a ten? Can't Doyle not have a ten? Wouldn't he check an overpair, like two aces, or bet smaller with an overpair because of that? Therefore, he has ace-king, I call, and Daniel Negreanu wins again."

But Doyle Brunson, who's made a living at poker for fifty years, remains a beacon of the old-school style, the exploitative game. Two extracurricular facts swirled around the hand above. One, Brunson had lost a huge hand shortly before, and therefore he may have been seen by the others at his table as being "on tilt," or "steaming," a poker phenomenon in which one becomes prone to unsound, rash decisions. Perhaps Brunson knew this. Two, Negreanu has a famous reputation for making "hero calls," risking lots of chips to catch other players bluffing. Perhaps Brunson knew this, too. Though his tactics may have been game-theoretically unsound, he was *exploiting* both the situation and the tendencies of his opponent. There is still some magic in that.

"This guy was at the top of the game for his entire career," Denison said, concluding his analysis. "Nobody is able to keep up with theory that well, to always be on the cutting edge of theory—there's always some new kid coming up with new theories that are going to be slightly better. Doyle has something else going on. I don't know what it is. It might be an understanding of his opponents. It might be an understanding of the way the table perceives him. It might be a general tells understanding that he can't fully explain. But there's something almost supernatural about Doyle that allows him to understand that this is a play that's going to work."

Back at their rental property in Vegas, despite the fact that poker plays a meaningful role in each of their lives and livelihoods, despite the powerful beauty of its math and the occasional old-school magic, the friends all sensed dread at the core of professional poker—and especially its modern incarnation.

"It is kind of shitty that your whole thing is taking someone else's money," Towner said. "You're literally taking money out of someone else's pocket. And, by definition, it's a negative-sum game rather than a zero-sum game," because the casino takes a cut out of each cash-game pot or each tournament entry fee.

"After a few years of playing professional poker, I really did feel soulless," Levy said. "I don't necessarily feel like I'm making the world a *worse* place by playing poker, but I do think there's a bit of a predatory element to it."

Of course there is. Definitionally there is.

"It's like an incredibly pure, microcosmic form of capitalism," Denison added. "Except the taxes are flat."

There are external and internal sources of poker dread. On the one hand, you're preying on weaker players. And on the other, this predation poses an opportunity cost: What else might you be doing with your time on earth? These factors combined can be dangerous.

"Professional gamblers in general, and poker players in particular, especially the young kids, the twenty-five-year-olds who have way too much money because they're good—they're really, really good—are also desperately unhappy." Levy said. "Like, *desperately*." He recalled an incident a few years before in which a young, high-stakes pro made a million-dollar bet with his roommate that he could run seventy miles in twenty-four hours. He nearly killed himself in the process, but he did it. According to Levy, he had done it just to feel something.

One engine of this dread has been technology. The academic computer science poker work has trickled down to the publicly available market in the form of computer programs called solvers. One of the most popular of these, PioSOLVER, has a premium version that sells for $1,099 and another, PokerSnowie, goes for $229.95 a year. Cheap, given the stakes at the WSOP. A player using such a program can enter the details of a hand—her cards, her position at the table, the size of her and her opponent's stack, and so on—and the program will spit out the game-theory optimal play. Perhaps the player should go all in half the time and call half the time, for example. A common question asked in the hallways of the Rio during the World Series is "Well, what does the solver say?" And while this has almost certainly raised the objective quality of the poker played there, questions remain about its effect on the subculture.

"I can't think of any of the crushers of recent years who's thirty-five or under and who seems like an entertaining personality at the table," Denison said. There is, for example, a German professional named Christoph Vogelsang—a young crusher—whom other pros have called the least exploitable player in the game. He has been known to wear a special hoodie, which he pulls over his face during hands, like a sort of mathematical turtle. Indeed, this approach to the in-person game has trickled down to the amateurs. Even in the low-stakes cash games I entered in Vegas, there were always players wearing the big headphones and the sunglasses. Schmucks, in other words. In seeking to emulate the soulless pro, exploiting every edge, these players cause the humanity of the game to bleed out onto the casino floor.

Here lies a paradox. On the one hand, professional poker needs engaging, *human* personalities in order to attract new players to repopulate its ecosystem. But today's best players are often bland acolytes of the silicon solvers. As the computers crowd out everyone else, the pros will only be able to feed on interested tourists like me, people with "real jobs," who enjoy the game despite their knowledge of the odds, and who must budget a sizable chunk of their book advance to play the WSOP in Vegas. It's possible that most poker pros don't think or care much about this. Just like most of them don't notice when a man pulls fifty thousand dollars in cash from his dingy khakis.

But there is no poker without money. The game makes no sense without it. Poker is bound together by risk, and that risk has to have bite. The chips have to mean something *outside* the game. Otherwise, you're just sitting at a table flipping over pieces of cardboard. Poker, therefore, is not self-contained. It's not a game of creation like, say, Go is. Go alone can give rise to valuable expressions of ingenuity; it needs no outside medium of account. Poker is a game of merchantry. It is a means to an end.

A related feature of poker creates another problem for anyone who wants to study the game at the highest level. When two top chess grandmasters play, their game is fully recorded, replicable and reviewable by other players and future generations. Indeed, volumes of collected games are a staple of the chess literature.[*] But poker, with the exception of some televised encounters, generates no comparable record. One player goes all in, another folds, the hands are tossed into the muck and a new hand dealt. No matter the brilliance of the play, no reliable record is created beyond the tallies of cash. There is no literature; there are no intellectual artifacts. The game continues, each play disappearing into a shuffled deck of cards.

---

[*] See, for example, Bobby Fischer's *My 60 Memorable Games* or Garry Kasparov's series *My Great Predecessors*.

DURING THE WORLD SERIES of Poker, a Carnegie Mellon computer scientist and his former student, then a Facebook AI researcher—the same duo behind the bot that defeated the pros in Pittsburgh—published a paper in *Science*. They had created yet another new AI, this one named Pluribus (Latin: "more"), that could defeat not just one other player but a *whole table* of top professionals in no-limit hold 'em.

"I think that this was the final milestone in poker," Noam Brown, the Facebook researcher, told me at the time. "I think poker has served its purpose as a benchmark and a challenge problem for AI."

I asked Tuomas Sandholm, the Carnegie Mellon professor, if he, too, thought the bots would kill the games they conquered.

"Unfortunately, there may be some merit to that," he said. "That would be very sad. I've come to love this game."

UNTIL ABOUT THREE-THIRTY on the morning I was due back at the Rio to continue my Monster Stack WSOP event, I was playing $1–$2 no-limit hold 'em in the poker room at Caesars Palace. As the hours passed like minutes, I kept telling myself that the late night was practice. It certainly was a human experience. I met the mayor of the village of Boyle, Alberta, population 845. I saw a man scream incessantly at a dealer with a particular turn of vulgarity I hadn't before heard: "Fuck you *twice*." I saw a man forcibly detained by a trio of yellow-shirted security guards and struggle to keep them from whatever was inside his backpack. I saw a line of beautiful people, blocks long, waiting to pay thousands of dollars for bottle service at a nightclub.

After an eight-hour session, I had made fifty-three dollars, not including the complimentary Jack and Cokes, and I was happy. I slogged back to the hotel through the neon-bright Vegas night, dodging the strip club touts and admiring the beautiful absurdity of the off-duty showgirls, cigarettes lit, enormous feathered head-dresses blowing and tilting dangerously in the breeze.

Whatever dread has been visited upon the professional game by the machines, the amateur game is still available and delight-ful for dabblers like me. If we're content to win or lose fifty-three dollars at a time, the game is still fully available to us—its mental challenge, its psychological rewards, its lure that the right cards will come. We profit in enjoyment rather than money. In fact, perhaps being an avowed poker amateur has its own unique rewards. "One of my theories in games is much of the wonder and the pleasure is in figuring out for yourself—that's why you do it," C. Thi Nguyen, a philosopher at the University of Utah and the author of *Games: Agency as Art*, told me. "If I want to win, a computer has figured out the optimal strategy for me to win. I don't understand it, but if I fol-low these rules, then I'm going to win. I think that takes something really important away from us."

Three hours of sleep and an enormous seven-dollar coffee later, day two of the Monster Stack saw me relocate from my by-then-beloved table in the gigantic and utilitarian Pavilion Ballroom to the smaller and posher Amazon Ballroom, down the hall, with its special tables reserved for the ESPN telecasts. Most of my early time there was spent trying to control tremors in my hands. About three hours into the action, during which I hadn't won a single hand or even seen a single flop, I got my first playable cards: ace-king, unsuited.

Ace-king is an important and tricky hand in tournament poker. There is an entire book about optimizing it.* It's undeniably strong,

---

* *Optimizing Ace King: The Right Strategy for Playing Poker's Most Complex Starting Hand* by James Sweeney and Adam Jones, which I have not read, as will likely become clear.

what with its high cards—but it's not anything, not even a pair, when the hand begins. Especially unsuited. I had been bleeding chips all morning, folding my blinds and antes, and had about 45,000 of my 92,000 chips remaining, and it was currently costing me 7,500 in forced bets with every orbit of the deal around the table. In other words, I was in an uncomfortable but not quite yet desperate position, and I decided that this was, at last, my time to play. I sat in the middle position, and the player to my right, who had significantly more chips than me, roughly 200,000, raised the 3,000 blind to 7,000. I re-raised to 19,000. (In retrospect, this was a big mistake.) Everyone else folded. He called. There were now 45,500 chips in the pot and about 26,000 in my stack.

Trench warfare has been described as interminable boredom punctuated by moments of sheer terror. Poker tournaments, too.

The flop came queen, nine, four, with two hearts. I had the ace of hearts, but nothing else of note. The big-stacked player to my right, a predictable bully, immediately made a bet that would force me to go all in. This is a typical "continuation bet," as in a continuation of his aggressive action before the flop. This is also why my

19,000 re-raise was a mistake; I should've gone all in right then and there and put *him* to a decision, rather than the other way around. Anyway, there was now 71,500 in the pot, nearly three times my stack. I thought for as long as I'd thought in the seventeen hours I'd been playing in the tournament, maybe twenty seconds that felt like twenty minutes, and a creeping worry built inside me that someone would call "*Clock*," triggering the dealer to summon a floor manager, who would give me a verbal countdown, at the end of which my hand would be forcibly folded for me. More frightening than the poker or the money was this creeping fear of embarrassment, of a loss of all decorum in the midst of a welter of doubt. It didn't end up mattering; nor did whatever game-theoretic thinking I was attempting to do. Shortly thereafter I watched helplessly as my own right hand grabbed the rest of my chips and deposited them into a neat and gaudily colorful pile in the middle of the table. All in, as they say. The other player—about whom I knew and continue to know precisely nothing, including even his first name—quickly turned over his king-ten of hearts, and I slowly revealed my ace-king.

There were two cards to come. I was at least relieved to be "winning"—I had ace-high and he had king-high—but it was not in any meaningful way. He was on a flush draw. If another heart came, his five hearts would crush me. However, if *two* hearts came, then I'd have a better flush. So my nameless villain needed precisely one heart in the next two cards, or to hit a pair of tens and have me avoid hitting a pair of aces. Later, I ran the numbers: in this situation,

I had a 51.5 percent chance of winning a comfortable stack of some 100,000 chips and sailing toward the money—and a 48.5 percent chance of losing it all. It was down to a coin flip. I was, as cab driver Stanley had instructed, hoping on that river.

Needless to say, a single heart came on the river, giving my opponent a flush and draining the blood from my face. I blinked as the dealer pushed my chips to the other player, and I blinked again as he stacked them; there was nothing but green baize in front of me. There is typically little fanfare when a player is eliminated from a poker tournament; indeed, no one said anything. I stood up slowly and silently and walked away. As I passed the stanchions separating player and spectator, I glanced back, no longer a player but the onlooker in Cézanne's masterpiece—arms crossed, vaguely interested in the game, carrying just a hint of a smile on my face. It's a mean town for a loser.

SCRABBLE

With twenty-six soldiers,
I conquered the world.

–JOHANNES GUTENBERG
(APOCRYPHAL, PROBABLY)

THE 2019 NORTH AMERICAN Scrabble Championship was held in an enormous ballroom in downtown Reno, Nevada, the self-described "biggest little city in the world." At nine o'clock on a sweltering July morning, more than three hundred players from around the world sought refuge in its industrial-strength air-conditioning. They were seated, two to a board, with some fifteen thousand lettered tiles in total awaiting them in cinched cloth bags. In front of them were boards that would spin smoothly on ball-bearing turntables. Next to these were sheets on which they'd keep score and meticulously track every tile played. At their sides were clocks, each displaying the twenty-five minutes players would have per game to consider their moves.

One theory of the ultimate fate of the universe contends that it will all end in a Big Freeze. As stars deplete the fuel they need to burn, the universe will grow darker and colder, approaching an average temperature of absolute zero. The universe's entropy—its disorder—will increase without bound until everything that ever was disappears into an eternal state of incomprehensibly large, icy, undistinguished *sameness*.

The Scrabble players in Reno were doing their part to fight this unavoidable, if distant, fate. A well-played game of Scrabble moves

from a disordered soup of a hundred letters in a bag to a highly specific, ordered, and precise web on the board.

I pulled up a chair at Table 18, across from a biostatistician from
Pennsylvania who happened to be the twentieth-ranked Scrabble
player on the continent. At precisely 9:09 a.m. Pacific time, I drew
seven tiles from the bag, a single random selection of letters from
among the 3,199,724 distinct possibilities, and placed them in alphabetical order on my rack.

E, I, L, O, S, T, V.

I took a deep breath and began trying to find the order hiding
within.

IN THE SPRING OF 1998, one year after the IBM supercomputer
Deep Blue defeated the world chess champion, Garry Kasparov, a
stand-up comedian and an unemployed college dropout occupied
the top floor of the headquarters of the *New York Times* for a seven-
hour series of Scrabble games against a computer program named
Maven. The match took place on the occasion of the game's official
fiftieth anniversary. (In fact, the game dates to the Great Depression,
when it was originally named Lexiko and invented by a down-on-
his-luck architect.) The comedian, Matt Graham, and the dropout,
Joel Sherman, were friendly rivals and two of the best human Scrabble players in the country, the latter having won a world championship and two national championship titles. Maven, running on a
Toshiba laptop, had been developed by Brian Sheppard, a programmer who began tinkering with Scrabble in the early 1980s, when he
was an intern at IBM.

Undeterred by humanity's recent failure in chess, the Scrabble
players were optimistic. "We have a slight edge," Graham told
the *Times*. But Maven won, six games to three. Its technology
reassembled the chaos of the bag into such diverse human nouns

as TIRAMISU, a coffee-flavored dessert, and GROSZY, Polish coins.*

"With even tiles, I think we'd have an edge," Graham said after the fact, chalking the human defeat up to bad luck.

In the late 1970s, as a student at the elite Bronx High School of Science in New York City, Brian Sheppard had been the captain of the math team. "I was really, really good," Sheppard told me with a laugh. As often goes with the mathlete territory, he also had a yen for computer code. Sheppard didn't own a computer, but like the great Alan Turing working on his chess program decades earlier, Sheppard wrote code with a pencil and paper.

"Programming games has always been part of my life, since as long as I can remember," Sheppard told me. "The first program I wrote was a blackjack program that I copied out of *Beat the Dealer*. I had pages and pages of if-then-else statements. Even as a fifteen-year-old, I knew this couldn't be the right way to do this."

Sheppard's programming skills would grow more sophisticated, and his math prowess would bring him to Harvard and then to a summer internship at IBM Research. When Sheppard arrived at IBM, his adviser was out sick. Days and then weeks passed, and the adviser had not returned. Sheppard went up the rigid IBM chain of command, to his adviser's manager, asking him what to do. "Just go to the library and read," the manager said, assuring Sheppard that his adviser would return eventually. This offhand instruction would have a lasting impact on the game of Scrabble.

In the library, Sheppard ran across a description of an early Scrabble program. Few such programs then existed. One early (unnamed) program, created by two Indiana University computer scientists and

---

*It is standard Scrabble notation to capitalize words used in play.

described in a 1979 paper, ran on a Digital Equipment Corporation mainframe computer and played passably, despite its limited lexicon; there were no digitized word lists in those days. The appendix of the paper describing the program reports that a human "played several rushed rounds against the program and consistently scored lower than the program."

Sheppard immediately saw room for improvement. "I had no real interest in Scrabble as such," he said. "For me, the pace of play was always too slow." But this was a programming challenge he could tackle. "I didn't need a supercomputer. If I had a few megabytes of RAM, I could do this. So I wrote a program that summer, because my adviser never came back. It was a PL/I [an early IBM programming language] program, running on an IBM mainframe, and it played better than anything in the literature, and the summer was over and I went back to college."

Sheppard's account understates the labor involved. For two weeks that summer, he typed words from the physical Scrabble dictionary into the computer by hand. For another two weeks, he verified that the words were accurate. For another two weeks, he "really verified" them. And for three more weeks, he entered certain nine-letter words from the ninth edition of Merriam-Webster's *Collegiate*, as the Scrabble dictionary only went as far as eight-letter words.* Sheppard named his blossoming program Maven, choosing a Yiddish word meaning "expert" that he'd discovered in the Scrabble dictionary. Sheppard saw it as fate.

At first, Maven "was a reasonable program and it didn't do anything special," Sheppard said. But it taught him invaluable lessons. For one, knowing words was the most important component of

---

* Sheppard would repeat this process again later in Maven's career, typing in the Dutch dictionary for a match against the Dutch Scrabble champion. "That was a pain in the neck," he said.

Scrabble skill. The Scrabble dictionary is less a dictionary—as in a reference work containing definitions, etymologies, and usage—than it is a really, really long rule book. Each word is a rule: its appearance in the dictionary indicates its validity, and its absence indicates its invalidity. To play the game well you first have to learn tens of thousands of rules, a fact in sharp contrast to the elegant simplicity of Go. In fact, the central battle in a game of Scrabble is not between one player and the other but between each player and *the rules themselves.* "My program had more words [than earlier programs], so it played better," Sheppard said. "But even with the words, I could still affect the outcome by giving bonuses for different tile combinations. Simple things like keeping a blank: don't play away your blank unless you get a certain number of points." Sheppard's instinct to hoard valuable tiles would become Maven's main contribution to the game.

Most casual Scrabble players learn pretty quickly that while you could play, say, CAT for five points or CATS for six points, you're much better off scoring five with CAT and holding on to the S to make a higher-scoring play later in the game. S's are valuable. Determining *precisely* how valuable an S might be is central to Scrabble strategy. An early instructive volume on the game from 1986, *The Champion's Strategy for Winning at Scrabble* by a top player named Joel Wapnick, posits some precise figures. For instance, the book pegs the value of an S at between six and eight points and a blank[*] at around forty points.

In Scrabble, the letters left on your rack after you make a play are called your *leave.* AERST is a great leave because those letters work together beautifully, forming common prefixes and suffixes and often appearing in concert in words; something like IUUWV is a terri-

---

[*] The wild-card blank tile is most useful in making bingos—plays that use all seven tiles and earn a fifty-point bonus.

ble leave because those letters are both individually and collectively ugly. Using data from Maven's own games and the power of machine learning, Sheppard was able to compute the values of letters and combinations of letters in Scrabble more accurately than ever before. "I was looking for linear tile values," Sheppard said. "How much more should I score in order to play that tile versus keeping it in my rack." The value proposition gets fiendishly complicated. The first E played is worth something different from the second one played, not to mention the repeats on your own rack. "And it's not just tiles," he said. "I was looking for *patterns*. The Q and the U are a pattern."

Sheppard's calculations ran counter to the human wisdom imparted in Wapnick's book. Sheppard discovered that the expert's stated values were both internally inconsistent and miscalibrated. Armed with better statistical values, Maven debuted in public against strong human players at a tournament in the winter of 1986 in Waltham, Massachusetts. Much like the comedian and the dropout a decade later, the players at the tournament were "polite, but skeptical about the program's chances," Sheppard wrote. "Or doubtful, or downright dismissive." Yet in its first competitive game, against a top-ten player named Alan Frank, the program opened with two early bingos and cruised to victory. Maven finished the event with eight wins and two losses, including wins over two former national champions. Its two losses came thanks to a bug in its code and human operator error.

Sheppard's work caught the eye of Jonathan Schaeffer, the University of Alberta computer scientist who solved checkers. Schaeffer encouraged Sheppard to write a paper, and then a longer paper, and then, finally, some fifteen years after Sheppard left college, a doctoral dissertation, which he called "Towards Perfect Play of Scrabble."

Maven's strong play flew in the face of established Scrabble theory. Top players in the 1980s emphasized *turnover*—the idea that, all else being equal, playing more tiles on a given turn is better.

These players had observed (correctly) that the player who won a game tended to be the one who played more tiles. But translating this observation into a theory of strategy confused cause and effect. Sheppard (and Maven) realized that the player likely won not because she had played more tiles but because she had drawn better tiles and therefore was able to play more of them. Maven avoided turnover. It liked to *fish*—to play off just a couple of tiles, grooming its rack for big scores and bingos in the future.

Champion Scrabblers did not welcome Maven's insights at first. "There is a doctrinaire streak in many top players," Sheppard wrote, "and one good tournament was not about to overturn the theories that had brought them to the top of the game." Nevertheless: "My impression is that Maven was better than the humans of the day were, notwithstanding holes in its vocabulary."

Sheppard had no designs on the world of competitive Scrabble. Programming was his hobby and Scrabble was his medium. "I had no intention of ever getting a PhD," he told me. But Sheppard had noticed a pattern in computer games: hobbyists often outpaced the academics.

The next harbinger of Scrabble revolution was also a small, private project, released in 2006 by an undergraduate named Jason Katz-Brown and a software engineer named John O'Laughlin. "My family would play Scrabble when I was growing up, and I always hated it," Katz-Brown told me. "I was the youngest and I'd always lose. It was no fun." But after reading *Word Freak*—the delightful, spelunking account of the game's odd and thrilling competitive subculture by the journalist Stefan Fatsis—Katz-Brown quickly began memorizing Scrabble words. At MIT he would carry the dictionary in his pocket. Practicing against Sheppard's program helped Katz-Brown peak at a ranking of third in the country.

Katz-Brown and O'Laughlin's program, called Quackle, has become the intellectual engine of the modern game. Quackle's innovations were twofold. First, it went beyond the values of particular tiles on a rack (the *leaves*) to the values of any possible combination of tiles (the *superleaves*). Why stop at single letters or pairs when you can assign a value to every possible group of letters? By the mid-2000s, computing power had advanced sufficiently to make such calculations possible. Second, Quackle was free, public, easy to use, available for both Mac and Windows, and (thanks to the donation of a Scrabble-obsessed poker pro) open-source. In the subculture of competitive Scrabble, Quackle emerged as a sort of anagramming and word-placing demigod. Tournament players consult it the same way poker players look to the solvers: *What does Quackle say?* Thanks to Maven and Quackle, the average winning score in tournament Scrabble games has increased steadily since the 1980s, from about 390 to about 420 today.*

Katz-Brown is humble about his creation. "In Scrabble, to make a reasonably good AI is so easy. The move generation is very simple. The leave evaluation is simple—you just have the computer play itself a bunch of times. Once you do that, you can beat anybody except maybe Nigel Richards."

Nigel Richards, of course, is the greatest Scrabble player the world has ever seen. We don't know much about the man, an ascetic who typically shuns interviews. He has no television, no smartphone, and no internet presence. But we do know that he is a New Zealander who lives in Malaysia and that his other great interest is bicycling. He rode fourteen hours from Dunedin to Christchurch to compete in his first national championship in 1998. After winning the tournament, he rode back. To tournament Scrabble players, Richards is a shamanistic figure, the man with the bowl cut and wizard's beard and mystical control over the bag of letters and the

---

* This is also thanks in part to the addition of useful new words to the game's dictionary, such as QI and ZA in 2006.

board on which he plays them. He not only has the dictionary memorized but is also able, if you give him a word, to tell you the number of the page on which it appears. He's won four world championships (the only player to win more than one), five U.S. national championships, and has a lifetime scoring average of 448 points per game.

A Scrabble board after two strong players have finished a game might look, to the uninitiated, as though they had played in Martian. Here's a taste: in a single, randomly chosen game from a recent national championship, Richards played the following words: ZIBET (an Asian civet), WADI (a dry riverbed), PAIK (to beat or strike), INIA (parts of the skull), CALX (a mineral residue), and SERED (burned). That was an utterly pedestrian game. Other "Nigel stories" are legendary. For example, Richards once held a rack of ?CDHLNR with two disconnected O's and an E open on the board. (The "?" denotes a blank tile.) He could've played the eight-letter bingo CHILDREN. Instead, he played through the three scattered tiles, dropping down the ten-letter bingo CHLO-RODYNE. He once played SAPROZOIC through the word ZO. He once played DECAGONAL through the words GO and AL. In 2015, after studying a dictionary for nine weeks, he won the French-language world championship. He doesn't speak French.

Richards's feats, like Marion Tinsley's on the checkerboard, are awesome yet inscrutable. Like certain machines, their skill appears superhuman. We find ourselves wondering, *How do they do that?* Hard work, of course, was mandatory for both players: hundreds of checkers books or hundreds of thousands of words. "I'm not sure there is a secret," Richards once said. "It's just a matter of learning the words." Tinsley augmented his hard work with faith, believing that checkers ideas came to him "out of the clear blue sky." Richards wields a supreme detachment, a full devotion to the game but none whatsoever to its random outcomes. He was once asked, after winning a tournament, if he'd like to say a few words. "I don't know any," he said. Another player once told Richards that it was impossible to tell if he'd just won or lost a game. "That's because I don't care," Richards said.

According to Katz-Brown, Richards remains the only human alive still stronger than the machines—an ascetic human force of nature. Sheppard disagrees, favoring Maven: "I would happily play Nigel for any stakes that he set." Such a match is unlikely to occur; Richards never plays against programs.

MY OWN OBSESSION with Scrabble began in the summer of 2009 in the sweltering heat of Austin, Texas, where I was a graduate student studying economics. As a kid, I had always hated the game, much like Katz-Brown, associating it with interminable, low-scoring affairs at the kitchen table that I inevitably lost to my elders. But I also fell down a *Word Freak* rabbit hole. Stefan Fatsis painted a picture of obsessed geeks sleeping with the dictionary, traveling around the country to exciting tournaments. It was like an über-nerdy *On the Road*.

The problem when you start playing Scrabble—especially if you start as a kid—is simply that you don't know many words. The words are the rules, and so it's not just that you're bad at the game, it's that you don't even know what the game is. You spend a lot of time trying to figure out how to make a word, *any word*, with the tiles on your rack, and then trying to figure out where to play them, and discovering that the whole enormously frustrating effort was worth, like, six points. There is something magical, however, about realizing how to play Scrabble even one step above beginner: using the bonus spaces, creating overlapping words, hitting your first bingo. You also learn how to play defense. The first time you realize that your opponent is stuck with the Q and you make a crucial play to deny her the legal two-word layup QI, securing yourself the victory, well—that's magic. It was this sequence of unfolding skills that eventually endeared me to the game—I realized what this game is, that it is the creation of something from nothing. It felt valuable to learn and exercise a craft, even if it was "just a game."

This feeling is not unique to Scrabble, of course; it's ancient and universal. "This has to do with this larger, Aristotelian picture of the *flourishing life*," Gwen Bradford, a philosopher at Rice University who has studied games, told me. "It has to do with the exercise and development of our core human capacities, our characteristic capacities. There's rational activity or thinking on the one hand, but also wielding on the other. Exerting effort, engaging in activity, that's always good, because that's just what it is to be a human being."

Once you overcome the initial tedium, the game is thrilling. Anagramming is an addictive intellectual rush. Unscrambling AAABLOPR, DFGGHIOT, or EILLMNOU for the first time feels like exercising a minor superpower.* Once you know basic technique, games quickly become intense shootouts and rich contests of strategy. Falling into Scrabble is like learning a new language— unlocking vaults of pattern and recognition and meaning—except that the language was already your own.

Once you've leveled up with basic strategy, you are ready to unlock its innermost beauty. But to do so, one must study. One first learns the "twos," or two-letter words, the shortest playable words in the game. There are 107 of them these days. Many of them are already familiar: AN, IT, OF, WE. But many are not: AA, AI, XI, XU.† Then one moves on to the threes, of which there are 1,082. Many of these are also initially familiar: AND, CAT, THE, WHY. But many are also not: AVO, CWM, LAR, ZAX.‡ Then the fours,

---

* PARABOLA, DOGFIGHT, and LINOLEUM.

† Cindery lava, a three-toed sloth, a Greek letter, and a Vietnamese monetary unit.

‡ A monetary unit of Macao, a deep basin on a mountain, a tutelary spirit of an ancient Roman household, and a tool for cutting roof slates.

of which there are 4,218—AGLU, CORF, HOWK, QOPH.* And so on. While the long words are beautiful and often high-scoring, the short words are the nucleotides that hold together Scrabble's DNA. These short words are so important and familiar and commonly played by good players that they are like monkish prayers, repeated, internalized, and subconsciously incanted.

The Austin Scrabble Club met on Mondays in a dingy back room with dodgy air-conditioning in the Austin Recreation Center. There, a dozen or so players would pay a dollar to play three games, a fee that often left me short of quarters for laundry. I was nervous about transforming what had been a private fixation into a public performance. In my first game I picked up the letter bag from the wrong end, spilling tiles across the linoleum floor.

But I steadied myself. In my first night at the club, I played three bingos: ERODING, GEARING, and OUTSIZE, the last for 123 points. I was hooked. Finding order in the chaos, turning a heap of letters into a beautiful spider web of words on the board, was magical—and addictive. The best Scrabble players are like wizards, and I wanted to become a member of their order.

The feats of top human Scrabble players are difficult to comprehend. For starters, there is the sheer scale. One linguistic study has found that just two thousand root words provide coverage for around 99 percent of spoken English-language discourse. Other researchers have found that many adults have an overall vocabulary of some thirty thousand words. There are, however, *192,111* words in the latest edition of the Scrabble dictionary used in North American play†—roughly an

---

*An airhole through ice made by a seal, a wagon used in a mine, to dig, and a Hebrew letter.

†There is also an English-language dictionary used in competition outside of North America, such as for the game's world championships. Known as Collins, it contains 279,496 words, including juicy oddities such as JA and ZO.

order of magnitude more words than a typical working vocabulary. There are 56,875 seven- and eight-letter words alone, the words most often played for bingos and their valuable fifty-point bonus.

There are 391 words whose definitions refer to monetary units, from Albania (LEK) to Lithuania (LITAS) to Zambia (NGWEE). There are 448 that refer to mammals (e.g., QUAGGA), 846 to birds (WEKA), and 1,244 to fish (FUGU). In the realm of history, 78 nouns have to do with things in ancient Greece (e.g., PHYLE), 94 with ancient Rome (AUSPEX), and 136 with medieval times (KERNE). And 190 words refer to a branch of science (e.g., EKISTICS), 162 to politics (MUGWUMP), and 272 to religion (VODUN).

Top Scrabble players know them all.

Complicating this further still are maddening irregularities and complex relationships between the words. Consider just a few randomly plucked examples, starting with the seemingly harmless word MARKA. It is a monetary unit of Bosnia and Herzegovina and can be pluralized by adding an S. But it can also be pluralized as MARAKA, a word that does *not* take an S. There's also MARKKA, a former monetary unit of Finland. That can be pluralized as MARKKAA *or* MARKKAS. But, careful! MARKKAA does *not* take an S. Or consider TIYN, a monetary unit of Kazakhstan. It is pluralized by adding an S. But there's also TYIN, also a monetary unit of Kazakhstan, which does *not* take an S. It's crazy-making.

Any single word of the 192,111 can send a player as deep down a linguistic rabbit hole as she would like to go, through thick layers of definition, history, culture, immigration, war, conquest, colonization, appropriation, derivation, coinage, conjugation, translation, pronunciation, and selection. As the great player Marlon Hill once said about learning the Scrabble words' definitions, "If you are sane at all, it will drive you slowly insane."

To play the game well you needn't learn the definitions, of course, and success in the competitive game of Scrabble has nothing to do with one's everyday working vocabulary. Its best players tend not to be poets or English professors but, rather, computer programmers, mathematicians, musicians, and the otherwise technically inclined. These are the sort of people who can easily retain coded information and quickly turn it into ordered meaning. A number of the world's best English-language players come from Thailand and barely speak English. And recall that the world's best English-language player won the French-language championship without speaking French.

Most players study with the help of a computer program; Zyzzyva ("The Last Word in Word Study") is the most popular. These digital flash cards display letters in alphabetical order—that is, as an alphagram. During gameplay one does the same with the letters on the rack, tightening the connection to earlier study. For example, the program might display AAEFLMOT. Your job, then, is to try to mentally rearrange those letters into the word MEATLOAF. Or if it displayed AAGKNOOR, you'd try to find KANGAROO. AEIKRSTW becomes WATERSKI, ADELOPT becomes TADPOLE, DGMOPRU becomes GUMDROP, ABINORW becomes RAINBOW, and so on. Do this successfully a couple hundred thousand times and you're on your way to becoming a strong tournament Scrabble player.

In 2007, a player named César Del Solar created the website Aerolith—part study tool and part daily online competition. A player arrives at the site and selects a "word wall." The screen fills with fifty alphagrams—AGMNORU, ILSSTTU, EEEKLNX, and so on—which a player must "clear" by typing in the unscrambled words. The pace is swift. To succeed you have to solve an alphagram about every five seconds.* Top players can clear their boards much faster. A leaderboard displays that day's top performers; its

---

* ORGANUM, LUTISTS, KLEENEX.

Hall of Fame is a who's who of the competitive Scrabble world. I
have spent many hours on Aerolith. Once your brain is attuned to
anagrams, you start seeing them everywhere. When I see "New
York," my brain rearranges it into WONKERY. The "Hamptons"
become PHANTOMS. A street sign reading "right lane" becomes
EARTHLING.

Marlon Hill's warning of insanity aside, learning the definitions, even cursorily, of some two hundred thousand words is an
enlightening and democratizing experience. There is approximately
no thing or concept in the universe that will escape you if you read
through the Scrabble dictionary, and each thing and concept is presented on equal terms.

I delighted in the serendipity of the word study, but the more
compelling driver of my obsession was that Scrabble was a respite—
an escape, really—from the stressors of grad school and the real
world. Scrabble study is meditative, in a sort of Buddhist sense, and
cheaper than therapy. It was fun to play at a high level. I met good
friends at the club and won a small tournament or two. I began
to climb the ranks, but my ego became tied up in the game. My
mood swung on the outcome of each contest, which is heavily subject to chance, what with the letters emerging randomly from the
bag—sometimes you draw AERST and sometimes IUUWV.* I
lacked both the detachment of Nigel Richards and the faith of Marion Tinsley. My ranking plateaued at around 200th in the country. Studying became a chore. I stopped caring about the difference
between MARKA and MARAKA. In 2013, I graduated, moved to
a new city, and quit the game. My modest Scrabble prowess, such as
it was, became nothing more than a reliable cocktail party anecdote.

But in 2019, I dusted off my word list, fired up Zyzzyva and

---

* According to Quackle, the former draw is worth the equivalent of 31.2 points,
while the latter is worth *negative* 32.7 points.

Quackle, and prepared to play in the North American Scrabble Championship. A few weeks before I was due to fly to Reno for the competition, to train against some actual humans and talk about the state of the game, I met César Del Solar at the Chess & Checkers House in New York's Central Park. Here, when the weather is nice, he and his wife, Mina Le, run a small weekly Scrabble club. Le is a Harvard-trained otolaryngologist and Del Solar, who studied electrical engineering at Caltech, is a software architect. They're both strong tournament players and would both be competing at the national championship.

When I met them in the park, Del Solar was at work on a new project—an advanced machine-learning, neural-network Scrabble-playing program. He and his research partner, Jesse Day, another elite player, named it Macondo after a fictional town in Gabriel García Márquez's *One Hundred Years of Solitude*. It was already fast enough, running on an average laptop, to play hundreds of games against itself per second. Del Solar said he was "always" working on it. If he achieves his ambition, Macondo will become the greatest Scrabble player—human or machine—that has ever existed. He hopes that it will also reveal deep and as-yet-unknown truths about the game, disrupting the human status quo, as Maven did with leaves and turnover.

"Maybe it will teach us how to play," Del Solar said.

As we sat outdoors on a beautiful day, surrounded by games players, he explained his goals: "We want to build something that does what AlphaGo did for Go, starting from scratch, tabula rasa. If we made something that was clearly dominant over humans, I think that would be awesome."

Computers have already changed the human game—much as they did for chess and poker. In Scrabble, this has opened a generational divide. Thanks to the computers, "people have gotten a lot better," Del Solar said. "Whenever you go to a tournament, people just know how to play. There's a lot of kids who have grown up as Quackleheads."

Such mastery has its downsides. As games players driven by faceless computerized lessons improve, they tend to homogenize, converging to some silicon-dictated ideal, losing their individual human styles. When I got good at Scrabble, in many ways it ruined the game for me. I could no longer play with family and friends; the strange words that now seemed second nature to me felt to them like cheats. (Who could blame them?) I found it inspiring to watch great players strive for the zenith of the game, each carving out his or her own style in a beautiful expression of human ingenuity. But the more I mastered the game, the less social it became. I missed the feeling of playing against a fellow novice, figuring out the game together. That struggle is a human achievement, too.

I sat down across the board from Le to play the first game of Scrabble I'd played against a human in nearly four years. Despite my promising opening bingo from a rack of EEIRSUZ,* she beat me by about sixty points. The familiar frustration crept in, as Scrabble and my ego began to intertwine once more. I left and walked through the park, trying to enjoy the sunshine.

"I ALWAYS DID POORLY in the SAT verbal," the great American player David Gibson once told *Sports Illustrated*, "but about ten years ago a supernatural love for words came upon me. When you get changed, you can't help it. It's spiritual."

In the three months before the event in Reno, I managed to study just under thirty-five thousand different words—all the twos,

---

*SEIZURE.

threes, fours, and fives, and the more useful chunks of the sevens and eights.* Despite the fact that my official rating would've placed me as only the 280th best player in North America, I registered for the championship's top division; I was thus slated to play thirty-one games over five days against the best Scrabble players on the continent, putting me technically, if not realistically, in contention for the event's highest title. Fifty-four players entered the top division, including most of the continent's top-rated players and a handful of the game's all-time greats.

In the ballroom, a detail from my study came to my mind, the end of a rabbit hole that had begun with my looking up the word DAGOBA, which I'd learned is a Buddhist shrine, from the Sanskrit *dhātugarbha*, meaning "having relics inside." The Buddha, I'd then read, is said to have given eighty-four thousand teachings. This is a figure roughly equal to the number of two- to eight-letter words in the Scrabble dictionary. In *The Blue Cliff Record*, a revered collection of kōans compiled nearly a thousand years ago, a teacher gives the following instruction, which would have served just as well at the championship in Reno centuries later: *"Pick up the whole world, and it's as big as a grain of rice. Throw it down before you. If you're in the dark and don't understand, I'll beat the drum to call everyone to look."* That's precisely what the legion of Scrabble players in the Reno Ballroom, myself included, was trying to do as the championship began. To pick up the whole world from the chaos of those cinched bags—birds, mammals, monetary units, meatloaf, and all—as big as just a few little Scrabble tiles, and throw it down on the boards in front of them.

My entire time in that ballroom, staring at the chaos of my tiles, I could hear the drum beating.

---

* For scale, this book is roughly eighty thousand words long and contains about eleven thousand *unique* words.

WHEN I ENTERED the ballroom for Game One, it took my eyes
some time to adjust from the glare of the Reno morning. I found
my table, checked my pocket for my backup pen, wished my opponent good luck, took a final gulp of coffee, and shook the bag of one
hundred tiles, hoping they'd come out favorably. I drew my seven
tiles one at a time from a velveteen bag held in my other hand above
eye level, as the tournament rules dictate. They emerged as follows:

E, I, L, O, S, T, V.

A violet is a plant of the genus *Viola*, especially *V. odorata*. Violets
have, according to Merriam-Webster, "alternate stipulate leaves and
showy flowers in spring and often cleistogamous* flowers in summer." The word comes from Middle English, borrowed from Middle French, from *viole* and the Latin *viola*, meaning any of various
spring flowers, deriving from a base root *vi-*, "of Mediterranean sub-
stratal origin," and the Late Latin masculine nounal suffix *-et*. The
word's earliest citation listed in the *Oxford English Dictionary* is from
a fourteenth-century romance called *Arthour and Merlin*: "Mirie it is
in time of June, violet & rose flour Woneþ þan in maidens bour."

A player has twenty-five minutes to make all of his or her moves
in a tournament game, and my clock now read 24:32. My opponent,
Scott Appel, the twentieth-best Scrabble player on the continent,
had opened the game with MATH for eighteen points. After I'd
spent a few seconds anagramming, VIOLETS, through its millennia of evolution and horticulture and centuries of linguistic history,
appeared in my mind and quickly went down on the board—eighty
points. Appel would later counter with ENSNARE, and I would

---

*Meaning "having closed self-pollinating flowers." A valid, if unlikely, Scrabble
word.

hit back with IODINES and hold on. Final score: 403–379. Record: 1–0. Mood: relief.

SCRABBLE MEMORIZATION is difficult and draining for humans. It is a mentally and spiritually exhausting task. But it's trivially easy for a machine, especially in the era of digitized dictionaries. It's simple enough to load a computer with the Scrabble tournament dictionary, currently officially known as the NASPA Word List 2018 Edition, or NWL; the file is just 1.9 megabytes in size. I am not an especially strong programmer, it should be understood, but after a few minutes of googling (a valid Scrabble word these days) and some high school–level coding, I was able to cobble together a program that was orders of magnitude better than me on my best day. I felt both joy and despair. With just a few short lines of code, my computer was able to perfect the task I had spent thousands of hours practicing.

Suppose one wanted to anagram the promising letters AEGINRST. After months of dedicated study, a practiced player could quickly unriddle this elementary rack. After ten or fifteen seconds, for example, I was able to see seven valid words. Then I loaded my program and typed the following function:

```
getAnagrams("AEGINRST")
```

After I hit Enter, the program spat out ANGRIEST, ANGSTIER, ASTRINGE, GANISTER, GANTRIES, GRANITES, INGRATES, and RANGIEST. The process took my laptop 0.002 seconds, or about a fiftieth of the time it takes to blink. I had taken fifty thousand times longer to do the same task, on top of which I'd completely forgotten about ASTRINGE. It's simply not a fair fight. This aspect of the game, remembering and finding the words, which requires years of Scrabble-training effort to perfect, is precisely what computers are built for. But finding words in jumbles of tiles, while essential, isn't the only important Scrabble skill.

First, Scrabble, like life, is a trade-off between today and tomorrow—between spending and saving. It's what an economist would call a dynamic programming problem. Therefore, one must have an accurate sense of the value of the tiles and of leaves. One must be adept at "grooming" one's rack for big scores in the future, while also scoring as well as possible in the present. In my real life, I'm sure I spend too much and save too little. I'm not always as kind as I should be to my future self, a phenomenon regularly observed by behavioral economists. But over the Scrabble board, I am a relentless and calculating saver—*Homo economicus.* I am, dare I say it, a machine. I meticulously balance spending today (scoring points on this turn) and saving for tomorrow (preparing my rack for the next turn) because I want to win the game. Over the board, I exercise an agency largely foreign to me in the muddy real world outside of the game. I become mechanical and disciplined. Games provide clarified access to agency; they teach us real things.

Another skill is often called "board vision." The Scrabble board isn't enormous; it's fifteen squares by fifteen, as shown below, or the size of a weekday crossword puzzle. But the number of possible plays on it is enormous, and only one of them is best. There are seven letters on your rack, and words can be played horizontally and vertically. So, as a very rough upper-bound estimate, there are $15 \times 15 \times 7! \times 2 = 2,268,000$ possible placements of tiles that a player might have to check for validity and consider playing. Also, a bit like in Go, you are competing for space—triple-word-score squares, bingo lanes—with your opponent. Therefore, a keen sense of the board and its potentials and hot spots is crucial.

Another skill comes at the end of the game. As each match begins, Scrabble, like poker, is a game of imperfect information—you don't know what letters your opponent has or what tiles are left in the bag. But players are allowed to track the tiles on a score sheet as the game is played. Toward the end of the game, the bag of tiles empties and all the remaining letters are on the players' racks. If a player tracks the tiles accurately, he will know *exactly* what his opponent holds at the end of the game. In the endgame, Scrabble becomes a game of *perfect* information. It therefore becomes more like chess—governed by the if-I-do-this-then-they'll-do-that logic of game theory. Even the computers struggle at this stage. Top players have found major flaws in how Quackle plays the endgame. They claim to be able to exploit these weaknesses and grind out good records. Brian Sheppard claims that Maven plays most if not all endgames perfectly—a feat it finally accomplished at a real cost to its creator. "You have to be insane to write code like this," he told me with a laugh.

Scrabble, probably chief among the games in this book, is not a test of a single type of skill but is, rather, a sort of brainy heptathlon of tests of various skills: memorization, anagramming, calculation, spatialization, long-term strategizing, game-theoretic tactics, bluffing, and the ability to roll with an ever-shifting meta-game. "What makes any game good, in my opinion, is a very healthy dose of luck combined with the feeling that you're in control," the former Scrabble world champion and poker pro David Eldar told me. "I don't think it really matters how much skill there actually is. I think people just like to feel like they're in control. Scrabble is very good at giving you the feeling that you're in control." Indeed, you are in control of a number of the game's levers and dials at once. Aesthetically, a game is something like a city. It is a designed place where you go to exercise agency—where you are in control. Scrabble, then, is a bit like New York City. It's serendipitous, engrossing, rich—and at times overwhelming.

I needed a guide. As I prepared for Reno, I consulted with Kenji Matsumoto. Matsumoto, who'd long been ranked in the country's top ten, self-published a book called *Breaking the Game*, which I had been keeping in constant tow during my preparation. The volume promises to introduce its reader to "strategic concepts largely used by only the best players in the world," and it features both the pseudoscientific prose and vague reassurance of a self-help book. In its introduction, Matsumoto writes, "While often brilliant, human thought is inconsistent. Success depends on your ability to harness the power of your mind. This requires using your cognitive ability to make good *choices*." I loved it. I wanted to make good choices.

Matsumoto casts himself as a technocratic Scrabble sage, a sort of Neo from *The Matrix*, awake to the deeper truths of the game. He studied game theory as an undergraduate and brings that quantitative disposition to his favored game. "I believe that my academic background gives me a unique ability to provide expert Scrabble analysis," his website declares. He says he advises several top-twenty players and, moreover, that the national championship's top seed wouldn't be at that elite echelon without Matsumoto's counsel. His book discusses "entropy," "synergy," "volatility," "permutation," and "ghost tiles"—concepts mostly alien to me and certainly alien to most players around their kitchen tables at home. Over fifteen of its pages, he discusses in detail the pros and cons of each tile, one by one, from A to Z to blank.

When we spoke, Matsumoto himself hadn't played a major tournament in almost four years. But he, too, was undertaking a rigorous and spartan training regimen. He was in the midst of a series of hundreds of games against Quackle—a series in which he claimed to maintain a .500 record. He was planning to play in the Reno championship because he happens to live there, in his parents' vacation house. He moved there "for poker mostly," though he claims not to love that game.

Unfortunately, despite Matsumoto's valiant and largely solo efforts, the state of understanding of Scrabble theory remains in its infancy. "Scrabble is definitely going to be the most underdeveloped game that you talk about in your book, by far," he told me. "I don't know of a single established game, at all, where we know less about what we're supposed to be doing than Scrabble."

Matsumoto compared his field to the recent evolution of poker strategy. A couple decades ago, the top poker players "didn't know what they were talking about on a math level—they didn't even try." But now poker is dominated by the mathematically and computationally inclined. The same is becoming true in Scrabble. "The availability and commonplace of computers is the single biggest factor" in the strategic seriousness in Scrabble today, Matsumoto said.

Matsumoto is also prodding at our understanding of "the way that boards evolve"—that is, the manner in which words radiate from the center to the edges during the game. "People used to view

Scrabble as a very chaotic game, and [assumed] that there was no real order in terms of how the board would start from the center and expand outward. Just the same in Go—there's some parallels in those games and it used to be thought of as chaotic as well." Matsumoto believes we may soon discover a deeper understanding. Just as a theory of geology might explain the flow and branches of a river, game theory might explain the flow and branches of words. Perhaps this knowledge could be exploited to win championships. But for all this theorizing, there didn't seem to be that many answers yet.

I asked Matsumoto for one piece of sage strategic advice—something from the expert that I could actually use in Reno. What one thing should an intermediate player like me do over the board against the continent's best?

"Play aggressively," he said. "It's really hard to combat aggression."

"Hey, maybe we'll play each other," I suggested as the realization hit me.

"I don't want to think about who I am playing," Matsumoto said.

CLINGING EARLY in the tournament to a winning 4–3 record, I played Mike Frentz in Game Eight, a top-twenty-five player, recognizable thanks to his favored fedora. In what I took as a good omen at the time, I opened the game (aggressively, I thought) with the word FARTED for twenty-eight points. Frentz, however, would soon get down a high-scoring bingo of SECTION, which I'd counter with my own ALUMINE. But late in the game I trailed by about fifty points, and badly needed to bingo again. I held the promising rack ?ENOORS. There are plenty of seven-letter bingos possible with this rack (SNOOKER, ENROOTS, ONEROUS, etc.) but the issue was that there weren't many places to play them, as you can see in the diagram below. (APNEIC is an adjective and doesn't take an S on the end.) There was, however, I believed, a winning play.

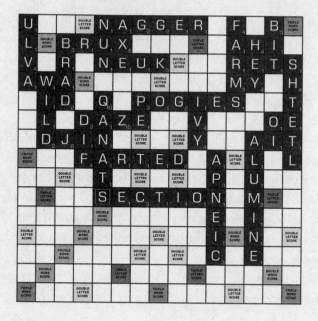

Three potential bingo spots had caught my eye: one overlapping along the right side of the vertical ALUMINE, one through a vertical E *and* T in the center that were separated by one open space, and one through a horizontal I and N in the lower right that were also separated by a space. Desperate and running low on time, I declared my blank an H and played the masterstroke HONORES in the first spot, simultaneously forming UH, MO (short for "moment"), IN, NO, and ER, for seventy-nine points and a near-certain victory. Huzzah! There was just one problem: HONORES is not a word. Frentz quickly challenged it. When a word is challenged in a Scrabble tournament, the players get up and march expectantly to a special laptop nearby. The challenger types the word into an adjudication program, and the challenged player hits Enter. In this case, the screen flashed red with a large X, meaning the word was no good. We returned to the board, where I sheepishly removed my tiles and Frentz sailed to victory. After the game we consulted the software. Indeed, I'd actually had *two* playable bingos through that disconnected E and T: the nine-letter OESTROGEN and OES-TRONES. Finding their order in the chaos would've won me the game. Quackle and Nigel Richards certainly would have. I did not.

Final score: 293–380 (ouch). Record: 4–4. Mood: slowly souring.

EARLY ON THE SECOND DAY, having split my previous eight games evenly between wins and losses, and I was paired for Game Nine against the eleventh-ranked player on the continent: my erstwhile Scrabble strategy guru, Kenji Matsumoto. With trembling hands—high on caffeine and nervous to be playing the man himself—I was able to bingo early in the game with the pedestrian LOCATING for seventy-seven points and added an overlapping play of ZAMIA (a tropical plant) making UM, LI (a Chinese unit of distance), and PA, for forty-four. Across from me, meanwhile, the board proved costive for Matsumoto. The words were not evolving in his favor, and he was unable to score well. He had a number of seven-letter words on his rack that simply couldn't find homes on the board. His frustration began to manifest, largely in the form of fidgets and sighs. Nearing an improbable victory late in the game, to rid myself of some duplicate consonants I played the word RUTTIER for just seven points. Matsumoto "held" the play, meaning he was reserving the right to challenge it. He began muttering to himself and twisting in his chair. I don't know exactly how long this went on, but it was at least a few increasingly awkward minutes. RUTTIER (which is a valid word) became the embodiment of this frustrating game, an expression of the unlikelihood of my defeating one of the top players in the world and Matsumoto's—the great theorist's—exasperation at that fact.

The capriciousness and stress of tournament Scrabble do take their toll. One afternoon in Reno, word quickly spread that a dermatologist from California had been ejected from the tournament and forced to forfeit his games for allegedly concealing a valuable tile on his lap.* And in the middle of another game, one of the top division's top seeds, a man not seemingly used to cardiovascular exertion, stood up and ran at full speed for fifty yards, from the playing hall into the lobby, and screamed, at full volume and high octave, the word "Fuck."

Eventually, Matsumoto let the play go without challenging, resigned to his unlucky defeat.

Final score: 366–343. Record: 5–4. Mood: cat who ate canary.

GAME SEVENTEEN FOUND me across the board from Matt Graham, the comedian who, two decades earlier, had lost that landmark Scrabble match to Maven in the headquarters of the *New York Times*. Next to him on the table was a plastic box containing bottles of something called D-cycloserine, a molecule that, online, is purported to enhance brain activity and learning; something called F-phenibut, another brain booster and the subject of many personal drug-experience website accounts that is said to aid memory; as well as a number of other unidentified substances, a measuring spoon, a coin, headphones, a bottle of water, and a colorful stuffed animal that Graham would soon wear around his neck. He'd get down the bingos CUMBERS, DISTOME, and GALENAS and destroy me, 358–505.

While sitting on a nearly *two-hundred-point* lead late in the game, Graham nevertheless meticulously re-counted every single tile that

---

* Cheating in competitive Scrabble is rare, but it happens. The most common form is using illicit means to ensure that you get the valuable blank tiles. These means might include hiding the blanks near you before the game begins or peeking into the bag while you draw your tiles, with your eyes obscured by the bill of a baseball cap, say. (This actually happened, leading to the suspension of an expert-level player.)

had been played—a process that I suppose was meant to ensure that he grinded out every point available to him but in reality just took several annoying and interminable minutes and nearly ended in me flipping the table over.

I did not. Record: 7–10. Mood: cloudy.

IN GAME EIGHTEEN I played Kevin Fraley, the continent's fiftieth-ranked player. He opened with BUM, and I held the rack ?DEIORY. After a couple minutes' hunt, I managed to find the only available bingo,* and I followed it soon after with bingos of SPANDRIL and LIMEADE (the anagram of EMAILED). I was seeing the words and I was seeing the board. I was exercising my minor superpower.

Until I wasn't. Entering the endgame, I had a nearly fifty-point

---

*JOYRIDE.

lead. I elected to play VISA on the upper left of the board, to get rid of my clunky V, thinking I'd have another turn to get rid of my last two tiles, an E and an N. I would not have such a turn. Through a disconnected I and G, Fraley played INGEST, also forming SPAN-DRILS, scoring thirty-eight points and ridding himself of all his remaining letters, ending the game. Had I myself simply put my own S on SPANDRIL, I'd have won. However, I wasn't completely sure SPANDRIL could be pluralized, or in fact that it was a noun at all, and if it wasn't and I tried to stick an S on it I'd lose for sure, and in any case I thought I'd win regardless. (A spandril is a space between two adjoining arches.) Instead, we tied.

Final score: 403–403. Record: 7–10, with one tie. Mood: border-line despondency.

ACROSS THE STREET from the Scrabble tournament sat the Silver Legacy Resort Casino. Inside the Silver Legacy Resort Casino was a poker room. And inside the poker room were Scrabble players. In fact, after a given day's tournament action, the Scrabble play-ers accounted for a majority of the poker players. I often counted myself among them. One top player whose Scrabble tournament had gotten off to a horrendous start took to playing poker in the mornings, evenings, and even during the tournament's lunch breaks. He'd rush out of the ballroom, suck down a cigarette, and rush across the street. He won as much money in the poker room, from what I could tell, as nearly anyone would win in the Scrabble tournament.

"Freedom, time, utility, chance—such concepts coagulate around the game player," the journalist Alexander Cockburn writes in *Idle Passion: Chess and the Dance of Death*, a passage also quoted in *Word Freak*. "Why do some players become addicted to the game of their inclination? Why does the long-distance runner torment himself with endless miles consumed each day; the racing-car driver confront death on such unfavorable odds; the gambler return to lose more; the chess player exhaust so many hours at his game? . . . Humanism has watered the pastures of leisure and of games with much uplifting speculation. But in the world of games lie areas of darkness, of taboos, of cruel instincts and vile desires."

Over the course of the Reno tournament I had rediscovered that sinister, vile desire in my own relationship to Scrabble. The longer the tournament went on, the tighter the outcomes of my games wrapped around my ego. A computer or a phenom like Nigel Richards accepts the mathematical realities of chance—the program simply performs a large number of simulations of the future and ascribes the results to an artifact of probability. Lacking this machinelike ability, I viewed every outcome, every randomly drawn tile, as meaningful, personal, and in most cases unfavorable. When I lost a game to the division's lowest seed after he drew both blanks and all the S's, I remembered why I'd quit the game all those years ago. The clash of my abundance of interest in the game and my lack of success at it was hard to reconcile. But why should those be reconciled? I appreciate the work of Cézanne and harbor no delusions that I ought to be able to paint like him.

GAME THIRTY-ONE. The final game, at last. By this point, my assigned location in the tournament had slid to the tables far in the back, where they housed the players with middling to poor records, and where I faced a man named Bond. Tom Bond. I wrote down no notes of interest about this particular contest other than my pedestrian losing score (367–395) and that I was ready to go home.

Final record: 13–17, with one tie. Final ranking: forty-second out of fifty-four players. Final mood: spent.

May the universe now die its entropic heat death in the Big Freeze. See if I care.

OVER THE COURSE of the thirty-one games I played in the championship, my thirty-one opponents and I combined for more than a hundred bingos—more than a hundred lovely, long crystallizations of language that we were able to pluck out of the random soup. More than a hundred things, actions, descriptions, and concepts that had wriggled their way through human history and onto our boards in a ballroom in Reno.

Theirs, in chronological order: ENSNARE, COAPTED, TIRADES, DANGLES, ROMANCES, SOREHEAD, VICTIMS, FRONDED, LANATED, AILERON, FLEABANE, RECARPET, SECTION, GESTATES, MISHEAR, SELLING, REBRACES (phony, challenged off), SINCERER, SAFROLE, OURANGS, ATELIERS, TIERCES, HOWDIES, OBTAINER, CONDORES, REASONER, SERIALS, IRONISED, SITUATE, ECOTONE, CUMBERS (valid word, erroneously challenged), DISTOME, GALENAS, PELOTAS, STIFLER, SEIZURE, ULLAGES, LEASHED, LITTERS, NOTICES, TRAPLINE, LEARNED, ENDITED, PSALTER, RAINILY, SECRETOR, EMULATOR, TONGUES, MARTINS, SUCKIER (valid word, erroneously challenged), MILTIEST, YELLING, ERELONG, ROOTLING, DRONERS, MAILINGS, DEMINER, and ORCINOLS.

And mine: VIOLETS, IODINES, TRIGRAM, PARADES, SPORTED, FORMATE, UNLOOSED (valid word, erroneously challenged), CONTUSE, LYSOGEN, RATIONS, ALUMINE, HONORES (phony, challenged off), LOCATING, WAITRONS, HANDLER, ENDOSTEA, BANDORE, RECUSING, GUTSIER, THIOUREA, ARGINATE (phony, stayed on), DOUSING, WENNIER (valid word, erroneously challenged), JOYRIDE, SPANDRIL,

LIMEADE, INTORTED, ARANEIDS, ASTRIDE, SESTINE, DIGLOTS, INSULAR, TEASELING (nine letters!), DRATTED, HOBNAIL, MOISTEN, MOTIONER, STANDING, ACCOSTED, EXAMINEE, AROINTED, OUTRIFLE (phony, challenged off), FLUORINE, BREADTHS, STUDLIER, CHOIRMEN (phony, stayed on—though it's valid in the *other* dictionary), EQUALIZE, QUINELAS, RECAPPED, ROBANDS, and ANDANTE.

As the Nevadan sun rose on the championship's fifth and final day, a loss-prevention specialist from Oregon named Carl Johnson and a collegiate harpist from Washington named Alec Sjöholm sat in first and second place. After their regulation games, they would play a best-of-three final and a champion would be crowned. The giant playing hall, which had once held hundreds of hopefuls in the various divisions, had now emptied, save for Johnson and Sjöholm, a handful of tournament officials, and me, gathered in a corner of the ballroom. The rest of the field watched on closed-circuit monitors in a room across the street. Video cameras were trained on the premium two-hundred-dollar rotating acrylic Scrabble board, as well as on the players' faces and racks. They drew yellow injection-molded, lettered tiles from a repurposed purple felt Crown Royal bag. A pair of annotators dutifully noted and keyed into a laptop each player's letters and plays for the game's internet broadcast. They split the first two games, 1–1.

In the decisive final game—a classic, pendulous display of expert word knowledge—the players, like two heavyweights, traded exploratory jabs for the first few moves, with words including VOTER and WUD (an adjective meaning insane). And then the bingo haymakers came. Sjöholm took the lead with RENTIER (one that receives a fixed income). Johnson took it back with RESOJET (a type of jet engine). Sjöholm took it back with PLAY-

GOER (one who attends the theater). Johnson took it back with SEDITION (incitement of rebellion), followed for good measure by XYSTOI (roofed areas where athletes trained in ancient Greece). But Sjöholm took it back for a final time with MOON-SAIL (a light, square sail). He held on to win, 445–412, and a new champion was crowned.

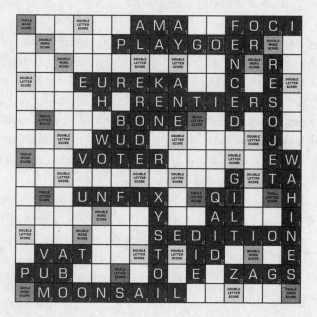

"Congratulations, Alec," Johnson said to a stoic Sjöholm. "You played beautifully."

"Beauty" is, of course, exactly the right word. Aristotle says in the *Poetics* that "to be beautiful, a living creature, and every whole made up of parts, must . . . present a certain order in its arrangement of parts." Sounds like a Scrabble tournament to me.

As the final players exited and the venue staffers cleared away the last of the tables and chairs and vacuumed the carpet for whatever group would occupy the ballroom the next day, they were really clearing out the remnants of a sort of particle accelerator. For five days in Reno, human brains working at high speeds had collided, and from their clashes had emerged those remnants of history, culture, nature, art, science, evolution, migration, war, commerce, and exploration that we call words, arranged beautifully, and in a certain order.

BRIDGE

For a long time she had refused to play
bridge. She knew she could not afford it, and
she was afraid of acquiring so expensive a
taste. She had seen the danger exemplified in
more than one of her associates.

—EDITH WHARTON, *THE HOUSE OF MIRTH*

ON MAY 2, 2015, a column was published on page C4 of the *New York Times* under the byline of Phillip Alder. It was in most ways an unremarkable piece. A search of the *Times* archive, for example, returns some 1,600 other articles written by Alder. This particular one was 682 words long. It ran on a Saturday. The weather in New York City was mild and partly cloudy. Next to it on the page appeared a middling review of an off-Broadway show. The column caused no international incidents, moved no stock indices, and occasioned no responses from elected officials. The next day, it filled recycling bins and was largely forgotten.

But in other ways, the piece was a death rattle. It was titled "A Final Column," and no bridge column has appeared in the paper of record since.

After the column ran, more than two thousand readers wrote to the paper's public editor, Margaret Sullivan. Two New Yorkers remarked that they were "disheartened, discouraged and taken aback. . . . Soon, the obits will disappear, and we won't even know if we're alive or dead." Sullivan replied that the column was a strain on the paper's copy editors, because "you have to play the game in order to check it and make sure it's right." It is a wonderful thing to picture playing cards being meticulously dealt on the *Times*' copy desk. But that delightful image aside, the bridge column, it seems, was killed because it made people play bridge.

Alder and I met for lunch recently on a gloomy afternoon not far from the old *Times* building. Just a few blocks from us, on West Sixtieth and Columbus, one could find the erstwhile Manhattan headquarters of the American Contract Bridge League. Alder, now in his late sixties, cuts the figure one hopes a bridge columnist would cut: bald pate, blue blazer over soft pink striped shirt, gray Hermès scarf, sneakers, British accent. Enamored with tradition, Alder wrote his earliest columns on a sticky typewriter he'd inherited from his grandfather. As a young man, bound for a top British university, he eschewed Oxford and Cambridge for a college in London. Why? "All the best bridge players were in London," he told me.

"Bridge is an intellectual, challenging pursuit with a lot of different layers," Alder continued. "It's like a jumbo-sized onion, more so than other games. There's a lot less luck in bridge than there is, for example, in poker. If you look at the World Series of Poker, the guys who are winning always have the wind behind them somewhere. It's an intellectual challenge, but it's also a more social game than chess, and not quite so stressful as chess. Chess, you make a mistake and it can cost you the game. Bridge, you get one deal wrong, you get it back on the next one—it doesn't terminate your chances."

New York Times bridge columnists form a small fraternity. Alan Truscott had the job for four decades before Alder, writing daily from 1964 to 1994 and then three days a week until 2005. Married to Dorothy Hayden Truscott, a world-class bridge player and teacher, Alan wrote a total of 12,750 columns for the paper. Alder called him the "Isaac Asimov and P. G. Wodehouse of bridge." Albert Morehead was the columnist before that, from 1959 to 1963. He was no less prolific. The author, coauthor, or editor of some hundred books, Morehead also oversaw the twenty-volume *Illustrated Encyclopedia of Knowledge*.

The card game bridge—or, more precisely, "contract bridge"—is necessarily a game of language. Its players craft intricate dialects to conjure meaning and gain competitive advantage. To fully exploit the game's rules, they rely on its literature. The bridge column as a genre attempts to reckon with an impossibly large set of intricate situations. Just as journalists write so that the public may understand a complex world, so bridge columnists write to make sense of the game. Indeed, for bridge players, their game *is* a faithful facsimile of many aspects of the real world. Unlike chess, it has randomness. Unlike backgammon, it has hidden information. And unlike poker, it is a game of teamwork. Bridge, like the real world, features alliances and discords, deduction and inference. The game requires memory and wisdom, prudence and risk, and empathy—for both friend and foe.

Bridge is played with a standard deck of cards and is a trick-taking game, much like its cousins spades, hearts, pinochle, and euchre—but it is the deepest, fullest, and most serious expression of the form. The richness that bridge offers, however, is countered by its cliff-steep learning curve. Full enjoyment of this game comes at the high cost of absorbing its many rules and conventions. With ten minutes of instruction, a beginner can play chess or poker in at least a rudimentary way. Not so with bridge. It would be like asking a toddler to play a game of charades.

"A passion for bridge is hard to explain to someone who doesn't share it," the *New Yorker* writer David Owen, himself a bridge player, once wrote. "One attraction is the sense of endlessly unfolding complexity: the more you learn, the less you feel you know."

This endless unfolding aroused great public fascination with the game, and this fascination, in turn, aroused public suspicion. One of the first articles concerning bridge in the *Times* appeared in the summer of 1907, when Theodore Roosevelt was president and the country had forty-five states. It opened with an ominous thought: "There must be some truth in the tales of the ravages of the game of cards called bridge on the finances and morals of contemporary society." Another article that fall warned of "disconcerting rumors of the recent derangement of bridge ethics, in the play of persons presumably respectable." A 1930 article cited a psychologist who argued that bridge players "are usually sufferers from an inferiority complex who find in the game an easy way to satisfy their striving for superiority."

While the dread about the game's corrupting influence abated, its undeniable attraction for a certain sort of player lingered. "Bridge is addictive, and I got addicted," Alder said.

Most columns Alder wrote were illustrated with a diagrammatic card table. The hands were printed along the four sides, labeled North, South, East, and West—a lovely idealization of the game as popularly imagined: playing cards on a felt table, perhaps ringed with martini-shaker condensation and dusted with cigarette ash. The columns are case studies, analyzing the play that occurred at some real event, played by some real humans. They include copy inscrutable to the outsider: "After East's unwise bid, West led a low spade. East won with his ace and shifted to the diamond king, which declarer ducked. East, aware that he had no entry, now led a club to dummy's jack." And lessons: "West's intervention with 4–4 in the majors at unfavorable vulnerability isn't recommended. But it could have worked well if East had bid one diamond, not one spade. As it went, though, West's bid helped Manley to read the deal perfectly."

For decades, tens of thousands of columns like these appeared in the *Times* and other papers, each shining a narrow ray of light on the game. Combined, the columnists and even just a handful of other notable bridge authors produced hundreds of thousands of pages' worth of books, articles, and columns. In addition to the *Times* column, there's Charles Goren's famous 420-page *The Elements of Bridge* and his 561-page *Goren's Bridge Complete*. There's Alfred Sheinwold's classic *5 Weeks to Winning Bridge* (548 pages). And there's *The Bridge World*, the game's venerable magazine, founded by Ely Culbertson and published since 1929.

These works have given life to the game and shepherded its fans through a century-long story of moral panic, social craze, Gilded Age lucre, and Goldman Sachs money. And, like every other game in this book, they have inspired MIT engineers and other obsessive geniuses who have tried to conquer the inscrutable and addictive pastime with machines.

Bridge reveals in stark terms the difference between the human approach to games (and to life) and that taken by computers. Humans become good at games through theory—through writing that seeks to explain important concepts and filter endless possibilities. Humans think in anecdote and narrative. Computers, on the other hand, become good at games through raw computation—through speedy search and evaluation of a game's large decision tree. Unique among games in this book, bridge remains one of a dwindling set of pursuits where the human approach is thus far superior.

That no computer has yet mastered the world inside of bridge, however, may say more about the state of the game than it does about the unique talents of the humans who play it. While its devotees proselytize the game, there is little incentive, monetary or otherwise, to conquer the world of bridge with artificial intelligence. Bridge—along with those who play it and write about it—is dying.

"When my generation dies," Alder said, "in the next twenty years or so, there's going to be this huge void, and I think bridge in this country will be in big trouble. Which is a pity."

THERE ARE ABOUT 53 billion billion billion possible deals of a single hand of bridge.* That number is far larger than the number of stars in the universe. Even a prodigious dream team of Morehead,

---

* To calculate this, take the factorial of fifty-two cards in the deck and divide it by the factorial of thirteen cards in one player's hand raised to the power of four hands being dealt.

Truscott, and Alder, hammering out a column every second on their typewriters, would need billions of times the age of the universe to describe them all. Not only that, there are more than a thousand billion billion possible auctions that can take place before the cards are even played. Auctions? I'll explain. The basic rules of the game of bridge are fairly simple, emphasis on "fairly," and I will try to do them succinct justice in the following two paragraphs. The game unfolds in two stages: the auction and the card play.

First, a player deals all fifty-two cards in a standard deck, thirteen apiece, to two pairs of teammates who sit across the table from each other. At this point, one knows the contents of only one's own hand but would badly like to know the contents of the other hands. Then, beginning with the dealer and orbiting around the table, an auction takes place. Each player places a bid—"One spade," say, or "Two hearts"—or passes. The number in a bid, plus six, is the number of tricks that the bidder is pledging his team will win. The suit in the winning bid will become trump—the suit that bests all other suits for the rest of the hand. Each bid must be higher than the bid that came before, and from low to high, the suits are ranked clubs, diamonds, hearts, spades, and "no-trump." (No-trump is exactly what it sounds like and presents the most austere test of card play.) So, for example, "three spades" bests "three hearts" bests "two no-trump" bests "two spades," and so on. Instead of bidding, a player may also "double," increasing the stakes of the hand, somewhat akin to the process in backgammon or poker; one might do this if one thinks the other team won't be able to make its contract. A double can be redoubled, but any new bid cancels out these increases in stakes. Once three players in a row pass, the final bid becomes the contract. (Hence "contract bridge.") If East placed a final bid of "Five hearts," for example, then the East-West partnership is obligated to win eleven of the thirteen tricks, and hearts is trump.

After the auction comes the card play. One of the players on the

team that won the auction—whoever bid the contract's suit first—is
called the declarer, and his partner is called the dummy. As soon
as the first card is played, the dummy's hand is turned faceup on
the table for all to see. The other two players are known as the
defenders. Players go around the table, led first by the player to the
declarer's left, each playing a single card, following suit if possible.
The highest card of the suit led in a round wins that trick, unless of
course the trick is trumped, in which case the highest trump card
wins it. Whichever player won the trick leads the next trick. The
declarer gets to play the cards from the dummy hand when it's the
dummy's turn, too. If the partnership that won the auction suc-
ceeds in getting the number of tricks to which they were obliged
(or more), they get points. If they don't, their opponents get points.
A number of important nuances and complications aside, those are
the very basics.*

Bidding in a bridge auction is the crux of the game—indeed, its
defining characteristic—and serves two main purposes. On the one
hand, it's *competitive*. Like in an auction for a painting at Sotheby's,
my bidding might deter you, and yours might deter me, and yet we
both want the painting. (In bridge, the prize is the points you notch
if you win the number of tricks promised in the bidding.) On the
other hand, it's *constructive*. The auction facilitates the flow of information. And from the simple set of bidding rules above has sprung
a forest of languages, a gaming Tower of Babel, known in bridge as
conventions.

An essential goal of bidding in bridge is to communicate to
your partner what cards you hold in your hand. You can't just come
out and tell them, of course—that would be cheating. Rather, you

---

* The official "laws" of bridge, as published by the American Contract Bridge
League, are 157 pages long and govern such contingencies as "gratuitous comments
during the auction" and "play by offending side before assessment of rectification."

must use the artifice of conventions to pass this information across the table. In Morse code, you send dots and dashes. In flag semaphore, you hold up two flags. And in bridge, you bid a number and a suit: "Two clubs." While a bid of "two clubs" may at first seem to indicate that a player has a strong hand in clubs, it may in fact have nothing to do with clubs or the number two at all.

In bridge conventions, the numbers and suits operate sort of like the ones and zeros in binary code, combining in different ways to express complex ideas. One of the classic conventions is called Stayman, after Sam Stayman, who wrote about it in *The Bridge World* in 1945. In Stayman, a bid of "two clubs" is actually a query. It asks that player's partner whether she has four cards in a so-called major suit, hearts or spades. A response bid of "Two hearts" or "Two spades" means yes; a response bid of "two diamonds" means no. Another popular convention, called Blackwood, after Easley Blackwood, who invented it in 1933, helps players learn how many aces and kings her partner holds. It is triggered when one partner bids "Four no-trump," thereby asking the ace question. When that happens, the other partner responds, answering the question: "Five clubs" means no aces or four aces, "Five diamonds" means one ace, "Five hearts" means two aces, and "Five spades" means three aces. The first partner can then ask again: "Five no-trump" means "How many kings do you have?" Again, the partner's next bid answers that question in the coded, artificial language of numbers and suits. By (legally) exploiting the strictures of the game's rules, players can learn rather a lot about cards that were a mystery to them when the hand began.

These languages also have the equivalent of local dialects. There is also, for example, Roman Blackwood, Key Card Blackwood, Roman Key Card Blackwood, Redwood, Minorwood, and Voidwood. These introduce endless wrinkles and contingencies and questions that can be asked and answered. The American Contract Bridge League's 640-page *Encyclopedia of Bridge* includes a hundred pages in tiny print over two columns with capsule descriptions of conventions and systems. The names of conventions, at the very least, make entertaining reading, from Astro Cuebid, Bergen Drury, and Crowhurst to Wolff Sign-off and Woodson Two-Way. A 1981 book called *Modern Bridge Conventions* goes into more detail, covering just a small selection of conventions over its 244 pages.

Nevertheless, what even the best bridge players can express in these convention languages is constrained. There are only the four suits plus no-trump and the seven ranks (from one to seven, since you hold thirteen cards and it is your bid *plus six* that you are aiming to win) that you might bid, and you can also pass, double, and redouble. That makes just fifteen words you are allowed to utter during an auction. Moreover, the bids must always increase, further limiting the expressiveness of the language.

"The opening bidding is like talking in Swahili," Alder told me. "And when you start responding you're using Urdu."

Moreover, these languages must be common knowledge. You and your partner must reveal your dialect's structure and intricacies to your opponents, and players are allowed to ask questions of their opponents like "What did that bid mean?" Bridge is a game of communication but not of subterfuge. As such, the "gravest possible offense" in bridge, according to its official rules, is exchanging information with one's partner outside of what the rules allow—that is, outside of the formal and public bidding process. Illicit *language* is the cardinal sin of the game. Fraud and treachery: Dante's eighth and ninth circles of Hell.

BRIDGE LACKS an ancient lineage, hailing instead from Victorian times. The *Oxford English Dictionary*'s earliest citation is from 1843, when the word appeared in the memoirs of Sir James Paget, an English surgeon, the son of a brewer and shipowner, whose other legacy is as the eponym of Paget's disease, a bone deformity.

"We improved our minds in the intellectual games of Bagatelle and Bridge," he wrote. The earliest known description of the game refers to it as "Biritch, or Russian Whist." That description appears in a small booklet, published in London in 1886, a copy of which is now shelved at the Bodleian Library at Oxford, where it is attributed to one John Collinson. "There are four players as at short whist, the cutting for partners, shuffling and dealing is the same, *except that no card is turned up for trumps*," the booklet reads, emphasis in the original. "Biritch," it goes on to explain, was the original term for "no-trump." Another etymology, adorable though almost certainly apocryphal, has to do with a pair of Turkish bridge partners who lived on either side of the Bosporus. Every night, before their game, they'd need to decide who would be the one to cross the bridge.

Whist, the earlier card game mentioned by Collinson, predates bridge by hundreds of years and is still played in some circles today.* Whist is essentially bridge without the auction—trump is determined simply by flipping over a card—and without the dummy hand. In 1529, Hugh Latimer, the bishop of Worcester, delivered a sermon decrying a similar game called Triumph. "And whereas you are wont to celebrate Christmas in playing at cards," he told his parishioners, "I intend, by God's grace, to deal unto you Christ's cards, wherein you shall perceive Christ's rule." Latimer was later burned at the stake.

The precise historical progression from whist to bridge isn't well documented. Someone decided that an auction would make for a more interesting selection of the trump suit, and someone had the idea that the dummy hand should be flipped over. These presented two marked strategic improvements. First, rather than the trump suit being the result of mere chance, it became the endogenous result of

---

* Trick-taking card games have strongly regional loyalties in the United States. Where I grew up in the Midwest, for example, euchre and pinochle reigned.

the actions of the players. Second, with the exposing of the dummy hand, a rich asymmetry of information was created: the declarer knows all twenty-six of his partnership's cards, while the defenders have to work out half of theirs independently. This asymmetry positions bridge in the sweet spot between luck and skill and allows the declarer to pull off seemingly magical feats of card play. These rules of *auction* bridge, thus enriched, were delineated in English clubs by the early 1900s.

The game's more recent history crystallized around Harold Stirling Vanderbilt—railroad heir, yachtsman, and three-time defender of the America's Cup. Vanderbilt made his lasting contributions to the game in the Panama Canal aboard the SS *Finland*, an ocean liner bound for Havana in 1925. Dissatisfied with the scoring procedures of the intermediate game of auction bridge, Vanderbilt borrowed elements from a French card game called *plafond* to tweak the numerical rubric by which winners and losers were determined.

"Many years of experience playing games of the Whist family were, I think, a necessary prelude to acquiring the background and knowledge needed to evolve the game," Vanderbilt later wrote. "I called it Contract Bridge and incorporated in it, not only the best features of Auction and Plafond, but also a number of new and exciting features; premiums for slams bid and made, vulnerability, and the decimal system of scoring which by increasing both trick and game values and all premiums and penalties was destined to add enormously to the popularity of Contract Bridge." (A slam involves taking twelve or thirteen of the thirteen tricks; vulnerability is a situation where the penalties and rewards a partnership faces are sharply increased.) Indeed, the amended game was a hit. "More than any other man he merited the title of father of contract bridge," reads Vanderbilt's 1970 obituary in the *New York Times*, "a game that in two decades spread to beguile 40 million people around the world."

That mass beguiling was also triggered by Ely Culbertson, contract bridge's sui generis promoter and showman in the first half of the twentieth century—its P. T. Barnum and Don King, occupying much the same role as Prince Alexis Obolensky would for backgammon. Culbertson had lived what could modestly be described as a textured life. He plotted revolution in czarist Russia, flunked out of Yale, stowed away to Mexico, plotted further revolution, studied political science at the Sorbonne, and returned, broke, to the United States, where he played bridge in Greenwich Village cafés, developing revolutionary theories of bidding under Vanderbilt's new scoring system. In 1929, he founded *The Bridge World*. In 1931 alone, Culbertson published two books of bridge instruction; both became best sellers.

So popular was the game in the 1930s that Culbertson, to prove the superiority of his own bidding convention—his *language*—organized a challenge match against a rival that has come to be known as the Battle of the Century. The match, held over two months in late 1931 and early 1932 at the Hotel Chatham and the Waldorf-Astoria in New York City, was daily front-page news nationwide and the object of intense radio and wire coverage. The great sportswriter Ring Lardner reported in the *Times*, "According to the diffident Mr. Culbertson, this event is more important to the world at large than the signing of the Armistice on Nov. 11, 1918." Culbertson won.

In a promotional film recorded in 1932, Culbertson sits in a dapper suit at a table, fingering a deck of cards. He intones, in an inscrutable accent, "Twenty years ago in America, cards were called devil's tickets. Today, millions throughout the world use bridge as their favorite relaxation and pastime. Church communities encourage bridge because it is an intellectual game of skill." Bridge, he maintains, is "a powerful antidote against the poison of gambling, such as dice, games of pure chance, stock exchange, or any kind of a game where the most intelligent person is on a footing of equality before luck with a moron."

NEARLY A CENTURY LATER, the faithful still heed Culbertson's call, putting their intellects to the test. The American Contract Bridge League maintains a YouTube channel with thousands of videos, recorded at its sanctioned tournaments, most about five hours long, of raw, unedited footage shot from single, stationary, wide-angle cameras. The cameras are mounted at oblique angles high atop card tables. The most noticeable variation in the oeuvre is the decorative patterns of the hotel conference rooms' carpets. The videos, with antiseptic titles such as *2019 Spring NABC—Lebhar F 1/2 Camera 04*, are meant, like security camera footage, as indemnification—they are a record of play that can be consulted in the case of irregularities or accusations of cheating. There is a "video review form" in the Conduct and Ethics section of the ACBL's website.

I watched many of these videos, like a guard in a panopticon, seeking insight into those who devote themselves to a complex and dying game. In one such video, an elite player named Chris Willenken sits in what looks like the room where one eats a free continental breakfast. He wears a gingham shirt and glasses. His movements are sparse, he bids and plays his cards efficiently, and occasionally he puts his hands behind his head or stretches his arms. But the insipidity of the video belies the rich worlds unfolding on the green felt tabletop in front of him.

Willenken and I would later find ourselves together at another table, in a much louder room, drinking beers and talking about empathy. Willenken, a man in his early forties, unassuming, balding, and bespectacled, is one of the best players in America. We met in a bar on the Upper East Side of Manhattan, where he made his case that bridge is a marvelous model for life.

"I think it's difficult to capture how great and multifaceted a game it is," Willenken told me. Of all the popular games, he said, bridge "exercises the most skills" and, like Scrabble or chess, requires "the ability to see the board as a whole and how all the parts interact."

But it's not just versatility that hews bridge closely to life; it's also a game of compassion and communion. "Card play in bridge is *just* as complicated as chess is," Willenken said. "There are positions that, if I showed you, it would look like magic. But the game has so much more attached to it. There are these empathy notes. You and your partner will have to work out what you know that he knows, and what you know that he knows that you know, in order to determine the meaning of plays." In many other games, the relevant question usually centers on *what*. What does that pawn move do to the position? What checker should I move? In bridge, the relevant question often involves *why*. Why did my partner make that bid? Why did my opponent play that card? It is a game, as life often is, of interrogating motivation.

Willenken picked up the game from a book while on vacation during high school. At a summer home in the Poconos, he got hooked by its depth. "The game is so rich, you never get bored," he said. Years later, in the late 1990s, he got a job trading options on the floor of the American Stock Exchange, where the traders played feverishly, passing around tricky bridge hands like polling questions, in search of the best plays. "The skills of proprietary trading . . . and the skills of bridge have some overlap," Willenken said. "You need some pattern recognition, reasonably quick ability to do minor calculations, a general strategic approach, and the ability to not get distracted from that by short-term adverse swings."

Bridge's fidelity to these aspects of the real world—indeed, its effectiveness as a *model* of the real world—is obvious to those who play it. But that fidelity comes at the cost of complexity. Its high barriers to entry often place it just outside the pantheon of the great popular games, and its practitioners often find themselves in a defensive posture.

"When people think cards, they think games of chance," Willenken said. "People are coming to understand that Texas hold 'em isn't really a game of chance—it just looks like one." Willenken approaches bridge almost like a lawyer. Bridge, he says, is "presented . . . as a bunch of weird people who like to show up and toss cards, when in fact I've studied the game very hard—by talking with my partner, reading old hands, trying to understand people's proclivities, thinking about strategies that haven't been tried yet, thinking about game theory's role in it."

Edgar Allan Poe advanced a similar argument in his 1841 short story "The Murders in the Rue Morgue," referring to bridge's forebear, whist:

> Whist has long been noted for its influence upon what is termed the calculating power; and men of the highest order of intellect have been known to take an apparently unaccountable delight in it, while eschewing chess as frivolous. Beyond doubt there is nothing of a similar nature so greatly tasking the faculty of analysis. The best chess-player in Christendom *may* be little more than the best player of chess; but proficiency in whist implies *capacity for success in all these more important undertakings where mind struggles with mind.*

I've added the emphasis in the last phrase. Willenken believes that bridge is such a rich learning environment that it should be taught in schools, like chess. "I think that if parents knew what educational advantages bridge would bring, this would be a no-brainer," he said. "The fact is that raw computing power and linearity, which chess teaches, are a relatively small part of almost every real-world endeavor. Whereas linguistics and empathy and seeing the big picture are enormous parts of succeeding in the real world."

Many believe that success in bridge increases one's capacity for success in the real world. Bill Gates and Warren Buffett, not coincidentally, are perhaps its two most famous players. This extends to the logistics of the competitive game. Wealthy enthusiasts, successful in the real world, or at least the real financial world, fund the pursuits of bridge's great players. An elite bridge tournament, therefore, runs as a sort of parallel competition, real-world success leveraged into bridge-world success, which, the theory goes, increases the capacity for real-world success—a cash-and-cards feedback loop.

Why does it work this way? Willenken said I should go talk to Marty.

MARTY FLEISHER'S LARGE and handsome apartment is on the Upper East Side, on a tony block near Seventy-First Street and Third Avenue. I arrived on a chilly autumn evening. The doorman sent me up, and Fleisher, a compact man of about sixty with thick gray hair, greeted me brusquely in the hallway, asking me to explain myself. I said Chris Willenken had sent me. Seemingly satisfied, he led me into a back office, where we took seats on leather recliners. Bridge awards littered a large desk nearby. Fleisher began rehashing an irksome event at a local café.

"I was annoyed," he said. "I was walking home and I picked up a cup of coffee and I overheard one guy say to the other, 'I teach bridge for a living.' So I sort of looked at the guy on the way out and he said, 'You look familiar, do we know each other?' I said, 'I'm Marty Fleisher.' And he said, 'I don't recognize your name. Am I supposed to?'"

Fleisher paused, scoffed, and continued.

"*I won the world bridge championship.* Can you imagine a guy who teaches chess for a living and he's never heard of Magnus Carlsen? It's just impossible, right?"

Fleisher is not only a champion player of the game but a financial facilitator of the game's competitive existence. The economy of professional bridge is unlike that of most other games. Rather than corporate or government sponsorship (like chess), entry fees from a large field (like Scrabble), or the steady losses of weaker players (like poker), bridge relies on patronage, and Fleisher is a patron. A team entering a top bridge competition typically has six members divided into three pairs, which combine for an aggregate score over a series of matches. One of those members—while still a decent or better player himself—pays the others to play on his team. Competitive bridge is a world of highly paid ringers and wealthy backers. And Fleisher is regarded as one of the most skilled backers in the game.

A former corporate lawyer, Fleisher made an enormous fortune with a business that owned life insurance policies on other people, despite, he says, knowing almost nothing about insurance when he began. About ten years ago, flush with cash, Fleisher told his wife, "Look, we could never spend all the money that I'm making. So I could just, like, retire now, but I don't think I want to do that. I think I'd like to have a bridge team."

"So I have a bridge team," he told me.

For patrons like him, having a team on the competitive bridge circuit is a bit like having a yacht in the America's Cup. Whereas Oracle billionaire Larry Ellison fields his dangerously fast wing-sail catamarans in San Francisco Bay at a cost of some $100 million, Marty Fleisher fields a team of five other bridge geniuses at small, green-felted tables around the world at a cost of perhaps a few hundred thousand dollars per tournament. What's in it for the bridge patron? A cocky sense of superiority, for one thing. ("I think if you asked anyone, they'd say I'm far and away the best sponsor now," Fleisher said. "It's not only that I'm the best, it's that I'm a level, at least, above everyone else.") A sense of fun, excitement, and mental challenge for another. And, like going out to sea, it's an escape. "Going to these tournaments is like being in a cult for ten days," Fleisher said. "I'm a person who really pays attention to the news, and I was really involved in the election, but when you're at the bridge tournaments, they could be declaring war and you really don't care."

Specific questions about money were touchy. I was asked to turn off my audio recorder as Fleisher explained what he pays to hire his teammates. But later, back on the record, he estimated that in any major American tournament, there are at least fifty players being paid five figures by their sponsors for a few days of work. What little prize money there is in bridge is dwarfed by these fees; the sponsors pay for glory alone. In some cases, Fleisher said, the top bridge professionals are people with the skills to excel in traditionally prestigious careers—doctor, lawyer, financier—yet choose to eschew those careers for the game.

"The top bridge players could be divided into two groups: the real savants who probably couldn't do anything else and people who could be making a lot more money in business and law," Fleisher said. "So you really have to like to play and dislike work. Someone like Chris [Willenken] is a really smart guy, but he doesn't like having an office job. He's worked at a couple of hedge funds. I'm sure even by putting in a partial effort he'd be making twice or three times what he makes at bridge."

I began to wonder if perhaps I'd gone into the wrong line of work. But Fleisher left me with one last piece of his advice: "I speak to lots of young players who are trying to become professional bridge players, and I always say, 'You should do something else.'" Perhaps he was still sore about the café.

It would seem that with egos and bankrolls like Fleisher's out there, someone might've funded the construction of an AI tool to master the game. But no such tool exists. The game has thus far defied efforts to automate it—it remains a final frontier. True, with fewer players, waning cultural cachet, and no large purses to pursue, there are few incentives for the University of Alberta guys or Google's DeepMind to pursue a computer bridge player. Indeed, the person who ventured furthest toward this frontier sees bridge not as a sandbox to be conquered but, rather, as a mystery of the universe to be explored.

MATT GINSBERG had a traditionally prestigious career. He was an accomplished scientist, trained in astrophysics—the intricacies of space-time, vacuum Einstein equations, and nonlinear gravitons. He also fostered an academic interest in artificial intelligence. And through it all, bridge exerted its own sort of gravity. Since Ginsberg had long been a good rank-and-file player, it was only a matter of time before the game drifted into his scientific sights. While many humans have tried for a century to conquer bridge with obsessive study and deep pockets, twenty years ago Matt Ginsberg tried to conquer it with computer science, and he got closer than anyone ever had. Eager to learn more about his experience, and the slipperiness of bridge within the machine's grasp, I booked a ticket to the home in the Oregon woods where he lives and works.

Ginsberg is also an aspiring author. For my journey west, I packed his techno-thriller novel, *Factor Man*, a self-published tale in which a thinly veiled Ginsberg character reveals to a journalist that he has solved one of the hardest problems in computer science. The character has proven that $P = NP$, definitively answering one of the most famous open questions in the field.* As a result, his computer code can render every hard problem easy and, for example, make all internet encryption obsolete. For this work he expects to be paid some $100 billion. In essence, he's created God's algorithm, code so perfect that it could compose the most beautiful music you've ever heard or write the most moving novel you've ever read.

I also brought a fresh deck of cards.

The real Matt Ginsberg, who cuts a wiry figure somewhere between dashing professor and aging alpinist, lives in the foothills of the Cascade Range, on ninety remote acres in the vast wilderness outside Eugene. His house, attractive and well-appointed but modest amid its grand surroundings, sits at the top of a long gravel driveway that snakes through the trees. Horses roam in a pasture outside a barn just past the main house, which is ringed by orderly hedges and flower beds. On the opposite side of the house, or through its large windows, lies a stereoscopic valley, gorgeous and green. Every clear night, the Milky Way is visible in the sky above—"Like *this*," Ginsberg said, slicing the air above his head with an open hand as if creating the galaxy himself. When I arrived, his Tesla sedan was parked in the garage. Its license plate read, "P EQ NP."

Ginsberg's bridge journey started in the 1970s in Oakland, New Jersey, with a copy of the classic *5 Weeks to Winning Bridge*, which he first cracked open in high school. That was fifty years—or some twenty-six hundred weeks—ago. Over those many weeks, Ginsberg fostered a modestly successful bridge-playing career, a prestigious

---

* Those among the first to think about this problem, in the 1950s, could make up a mathematical murderers' row: Kurt Gödel, John Nash, and John von Neumann. "P" stands for polynomial time, and "NP" stands for nondeterministic polynomial time. Basically, the question is this: If it's easy to *check* whether a solution to a problem is correct, is it therefore also easy, with the right tools, to *solve* that same problem in the first place? E.g., it's easy to appreciate a great symphony. Is it therefore easy to compose one? A proof that P = NP would mean yes, it is.

academic curriculum vitae, a thriving business career, and the greatest bridge-playing computer program the world had ever seen.

Originally, he'd wanted to call his digital creation Goren in a
Box, after the prolific bridge writer Charles Goren, but he couldn't
secure the proper rights from the estate. He also considered Garozzo
in a Box, after the Italian thirteen-time world champion Benito
Garozzo. Ginsberg's list of names divulged his project: to re-create
human bridge intellect, distilled from endless hours of play and
study, and stick it all inside a computer. He eventually settled on the
name Ginsberg's Intelligent Bridge Player, or GIB.*

In 1977, when Ginsberg was a physics student at Caltech, he
wrote his first article for *The Bridge World*. It was a tidy two-page
piece about four bridge hands—itself an homage to another bridge
writer, Terence Reese†—for which he recalls being paid $150. He
sent that $150 right back to the magazine and ordered a lifetime sub-
scription, which he is still receiving. (The magazine, desperate for
the money to keep publishing, occasionally sends him notices, he
said, asking him politely to please discontinue his paid-in-full lifetime subscription and to consider paying annually instead.)

"I didn't even remember writing it," Ginsberg told me, as we
pored over stacks of old bridge articles and books laid out on his
kitchen counter. As we read, his pet cat rang a bell with its paw, as it
had been trained to do when it wanted to go outside.

Ginsberg completed his doctorate at Oxford when he was
twenty-four years old. His adviser was Roger Penrose, the renowned

---

* Ginsberg is also the creator of the best crossword-puzzle-solving AI program,
which he named Dr. Fill.

† An alleged bridge cheater, as it happens, thanks to the events of something called
the Buenos Aires affair, which were followed by the so-called Foster Enquiry.
Truscott, the *Times* columnist, wrote a whole book about it called *The Great Bridge
Scandal*.

mathematical physicist, hunter of black holes, winner of a 2020 Nobel Prize, and close friend to Stephen Hawking. Penrose and, therefore, Ginsberg are recent links in a chain of Oxbridge advisers and advisees that stretches back to Sir Isaac Newton. Under Penrose, Ginsberg studied something called twistor theory, a complex yet elegant mathematical approach to quantum physics and gravity. He attempted to explain the basics of twistor theory as we drove through the sun-dappled Oregon wilderness.

"Imagine a five-dimensional space," Ginsberg began. I tried. "The path of every ray of light can be represented in five dimensions. And it turns out, amazingly, that the five-dimensional space corresponding to light paths can be embedded in a three-complex-dimensional space, which is the minimum it could ever be.

"That is a *miracle*," he said, for which I could only take his word.

Twistor theory has faded from the physics forefront as leading thinkers have pursued string theory, supersymmetry, and quarks—though there have been recent efforts to reunite these fields.

"The math was gorgeous, and remains gorgeous, but it never really worked," Ginsberg said. "In my opinion, God probably made a mistake when he designed the universe using quarks instead of twistors."

"THE PROBLEM OF BIDDING at contract bridge is an 'intellectual' task which has never before been performed skillfully by a computer program," the computer scientist Anthony Wasserman wrote in 1970. The first attempts had come in the early 1960s, thanks to graduate students at MIT. In 1962, Gay Loran Carley submitted a master's thesis titled "A Program to Play Contract Bridge." His research was supervised by Claude Shannon, the man who first outlined a modern chess-playing program, in 1950. Carley's program was designed for the IBM 7090 computer, the most powerful data-processing system of its time, and similar to the computer used in the earliest man-machine checkers matches. It included "a large complex of bridge-oriented subroutines," and Carley concluded that a "program which plays acceptable, but not outstanding bridge has been developed"—only it was "essentially a long list of rules-of-thumb." Progress was slow. Even by the 1990s, one world-class player observed that the commercially available bridge programs "would have to improve to be hopeless."

Ginsberg drew from physics and twistor theory, with its elegant ability to simplify the natural world, to eschew these complex subroutines and rules of thumb. In many bridge columns, cards irrelevant to the particular hand are represented in print by an "x." For example, a king, a queen, and two irrelevantly small cards in spades might be written as ♠KQxx. For a human, this is natural shorthand, but a computer has no such instincts. Ginsberg realized that he should imbue a program with a similar sort of reasoning, teaching it to ignore vast search areas and thereby creating a concise version of the bridge universe for the program to analyze, just as he had before with rays of light.

A program such as the once-popular Bridge Baron contained a long list of types of plays that would be recognizable to a human or that might be listed in a bridge book. Rather than playing to a computer's strengths, this earlier method tried to replicate a human approach to the game. Ginsberg recognized its shortfalls. One needn't preload a computer with a taxonomy of human bridge knowledge, the ingenious finesses and squeezes and coups that fill the bridge books. In fact, that does your program a disservice. To predefine good bridge as what humans had already been doing verges on a sort of hubris. Ginsberg's breakthrough, he recalled to me: "We should just search!" And his program did just that, searching through deals and bids and combinations of cards played, learning what won and what lost, discovering what good play was for itself, unfettered by the human approach. The computer will find the known ingenious tactics, and perhaps others, on its own.

In the June 1996 issue of *The Bridge World*, Ginsberg laid out his plan. The article, "How Computers Will Play Bridge," included technical aspects, of course: a double-dummy analysis module, a library of a million deals, a bidding-system generator. But it also presented the high hurdles that remained. To analyze the number of possible play sequences in a given hand, for example, a computer would need about ten to the twenty-seventh power seconds—"well over the age of the universe!" Ginsberg was undeterred. "The problems that I have described are hardly insurmountable," he wrote. "Our time as world bridge champions is limited."

While that was overly ambitious, he did make progress. Ginsberg first described GIB itself in detail in a paper in 1999, by which point the program had already begun its short playing career. It won the 1998 and 1999 World Computer-Bridge Championships easily before retiring from the competition. GIB also made its own appearances in the bridge columns of the human world, including Phillip Alder's. One was headlined "A Case Study of the Mysteries of the Robot Thought Process."

When it was released to the wider world, the GIB software sold for $79.95. The July 1999 review of GIB in *The Bridge World*—titled "A New World"—was guardedly positive: "The best bridge-playing program we have seen." However, it was a program that only "convinced us that it performs better than a human beginner." Not to mention: "It sometimes takes actions that strike us as weird."

One of GIB's key selling points, though, was its ability to overcome another human trait: the proclivity to cheat. In the late '90s, bridge, like most other games, began to move online, which was an especially well-suited venue for its aging and increasingly immobile player base. However, in a game of private information and coded communication such as bridge, online play makes cheating easy. I could, for example, simply call up my partner on the phone and tell her exactly what cards I was holding. The GIB-powered robot players, on the other hand, facilitated honest competition: I can partner with a robot and you can partner with a robot and we can compete against each other, as hybrid pairs, in good faith.

A quick logistical explanation of the lengths to which brick-and-mortar bridge events go to forestall cheating: For casual players, the only equipment bridge really requires is a deck of cards and a scrap of paper. But for serious tournament players, there is a bunch of requisite paraphernalia. There is the diagonal screen above the table to visually separate partners. There is the bidding box to facilitate the bidding. There is a door in the screen through which a tray holding the bids is passed. There are convention cards, on which a partnership must disclose to its opponents the bidding method it will use. There is a board to hold pre-shuffled decks securely and secretly. All of this gear is basically meant to prevent cheating, which is nevertheless the inevitable result of a complex competition between humans.

Broad American public attention has been focused on the game of bridge once in recent memory,* in 2016, and that was because people were caught cheating. Magazines flocked to the scandal—*The New Yorker*, *Vanity Fair*, and *Rolling Stone* all ran lengthy features within days of one another. A sociological principle called Sayre's law holds that disputes in academia are so bitter because the stakes are so low. A similar dynamic prevails in the world of bridge. It's captivating to watch tempests wreak havoc within teapots.

The accused 2016 cheaters were Lotan Fisher and Ron Schwartz, teammates and junior world champions out of Israel. Their quick success on the senior circuit came as a surprise. Bridge, unlike chess, does not have prodigies, for much the same reason that there are few

---

* Or perhaps twice, if you count the 2019 doping scandal wherein a top Norwegian bridge professional failed a drug test. The test revealed that the player had taken synthetic testosterone and clomifene, typically a fertility medication for women, but it can increase testosterone levels in men.

great teenage novelists. Human skill at bridge is deeply rooted in experience—in the game's language and literature.

Fisher and Schwartz's unlikely success brought suspicion and scrutiny. A website (bridgecheaters.com) was created, and YouTube videos of their games were uploaded. Collaborative international detective work commenced. Soon their method was revealed. After the deal, Fisher and Schwartz would clear away the tray and the board, a rote bridge-tournament chore. But they cleared it with a purpose. Sometimes they'd put it on a nearby chair, or sometimes leave it on the table, and sometimes in slightly different positions. Each of these meant something, signaling forbidden secret information to the other partner. "If Lotan wanted a spade lead, he put the board in the middle and pushed it all the way to the other side," one amateur investigator told the *New Yorker.* "If he wanted a heart, he put it to the right. Diamond, over here. Club, here. No preference, here."

Cheating is a curious concept. A successful cheater seems to win as if by magic—just like an effective AI. (We observe this phenomenon in backgammon, too.) And there is a deeper, epistemological side to bridge cheating. Suppose, for example, that we humans don't really know how to play bridge all that well, in the grand scheme of things. (A phenomenon also observed in Go.) Further suppose that some humans are eventually able to exploit the knowledge generated by an advanced AI, incorporating it into their own game. Now one of two things may happen, Willenken had explained to me over our beers. No. 1: a partnership comes out of nowhere and does amazingly well because the partners have decided to cheat. The relevant authorities get together and throw the cheaters out. Great result. No. 2: a partnership comes out of nowhere and does amazingly well because the partners have realized, through the benefit of the advanced software, that everybody else is playing bridge suboptimally. The relevant authorities get together, decide they are cheating, and throw the cheaters out. Not-so-great result. In a hypothetical world of advanced AI, legitimate radical human improvement can look like subterfuge.

Artificial intelligence affects the human world in a variety of unpredictable ways. It can help you cheat at games, but also prevent others from cheating. It can spark inspiration and dread. It can enrich the viewing experience of an elite competition, but it can also deaden the viewer's own understanding. Its deep theoretical insights are astonishing, but often beyond our animal grasp. It can be used to train and analyze human performance, but can also reveal how mediocre even our best performers actually are.

In the broader "real world," artificial intelligence's impacts are and will be just as varied and unpredictable. As Ginsberg and I were driving along the Oregon highways, our conversation became humanistic. For him, the triumph of computers over humans in our most cherished games serves, more than anything else, as an object lesson. Long-haul truckers rushed past us going south as we headed north on narrow mountain roads. Ginsberg, taking one hand off the wheel to gesture, said that theirs would be among the first jobs to go, rendered obsolete by the rise of artificial intelligence and automation.

"We're going to have to make some profound societal changes to live in a world where many people are no longer capable of adding value," Ginsberg said. "People need to know that that's coming, and that being smart and being strong are not necessarily going to protect you from the changes that are coming. One of the things that is good—about Watson, about Deep Blue, about Chinook, about AlphaZero, about the poker machines—is that they show people how different this world is going to be." In Ginsberg's mind, this was a good thing, as it would inspire us to adapt on a personal level, and to write laws to help us adapt on a societal level.

The likely response to a changing world? Half-human, half-machine centaurs. Chess grandmaster Garry Kasparov has famously

organized what he calls "advanced chess" matches, allowing players to play alongside a machine. As he concluded in the *New York
Review of Books* in 2010, "Weak human + machine + better process was superior to a strong computer alone and, more remarkably,
superior to a strong human + machine + inferior process." Humans
and computers have starkly different strengths, and the combination
of those strengths can yield more powerful systems still—human
intuition combined with computer calculation.

"It's going to mean, and I think this is unambiguously true, the
way to contribute to human society in the future is going to be to
cooperate with a machine—to be the human piece of a hybrid,"
Ginsberg said. "Like the fact that I'm hitting the brakes here," he
added, as his car's algorithmic antilock system kicked in and we
avoided a crash. Those who are able to work with and alongside
the machines will thrive. The supremacy of automation and even
the arrival of the technological singularity—runaway machine
superintelligence—are inevitable, Ginsberg said. But they won't be
catastrophes. They will simply be new problems to be solved—new
games to play.

AT CHURCH, EVERY SUNDAY, Ginsberg sits in the front row. "So
God can see me," he explained as we strolled down the aisle of the
large commercial garage that had been converted into his church's
sanctuary. The sermon that day, given by a pastor named Tim, in
jeans and a T-shirt, had to do with how Jesus Christ likes to "mess
with" people, even the people he loves—Jesus being the most impish third of the Holy Trinity. Ginsberg's choice of church fit with
his empirical cast of mind. He sent a questionnaire to candidate
churches nearby, asking them, for example, how old they thought
the earth was (Thousands of years? Millions? Billions?) and whether
or not they subscribed to the theory of evolution. The church in

which we sat had answered satisfactorily. "If they don't believe in evolution, they won't be ready for whatever comes next," Ginsberg said. "I don't know what that is, but they won't be ready."

Ginsberg's novel, *Factor Man*, references God's algorithm and its ability to compose beautiful music, and our discussion of twistors and string theory referenced God's possible mistakes. I began to wonder, To what extent does Ginsberg's scientific work overlap or intertwine with his faith? And to what extent, therefore, is an artificially intelligent bridge player a gift from or a paean to God? As we sat in his kitchen later that morning, a minor tiff erupted between Ginsberg and his wife, Pamela, having to do with dirty dishes and smartphone distraction. "This is the fundamental problem with the world today: it is impossible for any individual to be as entertaining as the internet," Ginsberg said. It seemed like a good enough time to interrupt with my queries about religion.

"I'm a mathematician," he answered. "That's really what I am. And I believe that when I say 'mathematics' and when Pam or Tim says 'God,' we are talking about the same thing. And I mean the *very* same thing. In both cases we are talking about the stunningly beautiful order that underlies the universe."

On four wide shelves in Ginsberg's library sit custom-made bound editions of every issue of *The Bridge World*, dating back to 1929—an austere physical testament to the game's language and literature. The volumes themselves, organized chronologically, tell a story of the history of bridge. They start out large: weighty tomes to match the popularity and subscription revenue commanded by the game. They then shrink, as the game did. And finally, they become large once more, the magazine switching to a large-print typeface to cater to its aging readership. Above those on another shelf are yet more bridge books, and below them are three-ring binders, one of which contains documents describing, in hundreds of pages of typescript, details about "controls" and "stoppers" and "naturals" and "openers," the custom bidding system that Ginsberg himself used when he was a (human) player.

There are certain languages, such as Aru in Indonesia or Nivkh in northeast Asia or Yaaku in Kenya, that are spoken today by no more than a few dozen people. There are languages in the game of bridge that are spoken by far fewer. The intricate bidding system described in a blue binder on Ginsberg's bottom shelf is one of those languages. It doesn't even have a name.

Ginsberg is no longer interested in bridge, or in reviving its endangered languages. "It's not a game anymore," he said. Hold 'em pushed it out. Bridge couldn't match poker's television appeal. Ginsberg's attentions have turned to "bigger" questions now. The P versus NP problem, for example. And American presidential politics.

Ginsberg has envisioned, and described to me in detail, an AI system that would enable a campaign to spend its resources efficiently in the battleground states of the Electoral College.* While the Democratic National Committee had failed to express early interest in Ginsberg's idea, he said, he wondered how much the parties might eventually pay. He was so convinced of his hypothetical system's efficacy that he worried what he'd do if the system was put up for auction—a possibility he had written into the plot of his novel—and the highest bidder was the House of Saud. Or Vladimir Putin.

These aren't the limits of his ambition. He once told me that he was going to "revolutionize sports" via a camera-and-software system, funded by a billionaire, that could literally predict the future. And he confided during a recent phone call, in a calm and serious tone, that he'd just come up with a surefire way to solve climate change.

---

* This exact problem was also cited as a potential future application of the poker-playing bot Pluribus.

But it's not power or money that drives Ginsberg. Rather, it seems to me, he's motivated by an anxious desire to avoid the mundane. This is a desire shared by his hero, the late impish theoretical physicist Richard Feynman. Feynman, who worked on the Manhattan Project and won a Nobel Prize, was famous for his brainy pranks and colorful, if problematic, habits—like breaking into coworkers' safes at Los Alamos National Laboratory, for example, conducting science in strip clubs, and playing the bongos. The pair met at Caltech, where the academically disillusioned Ginsberg sought solace and advice from the renowned idol.

"The reason I was unhappy is that I viewed myself as an artist," Ginsberg said. "I solved problems by insight, while everyone at Caltech solved problems by fortitude. I was incredibly sad." He was burned out and unhappy, and so was the legendary Feynman after the Manhattan Project. Feynman was spending much of his time idle, reading *Mad* magazines. Ginsberg approached him and explained his strife. "He got it completely and immediately," Ginsberg said. "I didn't know if I wanted to remain a scientist, and he convinced me that I did. He was completely infectious."

In his lectures, Feynman would ask students, "What do we mean by 'understanding' something?" And he'd answer, "We can imagine that this complicated array of moving things which constitutes 'the world' is something like a great chess game being played by the gods, and we are observers of the game. We do not know what the rules of the game are; all we are allowed to do is to *watch* the playing. Of course, if we watch long enough, we may eventually catch on to a few of the rules. *The rules of the game* are what we mean by *fundamental physics*."

Ginsberg and I drove up the driveway, toward the house atop the valley. "I don't want fame and I don't want power," he said. "I just want to be interesting."

On my last day in Oregon, we boarded Ginsberg's two-seat

experimental stunt plane, named *Air Force Epsilon*. (Ginsberg also once wanted to be president.) We flew around for about a hundred miles. Below us was a distant and gorgeous bounty: a sapphire-clear glacial lake, centuries-old firs, ancient volcanic peaks, bears, cougars, deer, rivers and reservoirs, birds, and even in this wilderness a complex and delicate system of human infrastructure and technology. Geology moved slowly and life quickly. It was a long and striking menu, laid out neatly on Earth's table below us, of the beauty created by God. Or physics. Or mathematics. Or dumb luck.

Like the deal of a hand of cards.

"It just smells so good up here," Ginsberg said, his voice crackling over my headset. "Isn't it gorgeous?"

It was.

In 2004, Ginsberg sold GIB to a popular bridge website for half a million dollars and quit the game. The money he made from his bridge program bought the grand piano that now sits in his living room. It was a Christmas gift to his wife. And it was the instrument on which their daughter would play beautiful music, above that sweeping valley, with the sunlight filtering in through the tall Ponderosa pines.

EPILOGUE

Win or lose . . . we're in the fuckin' greatest
game ever played.

—PETE ROSE, DURING GAME SIX OF
THE 1975 WORLD SERIES (HE LOST)

WHAT GOOD ARE GAMES? A game, the great Bernard Suits has told us, is simply "the voluntary attempt to overcome unnecessary obstacles." But surely it's more than that. As we've seen, games' adherents devote their lives—professional, personal, even mortal—to their chosen pursuits. Surely these lives aren't wasted. Games generate excitement, obsession, competition, and deep thought. Entire books are written about them. Surely this effort isn't wasted, or self-indulgent, or merely a frivolous result of boredom. I believe that from Suits's simple definition emerge things of real value.

Some philosophers hold that the value of games begins with their basic complexity and challenge. "Difficult activities are as such good," argues Thomas Hurka, a philosopher at the University of Toronto and a big fan of Suits's. Hurka has used Suits's analysis to plug games into a larger philosophical project. Marx and Nietzsche, Hurka points out, believed that "a central human good was activity that on the one side is necessarily directed to a goal but on the other derives its value entirely from aspects of the process of achieving it." Playing games—and the achievement of overcoming their difficulties—is therefore intrinsically valuable. And games' values are *modern* values: "process rather than product, journey rather than destination."

Gwen Bradford, the Rice University philosopher and a former student of Hurka's, told me that games are "little achievements." In Bradford's philosophy, achievement is good, per se—part and parcel of the flourishing life, the exercise and development of our core human capacities—and a game's Suitsian obstacles imbue it automatically with the structure necessary for achievement. "Every time you play a game, you're choosing to do something that is more difficult than it has to be," she told me. "Any game is like this. You can just arrange the pieces on the board to show a checkmate, but it's much harder to get them there by following these elaborate rules."

In her aptly titled book *Achievement*, Bradford explains that games generate value on their own, with no need for outside reward; games are self-sufficient. "My theory of achievement is that it's all in the undertaking," Bradford said. "It's the journey, not the destination. Cheesy, but it's true. Games are the paradigm example of this, because what you get when you play a game, even if you win, is absolutely nothing. It's this worthless satisfaction of some rules."

The value of achievement is exemplified in the extreme by the great masters in the preceding pages—Marion Tinsley, Magnus Carlsen, Lee Sedol, Masayuki Mochizuki, Nigel Richards—each of whom has played a difficult game with an unprecedented level of skill. The same could be said of hundreds of great computer scientists and engineers—from Ada Lovelace to Claude Shannon to Rémi Coulom—whose own tasks were no less complicated or difficult. These performers and toolmakers both are justifiably praised for their efforts and have been rewarded, implicitly and explicitly, for their overcoming great difficulty and complexity.

But most people, certainly me and perhaps you, are amateurs, hobbyists, non-masters. We are not so much achievers as we are *strivers*. The importance of striving in play and games is only just becoming understood.

"Games are a *wildly* understudied thing in philosophy," C. Thi
Nguyen, the University of Utah philosopher, told me. "Philosophers
have plumbed the depths of thinking about morality but have barely,
barely thought about the nature of play, which is, like, really weird."
In 2019, Nguyen published the first-ever article on games to appear
in the august *Philosophical Review*, a journal that has been in print
since 1892. Games, he argues there, are most striking and valuable
in their ability to capture human agency—intentional action. While
the rules and values of the real world are recalcitrant and sometimes unpleasant, the rules and values of games are fluid. Like clay,
they can be shaped and reshaped in any way you please; they can
be shaped by master designers into beautiful compositions. "There
are distinctive aesthetic qualities available primarily to the casually
active game player," Nguyen writes. "These are aesthetic qualities of
acting, deciding, and solving."

More than that, games are *art*, in the strictest sense. "Games are
part of our human practices of inscription," Nguyen notes. "Painting lets us record sights, music lets us record sounds, stories let us
record narrative, and games let us record agencies. That can be useful as part of our development. Just as novels let us experience lives
we have not lived, games let us experience forms of agency we might
not have discovered on our own." Aesthetically, games are less like
fiction, as is sometimes suggested, and more like cities—designed
spaces where we make choices.

Game designers endeavor to create a space where the rules of
the real world fall away and the rules of the game hold sway—
historian Johan Huizinga's "magic circle." It's where the fisherfolk of
Tlacuachero sat five thousand years ago; it's where Honinbo Shusai
lost his final match; it's where Marion Tinsley battled the machine.
It's also the space created when you set up a game board in your
living room. Huizinga writes in *Homo Ludens*, "Just as there is no
formal difference between play and ritual, so the 'consecrated spot'

cannot be formally distinguished from the play-ground. The arena, the card-table, the magic circle, the temple, the stage, the screen, the tennis court, the court of justice, etc., are all in form and function play-grounds, i.e. forbidden spots, isolated, hedged round, hallowed, within which special rules obtain. All are temporary worlds within the ordinary world, dedicated to the performance of an act apart."

The agencies we experience in these magic circles activate the good that lies within games. We take the lessons we learn there with us back to the real world. And games are medicine of a kind. By clarifying our vast, complex world, games can calm the existential worry caused by our muddy and unstable values.

For strivers, those of us who play games casually but have ambitions in some other realm, the pleasure comes from entering the magic circle and finding our footing. To blindly heed the advice of a computer as, say, professionals might do in poker or chess, is to cede the achievement—that is, to discard the value of play. A game is "a sculpted experience of beautiful struggle," Nguyen told me. This is not an experience that is diminished by the existence of superhuman players. "You have this AI built to do this thing really well," he added, "but it doesn't have any particular experience of it. I'm not sure what the purpose of that is. I understand why it's an excellent illustration of AI's potential. But from my perspective, when people are like, 'Oh my God, AIs can beat humans, what do we do about this?' I really think, 'It doesn't fucking matter.' I'm a rock climber, and AI being able to beat me at Go matters as much as a helicopter being able to beat me at a rock climb."

As we've witnessed, not every human has had such a sensible reaction. Usain Bolt surely doesn't care that a race car is faster than he is, but how do Garry Kasparov and Lee Sedol feel about artificial neural networks? There appears to be a deep difference between physical games and intellectual games, a sort of human intellectual exceptionalism. Why? "We don't care that a car is faster—it's just a different kind of creature," Bradford said. "Maybe that's part of it. Maybe part of it is accepting that there are different kinds of creatures from us. These minds, they think totally differently. Maybe our mistake was thinking that they are like us. They are like us; they're just not *totally* like us. And they may or may not be smarter than us just because they're better at chess."

Another way to think about these objects we call games is as elaborate tools for both machines and humans. For artificial intelligence, games are telescopes: narrow portals through which to glimpse a sliver of an alien, biological world. For humans, games are microscopes: enhancers of constituent truths about a world in which we already live.

Philosophers like Bradford and Nguyen don't worry much about the future of games under this technological assault; the games' experiences are still just as accessible to our human consciousness. Moreover, Bradford said, playing games could be "valuable" for a sufficiently advanced artificial intelligence in just the same way that it is "valuable" for humans. Nguyen does worry, however, about the technological *gamification* of the real world.

Modern AI systems require gobs of data to train, which makes easily collectible and cheap data attractive. These easy, quantified metrics can stand in for success in fields whose aims are in reality complicated and subtle: clicks for journalism, steps for exercise, box office for cinema, auction prices for paintings. Nguyen calls this "value collapse"—when rich, subtle values are replaced by simplified, quantified versions of those values. In games, this is OK—a success in a game is indeed simple to measure (win, loss, draw) and, indeed, this simplicity is why they've received so much attention from computer scientists. But for modern AI, serious, real-world tasks—facial recognition, self-driving—might as well be games, trained as neural networks are to maximize relentlessly some numerical reward. To a hammer, everything looks like a nail. In this sense, the impressive prowess of AI at games might be less success story and more caution-ary tale. Suppose a would-be auteur developed an AI to write a good series for Netflix. They used—sensibly, it may seem—engagement hours as part of their training data. But in so doing they've opti-mized their show for addiction, not aesthetic value.

"A Fitbit is not going to help you optimize a vastly beautiful run, because that's not the kind of thing that Fitbit can measure," Nguyen added. "It measures steps. I'm really worried about the input data for machine-learning networks. The games cases will mislead us with their sense of success, because that's one of the cases where the target is well defined." One can easily imagine far more sinister instances of value collapse, arising, for example, in the fields of government, medicine, or engineering.

The value of a sculpted, beautiful struggle isn't confined to tra-ditional board or card games. Once we look for them, we find games everywhere. Consider, for example, art appreciation. In science or medicine, we do well to defer to the judgment of experts. In art, we do better by trusting our own instincts and judgment. Why? I am, for example, no expert in rococo painting. I could read the guidebooks and catalogs and biographies, learn who the style's great painters are, memorize the titles of their masterpieces and what they depict, and I'd be in some sense a well-informed consumer of rococo without ever having seen a real painting—I'd have achieved something. Or I could go to a museum—or, better yet, to a palazzo in Venice—and experience the paintings for myself, and develop opinions of them and feelings about them for myself. I argue that the second option is strictly better. Might that be because art appreciation is a game? After all, why not? It's only the struggle to understand, a voluntary attempt to overcome an unnecessary obstacle, that truly produces joy from art. And if games are art, isn't the appreciation of games itself an art? Perhaps we're artists, you and I.

For Bernard Suits, games were the supreme good. He exhorted

their cultivation to prepare for a future Utopia, a time when all material needs would be met by advanced technology and, therefore, a time when games would be "perhaps our only salvation." Once all of the instrumental goods are provided, all that remains would be to nurture and enjoy the intrinsic good provided by games. It's an audacious but compelling argument—one I'm eager to accept as a lover of games, and it can't hurt to be prepared—though I am not convinced that the arrival of Utopia is impending.

Games, however, are also crucial in terrible crises, and their cultivation is perhaps our only salvation regardless of what the future holds. The reporting for this book was ongoing when the novel coronavirus began to spread and social distancing became the norm. As the pandemic ravaged the globe, we suffered and mourned, we cheered nightly for front-line workers, we masked up and sanitized, and we flocked to play games. Countless families and friends, mine included, kept in touch through board games augmented with video chat. A million new members joined Chess.com each month in 2020 after lockdowns began, and the chess miniseries *The Queen's Gambit* was a runaway hit. Backgammon Galaxy's servers crashed under the weight of record numbers of players. A new Scrabble site, cofounded by César Del Solar, was launched and flourished. At the height of the pandemic, more games were being played than at perhaps any time in human history.*

Games became solace. We players did not arrive in droves seeking difficulty or complexity, or a sense of achievement, or a frivolous

---

* And none of this is to mention other forms of play. The U.S. video game market, for example, set quarterly sales records throughout 2020. Sales of The Settlers of Catan more than doubled, and Hasbro saw a 20 percent increase in sales of games, including of Monopoly. The *New York Times* was inundated with unprecedented numbers of crossword puzzle submissions, and history's largest crossword event, Crossword Tournament from Your Couch, drew 1,815 competitors. There was also a global shortage of jigsaw puzzles.

distraction. We arrived, I believe, in search of agency that had been temporarily denied by sensible public health measures. We arrived to flex muscles that were atrophying. We arrived to spend a bit of time in the magic circle, consuming the art of games.

Today, game designers talk about crafting the "agential skeleton" that players inhabit during a game. That is, creating the "body" a person will inhabit while playing the game. The designers of the ancient games in this book are mostly nameless now, the games having taken their modern form over many centuries, thanks to countless hands. These games are mass historical collaborations. But why these games in particular? Why have they made their way onto these pages? "It's really hard to figure out, when you look at a rule set, whether or not that game will sustain generations and generations of play," Nguyen said. "I think the answer is almost evolutionary." These games, like other priceless relics, are survivors. A chess queen stands on a board the way *Nike of Samothrace* stands in the Louvre. "People keep asking why canonized art objects last so long," Nguyen mused, "and one answer is just 'There is no general answer.' Each one is a unique solution, and its uniqueness is what makes it good." The games in this book are their own set of canonized art objects, each one a unique expression of agency. For decades in some cases and millennia in others, members of the human race have inhabited their skeletons, each member in turn existing for a time in the same body, seeing through the same eyes, exercising the same will, experiencing the same world from within a magic circle.

ACKNOWLEDGMENTS

DESPITE JUST THE ONE name on the cover, no book is truly the work of a single person, and this volume is no exception. I owe a large debt to a medium-sized band of unthinkably generous and brilliant people who assisted at every point, from the development of the concept to publication. The traditional way to repay these arrears is with a few insufficient words at the back of the book—a tradition in which I will now participate, fully aware of its inadequacy.

You wouldn't be reading any of this without my frighteningly bright editor at W. W. Norton, Tom Mayer, who made this book both real and much better. Nor without my unrealistically talented and supportive literary agent, Alice Martell, who, despite her insistence to the contrary, is also the kindest person in the book business. Many thanks also to Nneoma Amadi-obi, the rest of the wonderful people at Norton, and the superlative copy editor Bonnie Thompson.

My deep appreciation for invaluable lessons taught is proffered to Chadwick Matlin, my longtime editor at *FiveThirtyEight*, and to Mike Wilson and Nate Silver, who took me to lunch one summer day in 2014, at the end of which I was inexplicably given a real writing job. Not only that, they allowed me—nay, *encouraged* me—to write about games. It felt and still feels like I was hallucinating.

I was blessed with two wonderful chronological bookends on the research and writing processes of this book. On one end, I thank Stefan Fatsis for deftly proving that games were something that journalists could and should take seriously; his encouragement at the earliest stage of this project was crucial. On the other end, I thank my fellow Nieman fellows at Harvard (emphatically but certainly not exclusively Rob Chaney, Alex Dickinson, Anne Godlasky, Natalia Guerrero, Gülsin Harman, Lucy Hornby, Johnny Kauffman, Ashwaq Masoodi, Andras Petho, and Alex Trowbridge), with whom I spent a dreamy year, undiminished even by a global pandemic, though it tried its damnedest; no one in the final throes of a book project could have asked for a more refreshing or invigorating group of colleagues and friends. The backgammon games were lucrative, too.

One plight among many of participating in a friendship with a writer is subjecting oneself to salvos of unsolicited drafts and complaints. With that in mind, I extend my deep gratitude to Emily Schmidt, an insightful and patient reader, expert librarian, and beautiful soul; Brin-Jonathan Butler, the best bar companion and worst Madden player I know; Christie Aschwanden and Anna Maria Barry-Jester, enviably skilled journalists, colleagues, and friends both; Sam Early, with whom I invented countless games as a kid; Andrew Paul, poker player and phrase turner extraordinaire; and Bret Sikkink, between whose kindness and brilliance I can't decide which to emphasize here.

Many of the ideas I've tried to develop in this book have been marinating in my human brain since childhood, whether I knew it or not. Such a childhood would not have been possible without my parents (and earliest editors), Phil Roeder and Mary Tabor, a visit to whose home cannot be escaped without at least one cutthroat game of euchre. Nor without the late Jack and Shirley Tabor, my grandparents. The poker games around their farmhouse kitchen table may have been for penny antes, but they were for keeps.

I am grateful to the Robert B. Silvers Foundation for a grant that supported this project when it was a work in progress. And to Gus Wezerek for his excellent assistance with some of the game diagrams.

Finally, I thank Steve Almond, Emily Bobrow, Mark Bognanni, Matt Canik, James Curley, Stephanie Finman, Andrew Flowers, Ryan Hayward, Robert Hess, David Hill, Caesar Jaramillo, Pamela Kinion, Maggie Koerth, Josh Levin, Steven Levitt, Pete Madden, Scott Moser, Myra and Oliver Peng (ages six and eight, they've asked me to point out), Mian Ridge, Alex Rivard, Hannah and Sam Roeder, Jennifer Schaeffer, Rob Schebel, Erika Schmidt, Nathan Sturtevant, Jonathan Tarleton, Geoff Thevenot, Amelia Thomson-DeVeaux, and Thomas Wiseman. They opened many doors for me, both figurative and literal, whether they know it or not.

SOURCES AND FURTHER READING

THIS BOOK IS BASED primarily on my interviews with expert games players and thinkers, along with computer scientists, historians, philosophers, anthropologists, archaeologists, psychologists, biologists, and other academics. Many of them are directly quoted within the preceding pages and many are not. It also draws heavily on my attendance at and participation in various games tournaments and games- and AI-related conferences and symposia.

And this book benefits immeasurably, of course, from the academic research of hundreds of people; many popular nonfiction books, biographies, and memoirs; a shelf full of reference volumes and textbooks; a pile of documentary films; and the contemporaneous news reports and feature articles of countless tireless journalists. I thank all their creators for their work.

The salient published works used in my telling of this story—and some that tell great stories themselves—are listed below. I hope the reader of this volume enjoys a selection of them if he or she wishes to explore this rich world and its offshoots further. Some general citations are listed first; the next sections are organized by game, in the order of the preceding chapters; and at the end, I've included further references for a few games that were mentioned only briefly.

GENERAL

Bashe, Charles J., Lyle R. Johnson, John H. Palmer, and Emerson W. Pugh. *IBM's Early Computers: A Technical History*. Cambridge, Mass.: MIT Press, 1985.

Bradford, Gwen. *Achievement*. Oxford: Oxford University Press, 2015.

———. "Kudos for Ludus: Game Playing and Value Theory." *Noēsis* 6 (2003).

Bremermann, H. J. "Quantum Noise and Information." In *Proceedings of the Fifth Berkeley Symposium on Mathematical Statistics and Probability*, 4:15–20. Berkeley: University of California Press, 1967.

Elias, George Skaff, Richard Garfield, and K. Robert Gutschera. *Characteristics of Games*. Cambridge, Mass.: MIT Press, 2012.

Feigenbaum, Edward A., and Julian Feldman, eds. *Computers and Thought*. New York: McGraw-Hill, 1963.

Finkel, Irving L., ed. *Ancient Board Games in Perspective*. Papers from the 1990 British Museum Colloquium. London: British Museum Press, 2007.

Huizinga, Johan. *Homo Ludens: A Study of the Play-Element in Culture*. London: Routledge & Kegan Paul, 1949.

Hurka, Thomas. "Games and the Good." *Proceedings of the Aristotelian Society* 80 (2006): 217–35.

———, ed. *Games, Sports, and Play: Philosophical Essays*. Oxford: Oxford University Press, 2019.

Nguyen, C. Thi. "Art Is a Game." *Forum for Philosophy* (blog), August 17, 2020.

———. *Games: Agency as Art*. Oxford: Oxford University Press, 2020.

———. "Games and the Art of Agency." *Philosophical Review* 128, no. 4 (October 1, 2019): 423–62.

Nietzsche, Friedrich. *The Gay Science*. Translated by Walter Kaufmann. New York: Vintage, 1974.

Piccione, Peter A. "The Egyptian Game of Senet and the Migration of the Soul." In *Ancient Board Games in Perspective*, edited by Irving L. Finkel, 54–63. Papers from the 1990 British Museum Colloquium. London: British Museum Press, 2007.

Roeder, Oliver. "The Bots Beat Us. Now What?" *FiveThirtyEight*, July 10, 2017.

———. "Computers Are Learning How to Treat Illnesses by Playing Poker and Atari." *FiveThirtyEight*, January 20, 2015.

Russell, Stuart, and Peter Norvig. *Artificial Intelligence: A Modern Approach*. 3rd ed. Upper Saddle River, N.J.: Pearson, 2010.

Samuel, Arthur L. "Computing Bit by Bit, or Digital Computers Made Easy." *Proceedings of the IRE* 41, no. 10 (October 1953): 1223–30.

Searle, John R. "Minds, Brains, and Programs." *Behavioral and Brain Sciences* 3, no. 3 (September 1980): 417–24.

Suits, Bernard. "Games and Paradox." *Philosophy of Science* 36, no. 3 (September 1, 1969): 316–21.

———. *The Grasshopper: Games, Life and Utopia*. 2nd ed. Introduction by Thomas Hurka. Peterborough, Ont.: Broadview, 2005.

————. "Is Life a Game We Are Playing?" *Ethics* 77, no. 3 (April 1, 1967): 209–13.

————. "What Is a Game?" *Philosophy of Science* 34, no. 2 (June 1, 1967): 148–56.

Voorhies, Barbara. "The Deep Prehistory of Indian Gaming: Possible Late Archaic Period Game Boards at the Tlacuachero Shellmound, Chiapas, Mexico." *Latin American Antiquity* 24, no. 1 (2013): 98–115.

————. "Games Ancient People Played." *Archaeology* 65, no. 3 (2012): 48–51.

Wittgenstein, Ludwig. *Philosophical Investigations.* Edited by P. M. S. Hacker and Joachim Schulte. 4th ed. Malden, Mass.: Wiley-Blackwell, 2009.

CHECKERS

Belsky, Gary. "A Checkered Career." *Sports Illustrated*, December 28, 1992.

Bloom, Allan, trans. *The Republic of Plato.* 3rd ed. New York: Basic Books, 2016.

Fortman, Richard L. *Basic Checkers.* 7 vols. Self-published, 1978–83.

Hopper, Millard Fillmore. *How to Play Winning Checkers.* New York: Simon & Schuster, 1940.

Pfeiffer, John. "Man vs Machine in the Checker Game of the Century." *Popular Mechanics*, August 1964.

Ryan, William F. *The Modern Encyclopedia of Checkers.* New York: William F. Ryan, 1940.

Samuel, A. L. *A Boy from Emporia.* Unpublished manuscript, n.d.

————. "Some Studies in Machine Learning Using the Game of Checkers." *IBM Journal of Research and Development* 3, no. 3 (July 1959): 210–29.

————. "Some Studies in Machine Learning Using the Game of Checkers II: Recent Progress." *IBM Journal of Research and Development* 11, no. 6 (November 1967): 601–17.

Schaeffer, J., N. Burch, Y. Bjornsson, A. Kishimoto, M. Müller, R. Lake, P. Lu, and S. Sutphen. "Checkers Is Solved." *Science* 317, no. 5844 (September 14, 2007): 1518–22.

Schaeffer, Jonathan. *One Jump Ahead: Challenging Human Supremacy in Checkers.* 1st ed. New York: Springer, 1997.

————. *One Jump Ahead: Computer Perfection at Checkers.* 2nd ed. New York: Springer, 2008.

Schaeffer, Jonathan, Joseph Culberson, Norman Treloar, Brent Knight, Paul Lu, and Duane Szafron. "A World Championship Caliber Checkers Program." *Artificial Intelligence* 53, no. 2 (February 1, 1992): 273–89.

Shuffett, Robert L. *Checkers, the Tinsley Way.* Independently published, 1982.

Weiss, E. A. "Biographies: Eloge: Arthur Lee Samuel (1901–90)." *IEEE Annals of the History of Computing* 14, no. 3 (1992): 55–69.

CHESS

Berliner, Hans J. "Chess as Problem Solving: The Development of a Tactics Analyzer." PhD diss., Carnegie-Mellon University, 1975.

De Firmian, Nick. *Modern Chess Openings.* 15th ed. New York: Random House, 2008.

Dottle, Rachael. "The Chess Boom Goes Digital After *The Queen's Gambit.*" *Bloomberg*, December 16, 2020.

Drasnin, Irv. *The Chip vs. the Chessmaster.* Documentary. Drasnin Productions, 1991.

Eales, Richard. "Changing Cultures: The Reception of Chess into Western Europe in the Middle Ages." In *Ancient Board Games in Perspective*, edited by Irving L. Finkel, 162–68. Papers from the 1990 British Museum Colloquium. London: British Museum Press, 2007.

Frey, P. W., ed. *Chess Skill in Man and Machine.* 2nd ed. New York: Springer-Verlag, 1983.

Hodges, Andrew. *Alan Turing: The Enigma.* New York: Simon & Schuster, 1983.

Hsu, Feng-hsiung. *Behind Deep Blue: Building the Computer That Defeated the World Chess Champion.* Princeton, N.J.: Princeton University Press, 2004.

Kasparov, Garry. "Chess, a Drosophila of Reasoning." *Science* 362, no. 6419 (December 7, 2018): 1087.

———. "The Chess Master and the Computer." *New York Review of Books*, February 11, 2010.

Kasparov, Garry, and Mig Greengard. *Deep Thinking: Where Machine Intelligence Ends and Human Creativity Begins.* New York: PublicAffairs, 2017.

Krabbé, Tim. "Stiller's Monsters, or Perfection in Chess." *Chess Curiosities* (blog), n.d.

Levy, David N. L., and Monty Newborn. *How Computers Play Chess.* New York: Computer Science Press, 1991.

Marshall, Frank. *The Man vs. the Machine.* Documentary. Kennedy/Marshall, ESPN Films, 2014.

Müller, Karsten, and Jonathan Schaeffer. *Man vs. Machine: Challenging Human Supremacy at Chess.* Milford, Conn.: Russell Enterprises, 2018.

Murray, H. J. R. *A History of Chess: The Original 1913 Edition.* New York: Skyhorse, 2015.

Newell, Allen, J. C. Shaw, and H. A. Simon. "Chess-Playing Programs and the Problem of Complexity." *IBM Journal of Research and Development* 2, no. 4 (October 1958): 320–35.

Poe, Edgar Allan. "Maelzel's Chess-Player." *Southern Literary Messenger*, April 1836.

Roeder, Oliver. "Computers Are Haunting the World Chess Championship (Which, Yes, Is Still Tied)." *FiveThirtyEight*, November 12, 2018.

———. "I Faced Off Against the World's Best Chess Player. You Will Totally Believe What Happened Next." *FiveThirtyEight*, May 14, 2018.

Sadler, Matthew, and Natasha Regan. *Game Changer: AlphaZero's Groundbreaking Chess Strategies and the Promise of AI.* New in Chess, 2019.

Shannon, Claude. "A Chess-Playing Machine." *Scientific American*, February 1950.

———. "A Mathematical Theory of Communication." *Bell System Technical Journal* 27, no. 3 (1948): 379–423.

———. "Programming a Computer for Playing Chess." *Philosophical Magazine* 41, no. 314 (March 1950): 256–75.

Silver, David, Thomas Hubert, Julian Schrittwieser, Ioannis Antonoglou, Matthew Lai, Arthur Guez, Marc Lanctot, et al. "A General Reinforcement Learning Algorithm That Masters Chess, Shogi, and Go Through Self-Play." *Science* 362, no. 6419 (December 7, 2018): 1140–44.

———. "Mastering Chess and Shogi by Self-Play with a General Reinforcement Learning Algorithm." *ArXiv:1712.01815 [Cs]*, December 5, 2017.

Silver, Nate. *The Signal and the Noise: Why So Many Predictions Fail—but Some Don't.* New York: Penguin Press, 2012.

Simon, Herbert A., and Allen Newell. "Heuristic Problem Solving: The Next Advance in Operations Research." *Operations Research* 6, no. 1 (1958): 1–10.

Soni, Jimmy, and Rob Goodman. *A Mind at Play: How Claude Shannon Invented the Information Age.* New York: Simon & Schuster, 2017.

Standage, Tom. *The Turk: The Life and Times of the Famous Eighteenth-Century Chess-Playing Machine.* New York: Walker Books, 2002.

Thompson, K. "Computer Chess Strength." In *Advances in Computer Chess 3*, edited by M. R. B. Clarke, 55–56. Pergamon Chess Series. Oxford: Pergamon Press, 1982.

Tomkins, Calvin. *Duchamp: A Biography.* New York: Henry Holt, 1996.

Turing, Alan M. "Computing Machinery and Intelligence." *Mind* 59, no. 236 (October 1950): 433–60.

Wilkenfeld, Yoni. "Can Chess Survive Artificial Intelligence?" *New Atlantis*, Spring 2019.

Wilson, Robert A., and Frank Keil, eds. *The MIT Encyclopedia of the Cognitive Sciences.* Cambridge, Mass.: MIT Press, 1999.

GO

AlQuraishi, Mohammed. "AlphaFold @ CASP13: 'What Just Happened?'" *Some Thoughts on a Mysterious Universe* (blog), December 9, 2018.

Associated Press. "Human Players Stop Machine in 'Go.'" *Times-News* (Idaho), November 26, 1992.

Bouzy, Bruno, and Tristan Cazenave. "Computer Go: An AI Oriented Survey." *Artificial Intelligence* 132, no. 1 (2001): 39–103.

Chen, Xiangchuan, Daren Zhang, Xiaochu Zhang, Zhihao Li, Xiaomei Meng, Sheng He, and Xiaoping Hu. "A Functional MRI Study of High-Level Cognition II: The Game of Go." *Cognitive Brain Research* 16, no. 1 (March 1, 2003): 32–37.

Coulom, Rémi. "Efficient Selectivity and Backup Operators in Monte-Carlo Tree Search." In *Computers and Games: 5th International Conference*, edited by H. Jaap van den Herik, Paolo Ciancarini, and H. H. L. M. (Jeroen) Donkers, 72–83. Berlin: Springer, 2007.

DeepMind. "The Google DeepMind Challenge Match, March 2016." https://deepmind.com/alphago-korea.

Fairbairn, John. "Go in China." In *Ancient Board Games in Perspective*, edited by Irving L. Finkel, 133–37. Papers from the 1990 British Museum Colloquium. London: British Museum Press, 2007.

Good, I. J. "The Mystery of Go." *New Scientist*, January 21, 1965.

Google DeepMind. *Challenge Match, 8–15 March 2016*. Game 1: "Dawn." Commentary by Fan Hui Go. Analysis by Gu Li and Zhou Ruiyang. Translated by Lucas Baker, Thomas Hubert, and Thore Graepel.

Graham, Elyse. "Adventures in Fine Hall." *Princeton Alumni Weekly*, January 10, 2018.

House, Patrick. "The Electronic Holy War." *New Yorker*, March 25, 2014.

Hsu, Feng-hsiung. "Cracking Go." *IEEE Spectrum*, October 1, 2007.

Huang, Dan. "How Much Did AlphaGo Zero Cost?" *Dansplaining* (blog), March 2018.

Huang, Shih-Chieh, and Martin Müller. "Investigating the Limits of Monte-Carlo Tree Search Methods in Computer Go." In *Computers and Games: 8th International Conference*, edited by H. Jaap van den Herik, Hiroyuki Iida, and Aske Plaat, 39–48. Cham, Switzerland: Springer International, 2014.

Johnson, George. "To Test a Powerful Computer, Play an Ancient Game." *New York Times*, July 29, 1997.

Kawabata, Yasunari. *The Master of Go*. Translated by Edward G. Seidensticker. New York: Knopf, 1972.

Kohs, Greg. *AlphaGo*. Documentary. Moxie Pictures, Reel as Dirt, 2017.

Kuang, Cliff. "Can A.I. Be Taught to Explain Itself?" *New York Times Magazine*, November 21, 2017.

Lasker, Edward. *Go and Go-Moku: The Oriental Board Games*. Rev. ed. New York: Dover, 1960.

Levinovitz, Alan. "The Mystery of Go, the Ancient Game That Computers Still Can't Win." *Wired*, May 12, 2014.

Lo, Andrew, and Tzi-Cheng Wang. "Spider Threads Roaming the Empyrean: The Game of Weiqi." In *Asian Games: The Art of Contest*, edited by Colin Mackenzie and Irving Finkel, 186–201. New York: Asia Society, 2004.

Lockhart, Will, and Cole Pruitt. *The Surrounding Game*. Documentary. Moyo Pictures, 2018.

Maddison, Chris J., Aja Huang, Ilya Sutskever, and David Silver. "Move Evaluation in Go Using Deep Convolutional Neural Networks." *ArXiv:1412.6564 [Cs]*, April 10, 2015.

Masunaga, Hiromi, and John Horn. "Characterizing Mature Human Intelligence: Expertise Development." *Learning and Individual Differences* 12, no. 1 (March 2000): 5–33.

Metz, Cade. "Inside the Epic Go Tournament Where Google's AI Came to Life." *Wired*, May 17, 2016.

———. "Making New Drugs with a Dose of Artificial Intelligence." *New York Times*, February 5, 2019, B1.

————. "The Sadness and Beauty of Watching Google's AI Play Go." *Wired*, March 11, 2016.

Müller, Martin. "Computer Go: A Research Agenda." In *Computers and Games: 6th International Conference*, edited by H. Jaap van den Herik and Hiroyuki Iida, 252–64. Berlin: Springer, 1999.

————. "Computer Go as a Sum of Local Games: An Application of Combinatorial Game Theory." PhD diss., ETH Zurich, 1995.

————. "Not Like Other Games—Why Tree Search in Go Is Different." In *Proceedings of the Fifth Joint Conference on Information Sciences*, edited by P. P. Wang, 974–77, Association for Intelligent Machinery, 2000.

Reitman, Walter, and Bruce Wilcox. "The Structure and Performance of the Interim.2 Go Program." In *Proceedings of the 6th International Joint Conference on Artificial Intelligence*, Vol. 2, 711–19. Tokyo: Morgan Kaufmann Publishers, 1979.

Roberts, Siobhan. *Genius at Play: The Curious Mind of John Horton Conway*. New York: Bloomsbury USA, 2015.

Rocke, Aidan. "The True Cost of AlphaGo Zero." *Kepler Lounge* (blog), March 24, 2019.

Sample, Ian. "Google's DeepMind Predicts 3D Shapes of Proteins." *Guardian*, December 2, 2018.

Silver, David, Aja Huang, Chris J. Maddison, Arthur Guez, Laurent Sifre, George van den Driessche, Julian Schrittwieser, et al. "Mastering the Game of Go with Deep Neural Networks and Tree Search." *Nature* 529, no. 7587 (January 2016): 484–89.

Silver, David, Julian Schrittwieser, Karen Simonyan, Ioannis Antonoglou, Aja Huang, Arthur Guez, Thomas Hubert, et al. "Mastering the Game of Go Without Human Knowledge." *Nature* 550, no. 7676 (October 2017): 354–59.

Strubell, Emma, Ananya Ganesh, and Andrew McCallum. "Energy and Policy Considerations for Deep Learning in NLP." *ArXiv:1906.02243 [Cs]*, June 5, 2019.

Tromp, John. "The Number of Legal Go Positions." In *Computers and Games: 9th International Conference*, edited by Aske Plaat, Walter Kosters, and Jaap van den Herik, 183–90. Cham, Switzerland: Springer International, 2016.

Zobrist, Albert Lindsey. "Feature Extraction and Representation for Pattern Recognition and the Game of Go." PhD diss., University of Wisconsin–Madison, 1970.

BACKGAMMON

Berliner, Hans. "Computer Backgammon." *Scientific American*, June 1980.

Bradshaw, Jon. "Backgammon." *Harper's*, June 1972.

Cooke, Barclay, and Jon Bradshaw. *Backgammon: The Cruelest Game*. New York: Random House, 1974.

Crist, Walter, Anne-Elizabeth Dunn-Vaturi, Alex de Voogt, and Nicholas Reeves. *Ancient Egyptians at Play: Board Games Across Borders*. London: Bloomsbury Academic, 2016.

Daryaee, Touraj. "Mind, Body, and the Cosmos: Chess and Backgammon in Ancient Persia." *Iranian Studies* 35, no. 4 (September 1, 2002): 281–312.

Emery, Walter B. *Nubian Treasure: An Account of the Discoveries at Ballana and Qustul.* London: Methuen, 1948.

Finkel, Irving L. "On the Rules for the Royal Game of Ur." In *Ancient Board Games in Perspective*, edited by Irving L. Finkel, 16–32. Papers from the 1990 British Museum Colloquium. London: British Museum Press, 2007.

Magriel, Paul. *Backgammon.* New York: Times Books, 1976.

McCorduck, Pamela. *Machines Who Think: A Personal Inquiry into the History and Prospects of Artificial Intelligence.* 2nd ed. Natick, Mass.: A K Peters, 2004.

McCulloch, Warren S., and Walter Pitts. "A Logical Calculus of the Ideas Immanent in Nervous Activity." *Bulletin of Mathematical Biophysics* 5 (December 1943): 115–33.

Menaker, Daniel. "The Backgammon Explosion." *New York Times*, April 28, 1974.

Pollack, Jordan B., and Alan D. Blair. "Why Did TD-Gammon Work?" In *Proceedings of the 9th International Conference on Neural Information Processing Systems*, edited by M. I. Jordan and T. Petsche, 10–16. Cambridge, Mass.: MIT Press, 1996.

Robertie, Bill. *How to Play the Opening in Backgammon.* Vol. 1: *A New Way of Thinking.* Arlington, Mass.: Gammon Press, 2020.

———. *Learning from the Machine: Bill Robertie Versus TD-Gammon.* Arlington, Mass.: Gammon Press, 1993.

———. *Modern Backgammon.* Arlington, Mass.: Gammon Press, 2001.

Roeder, Oliver. "The Man Who Solved *Jeopardy!*" *FiveThirtyEight*, April 24, 2019.

Shrake, Edwin. "Everyone for Backgammon." *Sports Illustrated*, May 4, 1964.

Silverman, David. "Largest Tax-Evasion Case in Area History." *Chicago Tribune*, August 18, 1993.

Soar, Micaela. "Board Games and Backgammon in Ancient Indian Sculpture." In *Ancient Board Games in Perspective*, edited by Irving L. Finkel, 177–231. Papers from the 1990 British Museum Colloquium. London: British Museum Press, 2007.

Subramanian, Samanth. "What We Learn from One of the World's Oldest Board Games." *New Yorker*, March 26, 2019.

Tesauro, Gerald. "Neurogammon: A Neural-Network Backgammon Program." In *International Joint Conference on Neural Networks*, 3:33–39. San Diego, 1990.

———. "TD-Gammon, a Self-Teaching Backgammon Program, Achieves Master-Level Play." *Neural Computation* 6, no. 2 (March 1994): 215–19.

———. "Temporal Difference Learning of Backgammon Strategy." In *Proceedings of the Ninth International Workshop on Machine Learning*, 451–57. Morgan Kaufmann Publishers, 1992.

Time. Modern Living. "The Money Game." February 19, 1973.

Voogt, Alex de, Anne-Elizabeth Dunn-Vaturi, and Jelmer W. Eerkens. "Cultural Transmission in the Ancient Near East: Twenty Squares and Fifty-Eight Holes." *Journal of Archaeological Science* 40, no. 4 (April 2013): 1715–30.

POKER

Bowling, Michael, Neil Burch, Michael Johanson, and Oskari Tammelin. "Heads-up Limit Hold'em Poker Is Solved." *Science* 347, no. 6218 (January 9, 2015): 145–49.

Brown, Noam, and Tuomas Sandholm. "Superhuman AI for Heads-up No-Limit Poker: Libratus Beats Top Professionals." *Science* 359, no. 6374 (January 26, 2018): 418–24.

———. "Superhuman AI for Multiplayer Poker." *Science* 365, no. 6456 (August 30, 2019): 885–90.

Brunson, Doyle. *Super System: A Course in Power Poker.* 3rd ed. New York: Cardoza Publishing, 2002.

Burch, Neil, Martin Schmid, Matej Moravčík, and Michael Bowling. "AIVAT: A New Variance Reduction Technique for Agent Evaluation in Imperfect Information Games." *ArXiv:1612.06915 [Cs]*, December 20, 2016.

Gibson, Richard. "Regret Minimization in Games and the Development of Champion Multiplayer Computer Poker-Playing Agents." PhD diss., University of Alberta, 2014.

Hughes, Robert. *The Shock of the New: The Hundred-Year History of Modern Art—Its Rise, Its Dazzling Achievement, Its Fall.* Rev. ed. New York: Knopf, 1991.

Janda, Matthew. *No-Limit Hold 'Em for Advanced Players.* Las Vegas: Two Plus Two, 2017.

McManus, James. *Cowboys Full: The Story of Poker.* New York: Farrar, Straus and Giroux, 2009.

———. *Positively Fifth Street: Murderers, Cheetahs, and Binion's World Series of Poker.* New York: Farrar, Straus and Giroux, 2003.

Moravčík, Matej, Martin Schmid, Neil Burch, Viliam Lisý, Dustin Morrill, Nolan Bard, Trevor Davis, Kevin Waugh, Michael Johanson, and Michael Bowling. "DeepStack: Expert-Level Artificial Intelligence in Heads-up No-Limit Poker." *Science* 356, no. 6337 (May 5, 2017): 508–13.

Nasar, Sylvia. *A Beautiful Mind.* New York: Simon & Schuster, 1998.

Nash, John. "Non-Cooperative Games." *Annals of Mathematics* 54, no. 2 (1951): 286–95.

Nash, John, and L. S. Shapely. "A Simple Three-Person Poker Game." In *Contributions to the Theory of Games,* edited by Harold William Kuhn and Albert William Tucker, 105–16. Annals of Mathematics Studies 24. Princeton, N.J.: Princeton University Press, 1950.

Roeder, Oliver. "It's Hard to Win at Poker Against an Opponent with No Tell." *FiveThirtyEight,* July 11, 2019.

———. "The Machines Are Coming for Poker." *FiveThirtyEight,* January 19, 2017.

Simonite, Tom. "A Poker-Playing Robot Goes to Work for the Pentagon." *Wired,* January 16, 2019.

Sklansky, David. *The Theory of Poker: A Professional Poker Player Teaches You How to Think Like One.* 4th ed. Las Vegas: Two Plus Two, 1999.

Sklansky, David, and Ed Miller. *No Limit Hold 'Em: Theory and Practice*. 2nd ed. Henderson, Nev.: Two Plus Two, 2006.

Sweeney, James, and Adam Jones. *Optimizing Ace King: The Right Strategy for Playing Poker's Most Complex Starting Hand*. Independently published, 2018.

SCRABBLE

Adolphs, S. "Lexical Coverage of Spoken Discourse." *Applied Linguistics* 24, no. 4 (December 1, 2003): 425–38.

Aristotle. *Poetics*. Translated by Malcolm Heath. New York: Penguin Classics, 1997.

Chaikin, Eric, and Julian Petrillo. *Word Wars: Tiles and Tribulations on the Scrabble Game Circuit*. Documentary. Seventh Art Releasing, 2004.

Cleary, Thomas, and J. C. Cleary, trans. *The Blue Cliff Record*. Boston: Shambhala, 2005.

Cockburn, Alexander. *Idle Passion: Chess and the Dance of Death*. New York: Simon & Schuster, 1975.

Fatsis, Stefan. *Word Freak: Heartbreak, Triumph, Genius, and Obsession in the World of Competitive Scrabble Players*. Boston: Houghton Mifflin, 2001.

Gordon, Steven A. "A Faster Scrabble Move Generation Algorithm." *Software: Practice and Experience* 24, no. 2 (February 1, 1994): 219–32.

Matsumoto, Kenji. *Breaking the Game*. Independently published, 2015.

Richards, Mark, and Eyal Amir. "Opponent Modeling in Scrabble." In *Proceedings of the 20th International Joint Conference on Artificial Intelligence*, 1482–87, 2007.

Roeder, Oliver. "What Makes Nigel Richards the Best Scrabble Player on Earth." *FiveThirtyEight*, August 8, 2014.

Shapiro, Stuart C., and Howard R. Smith. "A Scrabble Crossword Game-Playing Program." In *Computer Games I*, edited by David N. L. Levy, 403–19. New York: Springer, 1988.

Sheppard, Brian. "Towards Perfect Play of Scrabble." PhD diss., University of Maastricht, 2002.

———. "World-Championship-Caliber Scrabble." *Artificial Intelligence* 134, nos. 1–2 (January 2002): 241–75.

Thorp, Edward O. *Beat the Dealer: A Winning Strategy for the Game of Twenty-One*. Rev. ed. New York: Vintage, 1966.

Tierney, John. "Humankind Battles for Scrabble Supremacy." *New York Times Magazine*, May 24, 1998.

Wapnick, Joel. *The Champion's Strategy for Winning at Scrabble*. New York: Stein and Day, 1986.

BRIDGE

Berlekamp, Elwyn R. "Machine Solution of No-Trump Double-Dummy Bridge Problems." Master's thesis, MIT, 1962.

Carley, Gay Loran. "A Program to Play Contract Bridge." Master's thesis, MIT, 1962.

Clay, John. *Culbertson: The Man Who Made Contract Bridge*. London: Weidenfeld & Nicolson, 1986.

Colapinto, John. "Is the Competitive Bridge World Rife with Cheaters?" *Vanity Fair*, March 2016.

Collinson, John. *Biritch, or Russian Whist*. London: Blandford Lowe, 1886.

Culbertson, Ely. *Contract Bridge Blue Book*. New York: Bridge World, 1930.

———. *Contract Bridge Complete: The Gold Book of Bidding and Play*. Philadelphia: John C. Winston, 1936.

———. *Contract Bridge Red Book on Play*. Philadelphia: John C. Winston, 1934.

———. Speech given in London (?), 1932. *Pathétone Weekly*. British Pathé. https://www.youtube.com/watch?v=A_gPeb_mp-8.

Feynman, Richard P. *The Feynman Lectures on Physics*. 3 vols. Reading, Mass.: Addison-Wesley, 1964.

———. *"Surely You're Joking, Mr. Feynman!": Adventures of a Curious Character*. New York: W. W. Norton, 1985.

Ginsberg, Matt. *Factor Man*. Eugene, Ore.: Zowie Press, 2018.

Ginsberg, Matthew L. "GIB: Imperfect Information in a Computationally Challenging Game." *Journal of Artificial Intelligence Research* 14 (June 1, 2001): 303–58.

———. "GIB: Steps Toward an Expert-Level Bridge-Playing Program." In *Proceedings of the 16th International Joint Conference on Artificial Intelligence*, 1:584–89. San Francisco, 1999.

Goren, Charles. *The Elements of Bridge*. New York: Doubleday, 1960.

———. *Goren's Bridge Complete*. New York: Doubleday, 1963.

Keri, Jonah. "Tricks, Tics and Taps: Cheating Shakes Professional Bridge." *Rolling Stone*, March 9, 2016.

Manley, Brent, ed. *The Official ACBL Encyclopedia of Bridge*. New York: Crown, 1971.

Owen, David. "Dirty Hands: A Cheating Scandal in the World of Professional Bridge." *New Yorker*, February 29, 2016.

———. "Turning Tricks: The Rise and Fall of Contract Bridge." *New Yorker*, September 10, 2007.

Root, William S., and Richard Pavlicek. *Modern Bridge Conventions*. New York: Three Rivers, 1981.

Sheinwold, Alfred. *5 Weeks to Winning Bridge*. New York: Permabooks, 1960.

Smith, Marc. *Man vs. Machine: The Bridge Match of the Millennium*. Bridge Plus, 1999.

Vanderbilt, Harold S. *Contract Bridge: Bidding and the Club Convention*. New York: Charles Scribner's Sons, 1929.

———. *The New Contract Bridge: Bidding, the Club Convention, and Forcing Overbids*. New York: Charles Scribner's Sons, 1930.

Wasserman, Anthony I. "Realization of a Skillful Bridge Bidding Program." *Proceedings of the Joint Computer Conference*, November 1970, 433–44.

A FEW OTHER GAMES

Allis, Victor. "A Knowledge-Based Approach of Connect-Four: The Game Is Solved—White Wins." Master's thesis, Vrije Universiteit, 1988.

Buro, Michael. "The Evolution of Strong Othello Programs." In *Entertainment Computing: Technologies and Application*, edited by Ryohei Nakatsu and Junichi Hoshino, 81–88. Boston: Springer, 2003.

Gasser, Ralph. "Solving Nine Men's Morris." *Computational Intelligence* 12, no. 1 (February 1996): 24–41.

Ginsberg, Matthew L. "Dr. Fill: Crosswords and an Implemented Solver for Singly Weighted CSPs." *Journal of Artificial Intelligence Research* 42, no. 1 (September 2011): 851–86.

Hayward, Ryan B., and Bjarne Toft. *Hex: The Full Story*. Boca Raton: CRC Press, 2019.

Müller, Martin, and Theodore Tegos. "Experiments in Computer Amazons." In *More Games of No Chance*, 243–60. Cambridge: Cambridge University Press, 2002.

Romein, John W., and Henri E. Bal. "Awari Is Solved." *Journal of the ICGA* 25 (2002): 162–65.

Sturtevant, Nathan R. "On Strongly Solving Chinese Checkers." In *Advances in Computer Games*, edited by Tristan Cazenave, Jaap van den Herik, Abdallah Saffidine, and I-Chen Wu, 155–66. Cham, Switzerland: Springer, 2019.

Sturtevant, Nathan R., Ariel Felner, and Malte Helmert. "Exploiting the Rubik's Cube 12-Edge PDB by Combining Partial Pattern Databases and Bloom Filters." In *Proceedings of the Seventh International Symposium on Combinatorial Search*, edited by Stefan Edelkamp and Roman Barták, 175–83. Palo Alto: AAAI Press, 2014.

INDEX

Page numbers in *italics* refer to illustrations. Footnotes are indicated by *n* after the page number.